The World War II Bond Campaign

World War II: The Global, Human, and Ethical Dimension

G. Kurt Piehler, series editor

The World War II Bond Campaign

Lawrence R. Samuel

Fordham University Press
New York 2025

Copyright © 2025 Fordham University Press

Portions of Parts One and Three are reprinted from "Dreaming in Black and White: African-American Patriotism and World War II Bonds," in *Bonds of Affection: Americans Define Their Patriotism*, ed. John Bodnar (Princeton, NJ: Princeton University Press, 1996).

All rights reserved. No part of this publication may be reproduced, stored in a retrieval system, or transmitted in any form or by any means—electronic, mechanical, photocopy, recording, or any other—except for brief quotations in printed reviews, without the prior permission of the publisher.

Fordham University Press has no responsibility for the persistence or accuracy of URLs for external or third-party Internet websites referred to in this publication and does not guarantee that any content on such websites is, or will remain, accurate or appropriate.

Fordham University Press also publishes its books in a variety of electronic formats. Some content that appears in print may not be available in electronic books.

Visit us online at www.fordhampress.com.

Library of Congress Cataloging-in-Publication Data available online at https://catalog.loc.gov.

Printed in the United States of America
27 26 25   5 4 3 2 1
First edition

To my parents

When men are no longer united among themselves by firm and lasting ties, it is impossible to obtain the cooperation of any great number of them unless you can persuade every man whose help you require that his private interest obliges him voluntarily to unite his exertions to the exertions of all the others.

           Alexis de Tocqueville, DEMOCRACY IN AMERICA II

It's the average everyday Americans at home who are piling up these tremendous bond sales.... You reach these people because you are these people.

           Former New York governor Al Smith,
           speaking of Kate Smith in September 1943

★ ★ ★ **CONTENTS**

List of Illustrations ix
Acknowledgments xi
Introduction xiii

PART ONE
The Development and Marketing of World War II Bonds

Chapter 1. **The Voluntary Way** 3
Chapter 2. **Democracy in Action** 20
Chapter 3. **The Biggest Selling Campaign in History** 45

PART TWO
War Bonds and Labor, Class, and Ethnicity

Chapter 4. **On This We Are United** 77
Chapter 5. **Consent of the Governed** 94

PART THREE
African Americans and World War II Bonds

Chapter 6. **William Pickens and the Inter-Racial Section** 127

Chapter 7. **The NAACP and War Bonds** 152
Chapter 8. **African American Notables and War Bonds** 171
Chapter 9. **African American Investment in War Bonds** 186

Conclusion 207
Notes 219
Index 243

★ ★ ★ **ILLUSTRATIONS**

1. Schools at War display at a Los Angeles department store 34
2. Boy Scouts stuffing envelopes for bond solicitations 37
3. Girl Scouts selling bonds and stamps 38
4. Girl Scouts and girls of the Civilian Defense 38
5. Women's Division of St. Louis 39
6. Bond advertisement on a milk carton 49
7. Billboard advertising war bonds 53
8. Betty Grable and her bondbardiers 58
9. Bing Crosby 59
10. Helen Hayes and movie cast members 60
11. Hollywood Bond Cavalcade in Washington, D.C. 60
12. Movie fans buy a bond 62
13. War bond screening in Puerto Rico 63
14. Display window advertising "Yankee sub bonds" 67
15. Display window advertising "Axis Easter baskets" 68
16. Butcher advertising War Bond Day 69
17. Buying a bond in a New Jersey defense plant 89
18. Singer makes an appeal for bonds 90
19. B'nai Brith war bond booth 102
20. Selling war bonds during the Third War Loan 106
21. A family signs pledges for bonds 107

22. Opening a war bond booth in San Juan 108
23. Corporal buys a war bond 109
24. Members of the Klamath tribe buy bonds 110
25. Polish Alliance Society sells bonds 111
26. French Americans at a war stamp tea 114
27. Slovak War Mothers open a war bond drive 115
28. Paderewski war bond booth in Pittsburgh 116
29. Lithuanian war bond booth in Pittsburgh 117
30. Opening of the Serbian war bond booth in Pittsburgh 118
31. Chinese war bond booth in Pittsburgh 119
32. Russian war bond booth in Pittsburgh 120
33. Dedication of the Lebanese war bond booth in Pittsburgh 120
34. Lebanese Americans open their booth in Pittsburgh 121
35. Dedication of the Syrian booth in Pittsburgh 121
36. Dedication of the Victory Nationality Booth 122
37. "Nationality" Women in Defense float, Pittsburgh 122
38. Victory tea rally 123
39. William Pickens 128
40. Edgar T. Rouzeau confers with Arthur Sylvester 137
41. Receiving a War Bond Achievement Citation 174
42. Prisoner presented with war bonds 190
43. Pullman Porters Benefit Association buys bonds 193
44. Brotherhood of Sleeping Car Porters buys bonds 194
45. Dedication of Jeeps "purchased" by students 199
46. Taylors Musical Strings, St Paul, Minnesota 200

★ ★ ★ **Acknowledgments**

Many thanks must be expressed to those who played a vital role in making this book a reality. I am grateful to Charles McGovern at the National Museum of American History for his insights and for encouraging me to apply for a ten-week fellowship at the Smithsonian Institution. I also greatly appreciate the efforts of many others at the Smithsonian, the National Archives, the Library of Congress, the Treasury Department, and the Schomberg Center for their help in finding research materials. Special acknowledgment must go to Gary Gerstle of Catholic University, who planted the seed for this book by calling for more study in the area of World War II bonds.

Thanks also to the members of my committees at the University of Minnesota who offered constructive criticism at various stages of the project: John Fiske, Phil Furia, David Noble, Riv-Ellen Prell, and John Wright. I am especially grateful to Elaine and Lary May for hosting the American Studies dissertation group, to the members of the group, and to Rudolph's Barbecue for its excellent coleslaw. I am deeply indebted to Lary May for his vision, advice, and encouragement. This book would not have been possible without his unflagging support.

A number of anonymous readers were extremely helpful in reshaping and refining the work. Much thanks to Craig Gill at the University Press of Kentucky and to Mark Hirsch and Karin Kaufman of the Smithsonian Institution Press for their sagacity in the editing process. Finally, thanks to those who made the writing of this book a much more pleasant affair. A big Iconohug to Vickie Abrahamson and Mary Meehan, my partners in crime, and to Shannon Forstrom for her faith and laser printer.

★ ★ ★ **Introduction**

In May 1941, the first month of the U.S. Treasury's defense savings program, Adelard Courtemanche of Windsor Locks, Connecticut, brought the 11,250 nickels he had been saving for a new car to the local post office and purchased thirty defense bonds. In September 1943 Donato De Grossa, a sixty-three-year-old Italian-born shoe shiner in Philadelphia, celebrated the surrender of Italy by buying a $1,000 war bond. In 1944 an elderly African American woman in Los Angeles, with no sons or daughters to enlist in the armed forces, sold her $15,000 home and used the entire proceeds to buy war bonds.[1]

What motivated these and millions of other Americans to such extreme support for the war effort? How did first- and second-generation Americans view their ethnic identity in relation to such a patriotic cause? Why did the federal government aggressively pursue the African American market, and why did blacks eagerly respond? These and many other important questions arise within the intersection of the federal government's bond drives and Americans' experience during World War II. The cultural history of bonds reveals the paradigmic change in American nationalism that occurred during the war. War bonds both reflected and helped shape a new version of Americanism, steeped in the enduring paradox of "e pluribus unum," out of many, one. As a rare example of consumerism within the civic sphere, the buying and selling of bonds during

World War II helps us better understand national identity, that is, what it meant and means to be an American.

As any surviving home-front American could testify, government bonds and stamps were an indelible presence on the country's collective psyche throughout the war. Soon after the war ended, many in the media began to call the Treasury's bond program "the greatest sales operation in history." Eighty-five million Americans had purchased $185.7 billion in bonds, the largest amount of money ever raised for a war. Although the selling of war bonds was intended to serve economic purposes, specifically to slow inflation and help finance the war, the Roosevelt administration considered the campaign equally important from a psychological standpoint: it helped sell "the idea of the war" to a divided American people. The program was one of various avenues employed by the administration to create a more unified and harmonic nation, as displaying outward strength to foreign enemies relied upon lessening the domestic tensions among Americans along socioeconomic, ethnic, and racial lines. Grounded in public or private patriotic support for one's country, bond campaigns were viewed by government officials as an opportunity to bring together Americans from all walks of life. The Treasury's program was conceived, in President Roosevelt's term, as "one great partnership," offering all Americans a personal stake in the war.[2]

Backed by an unprecedented marketing effort, the bond program reached into virtually every aspect of American society throughout the war. World War II bonds represented the most tangible evidence of Americans' financial and moral stake in the war, the principal means by which those on the home front could take part in the war effort. Bond drives infiltrated everyday life, blurring the lines between the public and private arenas. The full power of the state was deployed to persuade all Americans—including potentially oppositional groups such as labor and African Americans—to literally and figuratively buy into the war through bonds. As Americans rallied together to win the war, prompted by bond drives and other forms of propaganda, a consensus, or what Alan Brinkley has called a "stable concert of interests among the state, business, and labor," emerged. Articulated in populist terms as the "American Way of Life," the consensus took on the form of a secular religion, fusing personal aspirations, nationalism, and consumerism. With the war positioned as a defense of the American Way of Life, a domestic ideology of nationhood was clearly defined and easily understood. The war was assigned the transcendent objectives of "the Good War": an opportunity to defeat fascism, defend and renew the faith in American democracy, restore the American economy, and reap the benefits of a new and improved consumer ethic. Although centered on defense, the wartime consensus was ultimately predicated on defending and preserving the ideals of the American Enlightenment and promised a prosperous and abundant postwar society.[3]

Due in large part to the coming and passing of the fiftieth anniversary of the war, revisionist historians are increasingly debunking the notion of World War II as the Good War and the idea that the war and postwar consensus represented blanket homogeneity. Much more attention is being devoted to the contradictions between America's claims of national unity and the racial, ethnic, and religious divisions on the home front. John Morton Blum was one of the earliest historians to recognize the tensions associated with these divisions, suggesting that "World War II posed a special test of the ability of American culture to accommodate to its inherent pluralism." America's awareness as a pluralistic nation had advanced immeasurably between the wars, largely a function of the Great Migration to northern cities by southern blacks and the New Deal bringing African Americans and other ethnic groups into power via the Democratic Party. As Depression-era populism raised the cultural status of "folk" peoples and traditions, the New Deal years provided a social climate in which pluralism could germinate.[4]

The Statue of Liberty was first recognized as an icon of American pluralism in the 1930s, an apt symbol of the elevation of the nation's multicultural identity during the decade. It was also in the 1930s that pluralism gained official status within academic and government circles. Although the concept of "cultural pluralism" was first suggested in 1915 and the term first used in 1924, it was not until the late 1930s that the idea achieved broad acceptance among intellectuals. Events in Europe had a direct effect on the views of social scientists and other "experts," reviving Horace Kallen's vague but compelling theory of cultural pluralism. Kallen envisioned the United States as a "federation of nationalities" united by voluntary participation within a set of "common institutions," a utopian synergy of difference and harmony. Shaped by Kallen's and many others' views, the idea of cultural pluralism gained broad circulation in American discourse. Prejudice became widely seen as a pathological condition contrary to the American creed, and a more liberal and tolerant attitude toward Euro-American immigrants and African Americans was espoused in popular rhetoric. Forced assimilation to an Anglo-Saxon identity became associated with theories of inherent racial superiority, an obstacle to positive intergroup relations or "brotherhood." America's uniqueness was that its citizens were bound together not by ancestral background but by belief in a common set of values.[5]

More important, cultural pluralism advanced beyond ideology and theory in the 1930s, shaping American politics and, in turn, community life. Ethnicity and race became linked to issues of class within the competitive dialogue of the New Deal, elevating the idea of pluralism to the center of American politics. For the first time the working class, composed largely of first- and second-generation Americans, emerged as a major coalition within the political arena of the 1930s. Through a combination of class-based rhetoric, economic programs, and support of labor, the Democratic Party successfully drew upon the loyalty of these Americans. The Roosevelt administration strengthened the autonomy of working-class, ethnic communities, providing a climate in which to seat a "hyphenated Americanism." Pluralism operated most dynamically at the local level, as thriving Euro- and African American communities redefined the culture of work and neighborhoods across the country.[6]

With American cultural pluralism cast in stark opposition to Nazi totalitarianism in prewar and wartime propaganda, the idea of democracy was raised to the status of a civil religion, invested with what Philip Gleason has called "the aura of the sacred." This change in American identity can be measured by comparing the country's tolerance for diversity in the two world wars. The "100% Americanism" programs of World War I demanded that white ethnic groups minimize any signs of foreign origin, whereas the country's ideological stance during World War II had to acknowledge that both ethnicity and race were integral parts of the American idea and experience. As demonstrated by the vivid cinematic image of the multicultural platoon, America's collective strength was a function of the diversity of its individual members. Pluralism emerged as the central character of American identity, in contrast to what Gary Gerstle called the dominant "class-based construction of Americanism" of the 1930s. The elevation of pluralistic democracy during World War II produced, according to Richard Polenberg, "a sharpened sense of ethnic self-awareness," as national loyalty was juxtaposed against ancestral ties. The ideological shift that occurred between the wars was reflected in World War II propaganda, which employed both a broad pluralistic tone and direct appeals to Euro- and African Americans. The war would exponentially advance the strides made by ethnics and blacks during the 1930s, raising their status as legitimate members of the national family tree. "Cultural pluralism in all its ambiguities and complexities," as Gleason claimed, emerged as "the crucial legacy of World War II in respect to American identity."[7]

As one of the cornerstones of the American home front, bonds played a key role in advancing the wartime pluralistic consensus society. Grounded in the ideals of "the voluntary way" and "democracy in action," the Treasury's program differed from other wartime avenues of state building, such as the Office of Price Administration (OPA) and the Red Cross, in that it was dedicated to nonpartisanship and nonelitism, intentionally designed to symbolize the country's democratic ideals. And unlike other forms of wartime sacrifice, purchasing bonds offered Americans a future, tangible return on their investment. War bonds were thus ideally aligned with the American creed of free enterprise, confirming one Treasury official's observation that "national defense seemed to combine in almost perfect measure the twin blessings of patriotism and economic prosperity." The blending of public and private interests that characterized the Treasury's bond campaign provides the opportunity to combine intellectual history—the modus operandi of propaganda studies—with a ground-level view. The arm of the state made an impact on everyday life at the individual, community, and institutional levels, with public policy translated into action among children, women, union members, ethnic Americans, and blacks. Because of this public-private dualism, many of the contradictions and limitations of the new Americanism—how society can be both unified and autonomous, how ethnic and racial identity can be expressed without the dimension of class, and how African Americans can be simultaneously included within and excluded from the consensus—became fully evident.[8]

Via war bonds and other forms of propaganda, the Roosevelt administration promoted a pluralistic brand of nationalism that inherited and leveraged the salient themes of the New Deal. The dynamics of bonds offers a means of directly understanding how the "bottom-up" nationalism of the 1930s was transformed into an official, "top-down" form of pluralism. Driven by the guiding principle of democracy, Euro- and African Americans became key parts of the wartime pluralistic equation. As authority shifted to the state through demands for national unity, the administration played a greater role in determining what was "acceptable" pluralism and what was not. Pluralism's roots in local, communal activities and institutions were transplanted to the consumption-oriented consensus of the American Way of Life. Depression-era class consciousness was significantly undercut and increasingly associated with un-American and potentially dangerous ideologies. War bonds acted as a catalyst in the shift from New Deal populism to a nationalism predicated on the common pursuit of affluence, linking pluralism to the universally shared desire for the good life.

With unity through pluralism the defining character of the Treasury's bond program, selling and buying war bonds were presented and perceived as opportunities to express national loyalty through the customs and codes defined by class, ethnicity, and race. Unlike in World War I bond drives, patriotism could be articulated in a variety of terms, not dictated by prescribed assimilation to an Anglo-American ideal. As a symbol of American democracy, war bonds helped to broaden the parameters of patriotism and national identity, accommodating the loyalties of the working class, Euro-Americans, and to some extent, African Americans. Within the nexus of bonds, virtually any form of group ritual or symbol was allowed to coexist when framed within the context of national loyalty, a dramatic difference from the Liberty Bond drives of World War I. Bond rallies were held at union meetings, Euro-American rituals, and African American civic celebrations. Only those practices which were believed to threaten the country's ability to win the war, that is, supporting the enemy or attacking the ideological principals of the consensus, were considered illegitimate. Although the wartime pluralistic consensus had some corrosive effect on the integrity of affiliation groups, as suggested by the decline of ethnic newspapers between 1940 and 1950, assimilation to mainstream American culture by the working class, Euro-Americans, and African Americans was voluntary, unlike in World War I.

Despite the greater pluralistic climate of World War II, the issues circulating around race were particularly complex. The "separate and unequal" treatment of African Americans during the war was clear evidence of the "official racism" endorsed by the Roosevelt administration. A government tolerant of, even subscribing to, discrimination toward a particular group of people was, of course, in direct contrast with American democratic ideals, which were serving as the backbone for the country's ideological war against Nazism. Unlike World War I, which was fought essentially as an Anglo-Saxon war, World War II was being fought on the grounds of defending New World democracy and liberty against Old World totalitarianism, fascism, and racism. Given the mission of the war to protect the inalienable rights of individual freedoms, exceptions of race were becoming increasingly difficult to defend. With Nazism cast in government propaganda as the antithesis to the Enlightenment-inspired principle of democracy, blacks leaders saw an opportunity to convincingly demonstrate the contradictions between popular rhetoric and African Americans' actual experience.[9]

Introduction

As race relations—what Gunnar Myrdal would call in 1944 "the American dilemma"—came to the forefront of the national consciousness, black leaders vowed not to slow their fight for equality as their predecessors had done a generation earlier. During World War I, blacks had demonstrated strong support for the war effort, but for the sake of national unity had postponed what W. E. B. Du Bois called their "special grievances." Expectedly, there was hope the Roosevelt administration and whites as a whole would see the parallels between Nazi racism and America's own oppression directed to fellow citizens based on skin color, and move toward a truly democratic society.[10]

Given their special interest in an Allied victory, a function of Nazi's overt racism, blacks' broad support of the war was, like that of most Americans, a demonstration of patriotism and loyalty to their country. However, although African Americans were indeed displaying a mainstream version of patriotism in their support for the war, this represented only half of their loyalties. Evidence of blacks' dual identity, what Du Bois termed "twoness" or a "double self," suggests that World War II's underpinnings—that of a unified and harmonious society joined to fight a common enemy—are faulty or, at least, only part of the foundation. Attitudes and behavior related to the other half of the Double V, victory over enemies at home, demand further attention in the continuing effort to redefine "the Good War" and recover important narratives of the present's past. As an articulation of the Double V, bond drives among African Americans illustrated that patriotism is not unidimensional but multivalent, accommodating an infinite number and variety of interpretations.[11]

Finally, the cultural history of World War II bonds helps us chart the trajectory of two defining themes of the postwar era. Widespread holdings of government securities were instrumental in linking wartime patriotism to the promise of postwar consumerism, most dramatically suggested by the image of a bountiful Thanksgiving dinner in Norman Rockwell's "Freedom from Want" war bond poster. As Frank Fox observed in his encompassing study of wartime propaganda, the right to both personal and national abundance was an integral part of the American creed the country was fighting to preserve. The idea that consumption could be a socially beneficial, even patriotic, act thus emerged not in the postwar years but during the war, spurred to a great degree by the consumer dynamics of bonds. As the clearest example of "investing in the future while the present was out of stock," war bonds purchased in the early 1940s were seeds of consumerism reaped in the early 1950s, when the securities reached full maturity and were redeemed. In addition, as recent scholarship is increasingly showing, the civil rights movement emerged not after but during the war. As the country prospered from defense production, blacks' demand for equal rights in jobs, housing, and recreation resulted in limited but important gains, laying the foundation for the full protest movement of the postwar era. The selling of bonds to and purchasing by African Americans were key to the fight for full equality during the war. The administration invited blacks into the consensus society through appeals for bonds, and African Americans obtained real economic power by investing in them. The World War II bond program helps us locate the beginnings of both the postwar consumption ethic and the civil rights movement, each an integral chapter of American social history.[12]

Part One of this book provides a broad overview of the Treasury's bond program of World War II, framing the campaign within the country's social, political, and economic climate. As in World War I, the administration implemented a bond program during World War II for both economic and ideological purposes. Versus the World War I campaign, which practiced Wilsonian "100% Americanism," however, the World War II program reflected the Roosevelt administration's attempt to achieve unity through pluralism. By reaching out to all segments of the population, including traditionally marginalized groups such as children, women, and farmers, the administration used bonds as a vehicle to strengthen morale and create greater domestic harmony. Offering all Americans a stake in the war via bonds was thus seen as a means to establish some common ground, a device to resolve or at least delay domestic tensions during the war emergency. The Treasury integrated bond appeals into virtually all forms of popular culture during the war, including music, literature, movies, theater, and sports. Retailers became an extension of the administration's selling program, merging privatized consumer culture with the war effort. Both the sheer volume of bonds sold and anecdotal evidence suggest that the World War II bond may indeed have been the most successful consumer product of a single time and place.

Part Two takes a close look at the bond activities of two groups considered essential to the program's success, labor and ethnic Americans. Although bond rallies occasionally functioned as opportunities to voice protest against corporate management or the government, unions and their members were responsible for a huge percentage of war bond sales. Through bond selling and buying, class tensions were largely defused (and labor power significantly weakened), important legacies for the postwar era. Rather than attempt to make ethnic Americans conform to a single definition of American identity, the Treasury took advantage of the loyalty of foreign-origin groups to their native lands. Bond drives became part of ethnic celebrations, a reason for those of common ancestry to come together to support their adopted country. Through bond rallies, the signs and symbols of foreign nationalities became linked to those of American patriotism, a successful reconciliation of ethnic Americans' dual identities. The government's bond program thus demonstrated the resiliency of national loyalty, and how it can be combined with ethnic identity to create a form of cultural synergy.

Part Three deals with the dynamics of the bond program relative to African Americans. William Pickens of the Treasury's Inter-Racial Section sold the idea of the war to African Americans through bonds, a difficult task given the vast contradictions between the nation's democratic ideals and its caste-like restrictions and obstacles. Pickens preached a form of civil rights grounded in the Double V, victory over enemies both abroad and at home, and positioned bonds as a rare opportunity that blacks should seize in order to realize the gains they deserved. Like labor, the National Association for the Advancement of Colored People (NAACP) strongly endorsed the program, believing that buying bonds on the home front was the best way to win the war overseas. Also like labor, however, the NAACP occasionally used bond drives as an opportunity to protest inequities and achieve greater social standing. Buying and endorsing bonds were viewed by the organization's leaders, Walter White and Roy Wilkins, as both a patriotic duty and a means to realize a more democratic society through greater African American economic power. Black government officials, academics and literati, entertainers, and sports figures also played an active part in making the bond program a success within the African American community. The endorsement of the program by a variety of notable African Americans, particularly Duke Ellington and Joe Louis, suggested that both the American dream and "democracy in action" were indeed possible. Although no records were kept according to race (a conscious decision by the government), sufficient evidence exists to know that African Americans accounted for a significant share of bond sales, perhaps higher than that of whites on a per capita basis. As in white ethnic groups, bond rallies became a source of communal celebration and pride, an opportunity to preserve an American identity that resided outside the dominant Anglo-Saxon archetype. Racial identity was expressed within the context of patriotism, again demonstrating the flexibility and adaptability of national loyalty.

The case of war bonds demonstrates that pluralism is indeed the crucial legacy of World War II. The state's brand of official pluralism effectively combined national interests with those of the working class, Euro-Americans, and African Americans, broadening the base of support for administration policy. Class tensions were dramatically eased, shifting American identity away from socioeconomic standing to a shared aspiration of middle-class materialism. While prescribing greater national unity and cohesiveness, however, the state tolerated, even encouraged, cultural diversity and difference in order to demonstrate the success of the unique American experiment. By accommodating alternative constructs of patriotism, war bonds most clearly represented the nation's motto of "e pluribus unum." The wide variety of ways that war bonds were bought and sold illustrated that Americanism was not necessarily assimilationist, that class, ethnic, and racial identity could augment, versus conflict with, national identity. With a newly defined, popular vision of the nation as pluralistic, the image of America as melting pot was temporarily taken off the burner during the war. Analogous to the ubiquitous multicultural platoon, war bonds symbolized that America's singular identity resided in its diversity.

PART ONE

★ ★ ★ **The Development and Marketing of World War II Bonds**

CHAPTER 1

★ ★ ★ **The Voluntary Way**

Just as the national deficit is today a charged political issue, public debt has long been at the center of the country's debate over the acquisition and allotment of economic resources. The largest source of public debt has been through the issuing of bonds, certificates that guarantee to the lender payment of the original investment plus interest at a future date. As the most tangible expression of partnership between the government and the American people, bonds represent an important and interesting chapter in the cultural history of the nation. In 1776, private citizens purchased more than $27 million in government securities from the newly formed United States Treasury to help finance the Revolution. During the Civil War, the Treasury used personal selling techniques for the first time to elicit financial support for the Union, and during the Spanish-American War, it first offered small denomination bonds, selling securities ranging from $20 to $300 to more than a quarter of a million people. In addition to financing wars, bonds have been used by the government to complete the first transcontinental railroad, build the Panama Canal, and acquire both the Louisiana Territory and Alaska.[1]

It was during World War I that bonds first played a significant role in the lives of many Americans. The goal of the Treasury was to raise as much money as possible in as short a time as possible, structured around limited drive periods known as Liberty and, late in the war, Victory Loans. To meet this goal, the administration led an aggressive marketing campaign to sell stamps and bonds to the American people. Promotional appeals such as "Save Your Child from Autocracy and Poverty" and "Surely Your Patriotism Equals the Cost of a Bond" were emblematic of the jingoistic tone of the program. Despite the heavy-handed campaign, however, banks and corporations ultimately accounted for a very large percentage of the total investment in the 1917–19 Liberty Loan drive. Relatively few Americans—about 350,000—had any experience owning government securities at the onset of the program, and many were uncomfortable converting a significant portion of their savings or earnings into what was to them a new and uncertain form of investment. This hesitation would, in retrospect, prove to be prudent, as negotiable-rate Liberty Bonds were worth less than their original purchase price when many chose to redeem them after the war.[2]

The aggressive tone of the World War I stamp and bond program reflected the foreign and domestic objectives the administration assigned to the war. President Wilson perceived World War I not only as a fight for American liberalism but as an opportunity to bring the country's divided factions closer together. With broad support of the war, Wilson believed, "nagging social conflicts would be swept away in a wave of patriotic unity," easing the administration's implementation of domestic policies. Overzealous organizations such as the Committee on Public Information and the American Patriotic League, however, pressured many Americans to adopt their ideological stance. The former, led by George Creel, distributed millions of pamphlets proclaiming the virtues of democracy over autocracy and orchestrated the efforts of some 75,000 Four-Minute Men. This small army gave an estimated 7.5 million public speeches at theaters, clubs, and concerts, preaching "100 percent Americanism" and urging listeners to buy Liberty Bonds. The American Patriotic League, with a membership of 250,000, was a quasi-official federal agency, the largest of various organizations created to promote Wilson's brand of patriotism.[3]

Wilson's attempts to defeat potential enemies within the country's borders was, as Leslie Vaughan wrote, a way of "strengthening solidarity among Anglo-Saxons, at a time when their cohesiveness was being challenged internally." The flood of Catholics, Jews, and non-English-speaking immigrants were perceived by many Anglo-Americans as "dirty, unkempt, unskilled and decidedly 'foreign.'" Wilson, like Theodore Roosevelt, believed that Americanism and ethnic loyalties were mutually exclusive, that practicing the former required giving up the latter. Within this nationalistic climate, Americanization programs designed to eliminate threatening ethnicity were adopted across the civic sphere, most evidently in public schools. Such crusades directed at new immigrants, however, did not achieve Wilson's vision of national unity, as ethnic groups became antagonized and alienated in this atmosphere. Instead of becoming a component of one's national identity, as Nelson Lichtenstein has noted, ethnicity became insularized, "a cultural mechanism of self-protection."[4]

With "100 percent Americanism" the dominant narrative of patriotism during World War I, however, great pressure was placed on individuals to purchase bonds or be labeled "slackers." A popular slogan of the Liberty Loan campaign was "Buy Until It Hurts," an indication of the popular sentiment surrounding the drives. Stamp and bond purchasers were urged to wear badges and medals as a sign of their patriotism, indirectly pressuring those who had not into buying them. Fear of being publicly shamed even drove many Americans to take out bank loans to purchase Liberty Bonds. In Philadelphia, the Liberty Bell was rung every night at nine o'clock, familiarly recognized as a "dirge for slackers." Along with clothing, one laundry service delivered cards reading "Buy Liberty Bonds today, because if the kaiser wins, good night shirt!" A personnel superintendent wrote in a report that "co-workers of any slacker use the necessary moral (and physical) suasion upon those declining to participate." As historians Charles and Mary Beard wrote, "Whoever refused to answer the [Liberty Loan] call was liable to be blacklisted by his neighbors or associate and enrolled in the Doom Book in the Department of Justice." Even Mennonites, who refused to purchase Liberty Bonds on the basis of conscientious objection to war in general, were intimidated or coerced into buying bonds, faced with the real threat of having their houses painted yellow or being tarred and feathered.[5]

Many of the huge number of Americans who had emigrated from Europe were put under particular pressure to demonstrate public support for the war, as overt signs of ethnicity were considered an indication of potential divided allegiances. Over the twenty-five years preceding the onset of World War I, about eight million immigrants came to the United States, most of them from countries involved in the war. Retaining loyalties to the Old World, the administration believed, was a catalyst for a divided population split along the lines of ethnic background. National origin was officially perceived as the basis for what President Wilson called "camps of hostile opinion, hot against each other." For these suspect groups, buying bonds, singing the national anthem in public, and displaying the American flag became important symbols of national loyalty, as well as measures of avoiding psychological or physical threat. Americans of recent foreign origin and their children were thus effectively forced to show their undivided allegiance to the United States through the purchase of Liberty Bonds. "Challenges [were made to] aliens or their descendants to 'prove their patriotism' by buying more bonds than they can afford," *Colliers* recalled.[6]

A relatively small but important part of the Treasury's campaign to sell Liberty Bonds during World War I was thus directed to ethnic Americans and, to a much lesser extent, African Americans. Bond promotion to ethnic groups often reflected the administration's philosophy of 100 percent Americanism, designed to pressure first- or second-generation Americans to show support for the war through the purchase of bonds. Posters with headlines such as "Are You 100% American? Prove It! Buy U.S. Government Bonds" (1917) reflected the suspicion the Wilson administration held toward ethnic Americans' national loyalty. Other posters, such as "Americans All!" (1919), listed an "honor roll" of ethnically diverse bond purchasers, including "DuBois, Smith, O'Brien, Cejka, Houcke, Pappandrikopolous, Andrassi, Villoto, Levy, Turorich, Kowalski, Chriczanevicz, Knutson, and Gonzalez." Rather than celebrating ethnicity or difference, however, "Americans All!" delivered the message that unity and conformity to the white Anglo-Saxon ideal was the appropriate means of achieving victory. Pluralism during World War I, and specifically in bond promotion, was thus defined in melting-pot terms, assimilation expected as the ultimate cultural destination of ethnic Americans.[7]

Bond promotion directed to ethnic Americans during World War I also depicted the immigrant experience itself on occasion. For the Second Liberty Loan, for example, the Treasury distributed posters that read, "Remember Your First Thrill of American Liberty. Your Duty—Buy United States Government Bonds" (1917), featuring an illustration of immigrants on the deck of a steamship looking toward the Statue of Liberty. Similarly, for the Third Liberty Loan, a 1917 poster with the headline "Remember! The Flag of Liberty. Support It! Buy U.S. Government Bonds" portrayed an immigrant family on a dock in front of a steamer. Another poster depicted a group of immigrants on line to buy war savings stamps from Uncle Sam, with Russians, Scots, Gypsies, Swiss, and Greeks clearly identifiable by their traditional Old World dress. These posters were intended not only to raise money to fund the war but also to create a sense of "patriotic unity" among recently arrived, still ethnically attached Americans. Recognizing that many immigrants did not speak English, the Treasury also distributed bond posters printed in foreign languages such as Italian, Czech, Russian, and Hebrew.[8]

Although not new immigrants, African Americans faced the possibility of further discrimination should they not show public support for the war. Given the social and political climate during World War I, the NAACP recommended that African Americans postpone their pursuit of equal rights and demonstrate support for the war by enlisting and purchasing bonds. W. E. B. Du Bois urged blacks to join whites in the fight for democracy, the appropriate decision at the time, given popular and official opinion regarding opposition to administration policy. Many African Americans expected that their support of the war effort would result in the administration's granting them greater civil rights after the war. The decision to align fully with the government during the war ultimately worked to their disadvantage, however, as no real gains resulted from this disruption of a nascent civil rights movement.

There were only minimal efforts by the Treasury to promote bonds to African Americans during World War I, as blacks could never conform to the dominant white, Anglo-Saxon vision of American identity. One poster of 1918, however, produced by Touissant Studios, featured a black American soldier from the Fifteenth New York Regiment charging into a German trench. The poster read, "We Are Doing Our Bit" and included facts about the Liberty Loan campaign.

In his history of the NAACP, Charles Flint Kellogg found that the organization supported the Fourth Liberty Loan drive, joining the National Association of Colored Women to sell and buy bonds in the South. Some white chairs of bond committees, Kellogg noted, refused to work with the African American women, but still, "good results among Negro citizens were reported." The Liberty Loan poster and bond drive demonstrated that African Americans were indeed contributing to the war effort, and that the Treasury wanted to persuade other blacks to enlist and purchase bonds. Although these were relatively minor efforts, the conscious attempt to reach blacks with the war bond message was an indication that the Wilson administration did indeed aim to win African Americans' national loyalty during World War I.[9]

In addition to the many social problems associated with World War I bonds, Liberty Bonds were negotiable, tied to fluctuating market rates. At one point, in fact, Liberty Bonds fell in value to a low of $82 for a $100 bond. Professional security dealers, eager to take bonds out of the hands of unhappy Liberty Bond holders, eventually made a handsome profit as market prices rose. Many Americans deservedly felt cheated by their Liberty Bond experience. Despite these major problems, however, bond campaigns during World War I were not without merit. Boy Scouts sold Liberty and

Victory Bonds and stamps, a forerunner to the extensive youth sales force employed in World War II. About $21.5 billion worth of Liberty and Victory Bonds were sold, a huge amount of revenue raised in just a two-year campaign. Most influential, the broad prosperity of the 1920s can in part be attributed to the postwar maturation of Liberty Loan investments among the wealthy, their capital gains effectively fueling the American economy.[10]

Outside the Liberty Loan program, the Vanderlip War Savings Campaign, formed in October 1917, was an effective, well-managed program before being merged with the Liberty Loan campaign in the summer of 1918. The campaign was orchestrated by Frank A. Vanderlip, a New York banker and expert in war finance, who modeled it after the British bond program. The goal of the independent Vanderlip campaign was to educate Americans on the value of thrift, with total sales of secondary importance. Unlike the Liberty Loan program, centered around the dominant white, Anglo-Saxon, Protestant American identity, the Vanderlip campaign honored ethnic loyalties alongside mainstream patriotic support. Ethnic Americans were appealed to in their own language, demonstrating that nationalism and pluralism were not necessarily mutually exclusive. A generation later, Treasury officials would incorporate many of the features of the Vanderlip campaign into the World War II defense bond program.[11]

Following the government's controversial bond program of World War I, no effort was made by the Harding, Coolidge, and Hoover administrations (all Republican) to offer bonds as a savings instrument to the smaller investor. In the midst of the Depression, however, Secretary of the Treasury Henry Morgenthau envisioned bonds could play an important economic role for the country as well as the ordinary citizen. Impressed with savings programs in place in Scandinavia, France, and England while on a 1934 trip to Europe, Secretary Morgenthau believed that a similar program could entice people to start saving again and, ultimately, revive Americans' faith in the national economy. For the Treasury's benefit, broader distribution of public debt would provide a safeguard against another economic collapse. Under Morgenthau's leadership, and as an amendment to the Second Liberty Loan Act of 1917, Congress authorized the distribution of Series A savings bonds on February 4, 1935, and sales of the bonds commenced March 1.[12]

Between March 1, 1935, and April 30, 1941, only one class of bonds was offered by the administration, although the series ultimately progressed from A to D. The bonds were partially tax exempt and had a ten-thousand-dollar maturity value annual limit. Despite having no sales organization in place, except the nation's fourteen thousand post offices, and no dedicated marketing campaign, sales of Series A bonds climbed. Encouraged by the potential of "baby bonds," Secretary Morgenthau created the Division of Savings Bonds in March 1936. In July, the Treasury began an aggressive direct-mail campaign to promote the program, sending out 125,000 pieces of mail a month. Already the largest direct marketer in the world, the Treasury next obtained taxpayer names and addresses, compiling a mailing list of 7 million people. Over the six-year campaign, the Treasury sent 30 million pieces of mail to the American people to promote United States Savings Bonds.[13]

With this unprecedented direct-marketing campaign as support, sales of U.S. Savings Bonds grew steadily from fiscal year 1935 to April 1941:[14]

Fiscal Year	Sales ($ million)
1935 (March 1–June 30)	63
1936	264
1937	515
1938	488
1939	688
1940	1,107
1941 (July 1–April 30)	824

Despite these respectable results, a closer analysis revealed that as during World War I, it was larger investors who accounted for most of Savings Bonds sales volume. Ninety-five percent of total revenues were in fact purchased in denominations of one hundred dollars or more, as wealthy individuals, banks, and corporations took advantage of the attractive interest rate and tax exemptions. With no field sales organization, no retail outlet except post offices managed by workers who were indifferent to the program, and limited advertising, the Treasury could not effectively persuade most smaller investors to buy bonds.[15]

Although the Defense Savings Program would not be formally launched until May 1941, there were earlier indications that the small investor would soon play a key role in the Treasury's bond program. In late 1939, America's stepped-up efforts in preparation for war began to have a direct impact on the Treasury's borrowing strategies and activities. First and foremost, it was clear to the Treasury that the nation's debt ceiling would soon have to be raised to support the potential cost of war. In 1940, actual defense costs were already accounting for 18 percent of the government's total expenditures (ultimately reaching a high of 92 percent of total expenditures in 1944). If history was a good judge, the potential cost for the United States of another world war would be huge. Treasury officials in 1940 began to plan for greater defense spending, which was predicated on raising the national debt ceiling. To help make its case, the Treasury estimated that the American Revolution cost $100 million, the Civil War, $7 billion, and World War I, $31 billion. A global war in the 1940s, the Treasury estimated, could cost the United States hundreds of billions of dollars. Backed up by President Roosevelt's Four Freedoms speech to Congress on January 6, 1941, Secretary Morgenthau went before the House Ways and Means Committee on January 29 to petition Congress for passage of the Public Debt Act of 1941, which would raise the national debt limit to $65 billion and give the Treasury broader authority to issue bonds. The act was passed in February, and with the passage of Treasury Department Order No. 39 on March 19, 1941, Secretary Morgenthau put the wheels of motion in place to sell defense bonds by creating the Defense Savings Staff.[16]

Beyond financing a potential war, a defense bond program was viewed by Treasury officials as a means to stem the rising threat of inflation. Inflation was perceived as an "insidious enemy," the home-front equivalent of a treacherous foreign foe. The analogy was extended as excess consumer spending power was labeled by the Treasury as "dangerous dollars." Both history and economic theory suggested that spiraling inflation would result from increased demand for consumer goods and rising prices as factories retooled for war-related production. As the cost of war rose, in the most simple terms, so would the cost of living. Therein resided the major paradox of wartime prosperity, that despite a rise in income, there is typically a shortage of consumer products and services. In addition to direct measures to minimize inflation, then, such as price and wage freezes, the Treasury planned to divert excess dollars from the economy, that is, to "immobilize" consumers' spending power. The government could achieve its two primary economic objectives—fund the war and stem inflation—simultaneously by taking money out of consumers' hands and putting it into its own.[17]

The key question for the administration was how to acquire funds, the two options being taxation or borrowing. As outlined in the definitive source at the time, John Maynard Keynes's *How to Pay for the War*, taxes were superior to borrowing over the long term in that the former required no payback by the government. Taxes, however, were slow to collect and inequitably assessed, whereas borrowing was immediate and enabled widespread ownership of the public debt. With 98 percent of Americans in 1940 having incomes of five thousand dollars or less, taxation would draw the bulk of funds from higher income groups, whereas borrowing could provide a revenue stream from all income groups. Although taxation was thus superior to borrowing in fighting inflation from a purely economic standpoint, borrowing represented a more "democratic" means of financing the war and minimizing inflation. From a lay point of view, bonds made one feel richer, whereas taxes made one feel poorer, and common sense suggested that gaining the support of ordinary citizens would be easier and more effective if Americans felt they were not only contributing to a national cause but also gaining financially. The decision to target bonds to a popularly based citizenry stemmed from economic programs of the New Deal and contrasted markedly with the Treasury's World War I bond experience, which was rooted in sales to banks and corporations.[18]

Expanding the promising if fledgling bond program was thus chosen by the Treasury over total taxation. Secretary Morgenthau determined that sale of securities in small denominations to private investors, versus banks, would not only raise funds but also act as a hedge against out-of-control inflation. By taking money out of the economy for an extended period of time through the purchase of bonds, Keynesian theory went, there would be less currency in the system to fuel inflation. As Alan Brinkley has noted, President Roosevelt was particularly sensitive to the issue of inflation, knowing that Americans held him personally responsible for high prices in the marketplace. As the nation slowly emerged from the Depression, both the prices of goods and services and consumer credit were rising, and gold and capital flowing out of Europe into the United States compounded the problem. By augmenting an aggressive borrowing program with other anti-inflation measures such as rationing and price/wage freezes, the Treasury believed, significant synergies could be created. The Treasury's defense bond program was thus conceived as one of a number of measures the administration could use to stem wartime inflation and lessen the threat of postwar inflation. During the war, the Office of Price Administration (OPA), created in 1942 by the Emergency Price Control Act, would function as the administration's primary agency working to control inflation.[19]

Together, higher taxes, OPA controls, and the Treasury's bond program were thus designed to work as a powerful combination of Keynesian theory applied to a wartime economy. Higher taxes, the OPA's price controls, wage freezes, and rationing would operate in marketing terms as "push" strategies—direct, legally enforced actions that contained laissez-faire marketplace supply and demand. The bond program, on the other hand, would work through "pull" strategies, designed around Americans themselves stemming inflation by voluntarily taking excess dollars out of what Katznelson and Pictrykowski called the "artificially overheated war economy characterized by shortages of consumer goods." From a macro standpoint, higher taxes, OPA measures, and the bond program would act symbiotically, a multipurpose package of Keynesian fiscal policy arguing for both "top-down" and "bottom-up" tactics. The Treasury's tiered plan to (1) tax heavily but not completely, (2) borrow as much as possible from nonbanks, and (3) borrow the rest from banks would make it a "people's war" without violating the American creed of free enterprise.[20]

Launching a full-scale effort to sell government securities to the average citizen was also viewed by Secretary Morgenthau as a way to bridge the historical divisions between capital and the state. Since the 1937 recession, a debate had raged among key administrative officials regarding how to get the country out of Depression. Morgenthau was convinced that private investors' reluctance to take financial risks was a crucial factor in the persistently lagging economy. Capital not unreasonably viewed New Deal administration policies as antibusiness and resisted expansion within what they perceived as a hostile, overbureaucratic climate. Throughout 1937 and 1938, Morgenthau led a personal campaign to reach out to big business in an attempt to establish a more stable and growth-oriented economy. Morgenthau believed that creating a sound economy was dependent on forming what Brinkley called a "stable concert of interests among the state, business, and labor." He sought to ease the burdens of governmental regulations on big business and the financial community in particular, so that corporate America would again be willing to invest and drive the nation's economic growth.[21]

With the defense bond program structured around a codependent, mutually beneficial relationship between the Federal Reserve and private banks, a unique opportunity to bring together government and business emerged. The Treasury's program could not only help the economy by fighting inflation but also act as a device to stimulate private interests in order to serve public ones. Defense bonds were thus an extension of what Robert Lekachman termed "commercial Keynesianism," the pursuit of economic growth through fiscal policy. Just as the administration chose to contract with private capital to produce defense equipment and materials, it established an alliance with big business through the promotion and sale of bonds. The bond program proved to ease New Deal antagonisms between business and the state resulting from social Keynesian policies, and to help build a wartime (and postwar) economic partnership. On an even larger scale, both public and private interests and traditional class divisions blurred as a result of the bond program's dual offerings of patriotism and financial gain. The administration's use of bonds to bring in labor interests would ultimately form a consensus triumvirate of government, capital, and unions during the war years.[22]

The economic deal thus struck between the government and the American people was that through a combination of higher taxes and loans from bonds the former would gain liquid assets for the present emergency without significantly disrupting the latter's standard of living. Excess money would be diverted from the marketplace to the government, creating a save-versus-spend ethos. This plan to temporarily postpone consumerism was the essence of what the Treasury termed "the voluntary way," the democratic idea that Americans were voluntarily contributing to the war effort. The voluntary way stood in contrast to nondemocratic compulsory lending or saving programs recommended by Keynesian theory (and briefly considered by Secretary Morgenthau in September 1942, when Treasury debt levels hit new highs). Morgenthau felt strongly that voluntary contribution was an integral part of the American Way, and was more effective on a psychological level than compulsory savings. Learning again from the Liberty Loan campaigns in which "top-down" pressure and coercion to buy bonds alienated many Americans, the Treasury was determined to sell bonds during the new crisis from the "bottom-up."[23]

Morgenthau's demand that the defense bond program remain voluntary stemmed from his populist perspective shaped by a career outside of Washington politics. From 1922 to 1933, Morgenthau was editor of a farm journal, *American Agriculture,* and served as the chair of New York state governor Franklin Roosevelt's agricultural advising committee from 1929 to 1933. A neighbor and close friend of Roosevelt, Morgenthau became secretary of the treasury when Roosevelt became president in 1935. Industrious, conservative, and with a rather gloomy disposition, Morgenthau supervised the financing of the New Deal's domestic programs, furthering his empathy for "the people." He firmly believed that a balanced budget was vital to the nation's economic stability, despite Roosevelt's actions to the contrary. As attention shifted from the domestic arena to the foreign in the late 1930s, Morgenthau translated his populist vision of economics from government spending to citizen participation in war finance. The defense bond program emerged as Morgenthau's primary articulation of economic populism, an opportunity for Americans to literally and figuratively invest in national and economic security. He believed the new program would hold special appeal for members of groups largely disenfranchised from the economic system, such as white ethnic and African Americans, many of whom still harbored suspicion toward banks. Bank failures during the Depression and discrimination by financial institutions toward the poor made federally backed, "democratic" securities a particularly attractive investment alternative for these groups.[24]

More broadly, the rise in average income was considered justification by Morgenthau and other Treasury officials for a "people's loan," a tithing as compensation for personal prosperity. Because it was the government that was responsible for the economic boom, the Treasury believed, the government could legitimately ask the American people for support in its time of need. Robert K. Merton has elaborated on this metaphor of tithing as compensation for wartime prosperity. Drawing upon Durkheim, Merton viewed the patriotism revolving around bond drives as sacred, operating on a higher plane than normal activities. Within this theoretical context, private gain is profane, representative of the opposing dimension within the Christian paradigm of heaven and earth. From this perspective, then, purchasing bonds was an opportunity to integrate sacredness into the profane world of consumer capitalism, a means to lessen potential guilt about financial gain resulting from the war buildup.[25]

As he had when creating the savings bond program in 1935, Secretary Morgenthau firmly believed that defense bonds' ideological role could be as important as their economic role, specifically by acting as a catalyst for national unity. In early 1941 Americans remained politically divided on both domestic and foreign affairs, a function in large part of the decade-long economic strain of the Depression. Many Americans were opposed to involvement in the European war, and polls showed that most Americans thought the war would be a short one. Morgenthau believed Americans did not fully grasp the country's stake in the war in Europe, and envisioned that bonds, and specifically bond drives directed to smaller investors, would be "a potentially unifying factor in a time of great public discord and uncertainty." Administrative officials conceived the Treasury's bond program acting as a "channel for unity" based around national defense, a catalyst for a more consensual society grounded in the pursuit of financial stability. Rather than attempting to resolve domestic conflicts, the administration would focus on the common goal of personal and national security. One Treasury official reflected that "national defense seemed to combine in almost perfect measure the twin blessings of patriotism and economic prosperity."[26]

Offering government securities to a broad group of potential investors was also consistent with Keynesian theory, which postulates that wars cannot be financed just by the wealthy, that some sacrifice by the working class is necessary. In order to make bonds more attractive to smaller investors, however, Secretary Morgenthau determined that they would have to be made less attractive to larger ones. Although some private investors were putting their money into savings bonds through the late 1930s, commercial banks represented the larger market because of bonds' tax-exempt status. Making government securities subject to federal taxes would deter commercial banks from monopolizing the bond market without seriously penalizing the small investor. In his speech to the House Ways and Means Committee, Morgenthau recommended that the tax exempt status of federal securities be eliminated. "Such preferential treatment to this ... class [large investors]," Morgenthau stated, "is incompatible with democratic financing of the defense program and should be removed." Changes in tax law passed as part of the Public Debt Act of 1941 made possible the offering of long-term bonds that would attract private investors and businesses while not alienating commercial banks.[27]

Although the mission of defense bonds was thus grounded in economics, specifically to raise funds to support the prewar buildup, curb inflation, and "store" surplus funds for the future, there was clearly an overt ideological role assigned to bonds as well. In his pitch to Congress, Morgenthau stressed that defense bonds could act as a vehicle to bring the country closer together. "It is the purpose of the Treasury," he declared, "to raise money for national defense by methods which strengthen the national morale." By investing in a government security, Morgenthau believed, Americans were more likely to align with the administration's political aims, particularly those related to foreign policy. As Secretary Morgenthau expressed it while the nation mobilized for defense, the government would "use bonds to sell the war, rather than vice-versa." Bonds would act as a physical reminder of the owner's stake in the European war, stand as a symbol of unity to potential enemies, and ultimately be the seeds for postwar economic prosperity should America enter the conflict. Unlike the World War I program, which was elitist and ultimately divisive, the Treasury's new program effectively translated New Deal populism into wartime capitalism and served as a tangible articulation of pluralistic democracy.[28]

Morgenthau's views regarding the propagandist power of bonds were significantly influenced by Peter Odegard, a political scientist on leave from Amherst College with whom Morgenthau consulted in March and April of 1941 as the Treasury waited for bonds and stamps to be printed. Odegard, an expert in public opinion and the dynamics of "pressure groups," recommended that the defense bond program be "a kind of campaign peculiarly adapted to the democratic pattern of American life, simultaneously exploiting and extolling American traditions and institutions." The new defense bond program differed from any other war financing plan because it eschewed involuntary methods such as taxation, forced savings, or coercion and because it was designed to permeate all aspects of everyday life. Odegard suggested that a bond sales campaign grounded in nationalism could erase defeatist attitudes still lingering from the Depression. "The first task in mobilization," he wrote, "is to enlist the latent energy of the general public." Linking defense bonds to values of strength and determination, Odegard believed, could help bring the country's divided factions—economic, political, and social—closer together, particularly when contrasted with Nazi totalitarianism. Odegard viewed the defense bond program as a means, versus an ends, of a more united America:

> Behavior begets belief quite as often as belief begets behavior. Public opinion is as much a product of what the public does as what it thinks. The experience of participation in a joint effort breeds community of purpose, conveys a sense of national direction, creates what is commonly referred to as morale. National unity is not so much the precursor as the product of united action.[29]

As the Treasury prepared to launch the defense bond campaign, the financial community looked on with bemused interest. For professional investors, government securities represented a means of making money, not a means of creating national unity or a primer in the value of thrift. With all the prepublicity, one did not have to be an expert in public opinion to recognize the cultural significance of the looming defense bond program. Two weeks before the May 1 kickoff, a reporter for the *American Banker* wrote:

> Now we are going to see the Treasury "package" its offer of paper promises for cash so as to appeal to other possibly greater stimuli—the emotions of Patriotism and Thrift.... It should be a general lesson in applied mass psychology and understanding of the way that human emotions can be used to persuade people to part with their money and save.[30]

In order to have all classes of Americans "part with their money and save," it was necessary for the Treasury to package a new line of bond products. Secretary Morgenthau, his staff, and hired advisors studied various savings programs, including the World War I Liberty Loan campaign, the Savings

Bond program, and plans in place in Great Britain and Canada. The team developed a portfolio of securities that incorporated what were considered to be the best features of the plans studied in order to meet the needs of a very wide group of investors. Designing products with particular types of consumers in mind reflected the strides made in marketing segmentation techniques between the wars. Parallel progress was made in advertising techniques, with World War II propaganda more effectively making use of emotional, "psychological" appeals.[31]

In contrast to World War I Liberty Loans, in which only one type of security was offered, three different types of securities were developed in order to segment the market according to investor size: stamps, the Series E bond, and the Series F and G bonds. Interest rates on the Treasury's new package of securities were slightly higher than those available at commercial banks, but safety was considered to be a more important criterion among both Treasury officials and consumers. Rather than fluctuating in relation to bond markets, the securities were priced at face value and earned interest until maturity. Bonds tailored to the investment needs of the "people" versus bankers reflected the antibusiness legacy of the Depression. The flagship product of the Treasury's defense bond program was the new Series E, priced at 75 percent of face value and returning a then respectable 2.9 percent interest rate. When held to full maturity of ten years, a bond purchased for $18.75, compounded semiannually, would be worth $25.00. Small denominations were considered instrumental to fulfilling the program's goals of reaching all classes of investors. Five denominations were initially offered: $25, $50, $100, $500, and $1,000, with two larger denominations, $5,000 and $10,000, offered later.[32]

Upon its introduction, the Series E bond was received favorably by the press and public. *Women's Home Companion* considered the 2.9 percent annual return to be the "best available on any obligation of comparable value." *Colliers* was somewhat less enthusiastic, but still endorsed the bond: "2.9% a year ... isn't wildcat interest but few other investments and almost no savings banks are paying any better nowadays." In designing the "new and improved" bonds, the Treasury knew that they would have to differ substantially from both World War I Liberty Bonds and the Series A–D savings bonds. Most important from the consumer's standpoint, the Series E's fixed interest rate contrasted with the variable rate of Liberty Bonds. The Treasury wanted to protect the small investor against the kind of financial risk associated with Liberty Loans, which had caused many to lose faith in government securities. Additionally, intermediate redemption yields were reduced sharply from the earlier savings bonds in order to encourage investors to hold onto the bonds until full maturity, and the limit on annual bond purchases was reduced from ten thousand to five thousand dollars. Finally, Series E bonds were issued only to individuals and could not be transferred or sold; if lost or stolen, the bonds could be replaced. All of these changes were measures intentionally taken by the Treasury to discourage larger investors from monopolizing the bond program. The Series E was, essentially, created as a security that would be considered "boring" to the professional investor yet very attractive to those who had little or no experience with government bonds, exactly the opposite of what was offered to Americans during World War I.[33]

Available in denominations of 10, 25, and 50 cents, $1.00, and $5.00, savings stamps were targeted to entry-level investors, that is, the underclass and children. Stamps were conceived as an "installment plan," in which purchasers could gradually work toward the $18.75 cost of a $25.00 bond. The ability to convert stamps into bonds when reaching the $18.75 level gave many smaller investors a reachable goal, a key principle of savings programs. The stamp program was a miniature version of the Treasury's payroll savings plan, each founded on the idea of making regular contributions to build a nest egg for the future. Savings stamps were primarily an educational and promotional device, designed to teach the principles of thrift and sacrifice. The stamps were never intended to generate a large amount of revenue, with the number sold considered more important than the dollars raised. Besides being an ideal program to sell the war to children—the aim of the Treasury's Schools at War program—savings stamps represented the idea that the defense program was for Everyman, not tailored to the interests of big business. Initially sold as postal savings stamps by the U.S. Postal Service, they were converted to United States savings stamps and sold through the Treasury beginning in September 1942.[34]

The third type of security offered, Series F and G bonds, were similar in concept to the Series E but earned lower interest rates, a clear sign of the Treasury's favoritism for the smaller investor. Targeted to larger investors, Series F and G bonds also differed from Series E in terms and purchase limits. Despite the bonds' limitations, the 2.5 percent return on F and G bonds was higher than the standard 1.5 to 2 percent offered on other government securities, which made the series attractive investments for banks and large corporations.[35]

Equally important to the investment aspects of defense bonds, easily affordable federal securities offered a safe haven for cash until the emergency was over. The failure of thousands of banks during the Depression obviously made many Americans consider alternative places to store their cash, and bonds being non-exchangeable and of value only to the purchaser were strong selling points as cash reserves began to build during the boom prewar and war years. With "investing in the future while the present was out of stock" the dominant consumer ethos, bonds became the sensible way to store extra cash and demonstrate one's national loyalty at the same time. For the Treasury, the only real danger was the possibility of sudden redemption by a large number of people. It was considered a risk worth taking.[36]

On April 30, 1941, the evening before the first day Series E bonds would be offered to the American public, President Roosevelt, Secretary Morgenthau, and the postmaster general announced the new bond program on the radio. The bonds were positioned as an opportunity to take part in the defense of America's pluralistic democracy. The climax of President Roosevelt's speech was his asking Americans to "join [him] in 'one great partnership,'" a clear sign of the administration's intent to use bonds as a vehicle to create greater national unity. In his speech, Secretary Morgenthau emphasized that defense bonds were created for "the people," not for the economical elite:

> Defense Savings Bonds and Stamps are not for the few; they are for the many. They are for the great mass of the people—for the laboring man, the skilled mechanic, the office worker, the employer, the housewife, the retired business man—even children can save their pennies to buy the stamps ... Let this be clear: your government is frankly seeking the current, regular savings of the people—all the people ... The Defense Savings Bonds and Stamps are presented as an opportunity ... for each citizen to buy a share in America.[37]

The next day, Secretary Morgenthau sold President Roosevelt the first defense bond on the Treasury's steps, the beginning of what would turn out to be called the "greatest mass selling achievement in history." Twenty years later, Morgenthau would thank Harold Graves and Peter Odegard for their contributions and declare that the defense bond program had acted as nothing less than "the spearhead for getting people interested in the war." As the tangible fusion of nationalism and consumerism, the defense bond would prove to play an integral role in the forging of the "American Way of Life" and the revival of American democratic capitalism.[38]

CHAPTER 2

★ ★ ★ **Democracy in Action**

Awarded President Roosevelt's most sacred blessing—endorsement over a coast-to-coast fireside chat—the Treasury's Defense Savings Program was officially launched on May 1, 1941. From the initial planning of the Defense Savings Program, it was understood that the Treasury's organization would consist of individuals and groups from across class and political lines. The staff of the Defense Savings Program thus directly contrasted with that of the World War I Liberty Loan campaign, which was led, and one could argue exploited, by professionals from the investment community. Government officials whose careers were forged during the New Deal wanted a more diverse, inclusive defense bond organization reflective of the pluralistic goals of the program. It was important that the "people," rather than just big business, be involved in delivering the democratic message embedded in defense bonds to all Americans. "I'm going to do it the hard way," Secretary Morgenthau said in the first weeks of the operation, "which is the democratic way."[1]

Versus the savings bond program, which relied on a "top-down," Washington-driven organization, the Treasury structured the Defense Savings Program with a small Washington staff and large field sales force. A staff of only forty, including stenographers and clerks, ran the program from Washington, supported by a huge number of volunteers in all parts of the country. In early 1941, the Treasury had compiled a list of roughly two hundred organizations considered instrumental to the program's success. These organizations represented a cross-section of American working life—business, labor, professional, farm, and education—as well as major "affiliation" organizations, such as women's, fraternal, civic, ethnic, and African American groups. Volunteers, who served as the field organization for the program, managing the bond campaign at the state and local levels, were recruited from these existing organizations. State committees operated as intermediaries between Washington and the people, implementers of specific programs on a grass-roots basis.[2]

The Treasury insisted that state chairs be named on a nonpartisan basis, that personal politics remain outside the realm of bond activities. The field organization thus reflected the Washington staff, which itself was bipartisan. Despite this policy, certain "outstanding citizens" declined the state chair post because of opposition to the Roosevelt administration's stance on a particular issue. It was considered important that leaders of the program agree on the administration's foreign policy, whereas seeing eye-to-eye on domestic issues was considered relatively unimportant.[3]

Harold N. Graves, a career bureaucrat, was chosen by Secretary Morgenthau to head the defense bond program. Named assistant to the secretary in March 1941, Graves was given the charge to study the savings bond program and put together a plan to market bonds tailored to the nation's defense needs. Graves was chosen over the longtime manager of the program, Jim Bryan, because of his experience and skill in bringing together disparate interest groups. Other key members of the Defense Savings Staff had long experience in the private sector. James L. Houghteling, named assistant to the secretary in July 1941, was chosen to head the National Organizations Division. Houghteling, a Yale graduate and "blue-blood Democrat," was formerly a banking and investment executive. He also happened to be the son-in-law of Frederick Delano, President Roosevelt's uncle and former editor of the *Chicago Daily News*. Eugene W. Sloan was selected as the staff's executive director in March 1941. Sloan, a Princeton graduate, had supervised the savings bond program since its origins in 1935 and was formerly a banking executive. Gale F. Johnston, named field director in February 1941, had been an insurance executive, and Harford Powel, named information director the same month, was a Harvard graduate who had a distinguished career in journalism and advertising with stints as editor of *Harper's Bazaar* and *Colliers*.[4]

After scouring the civil service lists, the Treasury looked to the private sector to fill jobs whose requirements often fell outside the realm of public administration. The Washington staff consisted of both volunteers (paid one dollar a year) and salaried employees (who usually took a substantial pay cut from their previous jobs). Although the leaders of the program were Ivy League–educated and had broad government and/or business experience, the staff as a whole was quite diverse. One member of the staff later recalled the eclectic mix of people in place:

> They came from everywhere and many diverse backgrounds. They came from business and the professions, from teaching and preaching and acting. They came from Foreign Funds Control, the Alcohol Tax Unit and the Secret Service, from the Departments of Commerce and Justice, from nearly every state and section of the Union. There were Irish Catholics among them, and Campbellites and Anglicans and Jews. No one knew for sure or cared what their political affiliations were. They included a rainbow of political colors, probably the largest group being Republicans, but all were agreed on one thing—the urgent need for national defense. Beyond that there were talents of every sort. Some were college graduates with more than one advanced degree. Others had stopped their formal education with the elementary school. There were lawyers, doctors, engineers, writers, "exploitation and promotion" men with talents that defied description, reformers and performers, advertising executives and newspaper reporters.[5]

With reporting lines vague and former business executives unfamiliar with governmental bureaucracy, the Defense Savings Staff became recognized as somewhat of a rogue organization within the more rigid defense administration. The objective of the Defense Savings Staff—to promote and sell bonds to the American people—also lent to the organization an air of informality and enthusiasm typically foreign to governmental affairs. The constant stream of celebrities into the Treasury building volunteering their time and effort to the cause also contributed to a circuslike atmosphere in the department. Early in the program, members of the staff were divided over what the organization's philosophy should be. One camp believed the organization should adopt a firm sales orientation, as if the Treasury were selling automobiles or chewing gum, another felt the staff's operative style should be moralistic or ideological, the group privileged to be leading a "great educational crusade to teach thrift." Although fighting inflation was the official, prescribed mission of the bond program, it was apparent from the start that within and outside the Roosevelt administration, there would be multiple interpretations of the societal role ascribed to bonds.[6]

In choosing state chairs for the field organization, particular care was taken to avoid accusations of Democratic partisanship. The increased inclusivity of Roosevelt's current administration was genuinely reflected in the Treasury's Defense Savings Staff for both symbolic and practical purposes. A bipartisan organization was essential not only to project an image of national unity but also to increase bond sales by appealing to a broader audience. "Above all it was necessary to avoid partisan considerations in the choice of . . . top state leaders," a Treasury official wrote. Although some senators and representatives pressured the Treasury to name state chairs who belonged to or at least were friendly to their own party affiliation, the Treasury "insisted on securing the best qualified men regardless of party." Bankers, newspaper publishers, and college presidents were most often picked to head state bond committees, with political affiliation not a determining factor. "In the entire history of our government it would be difficult to find a civilian organization of similar magnitude and scope from which partisan politics was so conspicuously absent," the same official wrote. "From beginning to end this policy of recruiting the best talent available without regard for party was scrupulously observed." Only hostility to Roosevelt's foreign policy was grounds for elimination from the Treasury's candidate pool, with isolationists screened out or, more likely, declining to serve.[7]

The creation of a distinctly bipartisan bond organization was consistent with the transformation of the political landscape in the late 1930s and into the war. Appointing conservatives to key Treasury posts and in the field was emblematic of the administrationwide "liberal diaspora" that accelerated as the nation prepared for war. Alan Brinkley noted that the Treasury was "invaded by corporate figures, conservatives, and reactionaries," with precious few New Dealers around by the end of 1943. As in other agencies, liberal New Dealers on the Defense Savings Staff complained that the organization was being "loaded with conservatives," but political differences were more often than not put aside and common ground found. The invasion of business executives within the Treasury was particularly heavy because of the department's new role as bond marketer, but was also a function of Secretary Morgenthau's personal mission to bridge the gap between government and capital. Morgenthau's vision of a "new liberalism," Brinkley wrote, required that the administration be "committed above all to a newer vision of a consumer-driven economy." Bringing in representatives from corporate America and going into partnership with big business through the selling of bonds were each strategies Morgenthau used to realize greater national security grounded in broad-based economic stability.[8]

In addition to its serving as a vehicle for a new brand of liberalism, the Treasury's bond program functioned as one of various avenues of the state-building process immediately preceding and during the war. The Roosevelt administration policed home-front activities through the Office of Price Administration, which regulated wages and prices and rationed goods. Consisting mostly of a voluntary "watchdog" force, the OPA administered retail and wholesale prices, monitored rents, and distributed ration coupons. Because the OPA interfered directly with the workings of the marketplace (its very intent), however, the organization was commonly viewed as intrusive and overly bureaucratic. The agency became a critical target among business people who objected to governmental price controls, politicians who resented its power, and consumers angry about inequities in the rationing process. Many felt that the OPA overstepped the boundaries of American government, and represented the potentially dangerous element of state power. From a people perspective, the OPA was essentially doomed to failure. Although purportedly nonpartisan, the OPA was led largely by upper-class Republicans, negatively labeled "volunteer housewives" by Deputy Administrator John Kenneth Galbraith. Failing to attract a pluralistic team of volunteers, marked particularly by an absence of African Americans, the OPA could not effectively enforce its power on a broad social level.[9]

Another principal organization mobilized to serve national interests was the Red Cross. Although private, the Red Cross functioned along quasi-official lines, providing the military with nurses and nurses' aides. Services the Red Cross offered included first aid, water safety, home nursing, nutrition classes, canteen operations, and accident prevention. D'Ann Campbell found that the organization allowed many American women to find "an outlet for patriotism that strengthened their private domain." By lifting morale and raising consciousness of the war effort, Campbell observed, the Red Cross succeeded in bringing the distant, remote war "to the local and personal" and added a dimension of patriotism to family responsibilities. Despite its strong effort and good intentions, however, the Red Cross also suffered from class and racial divisions. The organization's mostly middle-class volunteers were often alienated from its mostly upper-class staff, the latter having "elitist social pretensions" and disdain for its own volunteers. Worse, the Red Cross failed to adequately serve the black community and became a symbol of discrimination by segregating blood by race.[10]

Charged with the mission to reflect true "democracy in action," the Treasury organized Defense Savings Committees in some three thousand counties, sixteen thousand incorporated cities and towns, and twenty thousand unincorporated communities. The Treasury urged that representatives be drawn from all major social and economic groups, and that committees reflect the demographic makeup of a particular community. This policy generally did not present a problem, even in unusual situations, such as some committees in the Midwest being composed of what would otherwise be a disproportionate number of farmers. In areas of the country with a significant number of ethnic or African Americans, however, conflict occasionally arose. Ethnic groups in the Northeast, for example, insisted in some cases that committees include a heavy representation of first- or second-generation Americans to reflect their community's makeup. Jim Crow in the South made the situation even more problematic, as whites often refused to serve on the same committee as blacks. The role of women was equally unclear, with women included on major committees in some communities and forced to form separate ones in others. To help resolve these organizational issues, deputy administrators would eventually be added to many committees to work with particular groups, such as farmers, labor, women, schools, members of white ethnic groups, and African Americans.[11]

With the cooperation of key representatives from management and labor, particularly from the insurance industry, the Defense Savings Staff orchestrated a payroll deduction plan for the purchase of defense bonds, which would prove to be the source of a huge amount of bond revenues. Labor and corporate America each enthusiastically endorsed the plan early in the defense bond sales campaign. The American Federation of Labor (AFL) and the CIO agreed to support the sale of bonds to their members, William Green, president of the AFL, going so far as to say, "Nothing could be finer for national psychology at this time." On the corporate side, virtually every major company in the country began to institute a payroll savings plan by which weekly or monthly deductions could be made from employees' salaries toward the purchase of bonds. From literally day one of the defense bond program, there were signs that bonds would act as Morgenthau had envisioned, a central rallying point for both sellers and buyers in a united effort to prepare for war and defend American democracy. The Treasury's bond program created an unprecedented alliance among business, labor, and the state, bringing together these institutions to sell not only bonds but also the idea of the war to all Americans.[12]

Equipped with a national organization, the Defense Savings Staff spread the gospel of investment through all available channels. Rather than pay for advertising, the Treasury made the decision early in the program's planning stages to solicit free media space and time or else "borrow" space in other advertisers' ads. As in World War I, Congress did not want the American people's money going toward nonmilitary war costs. As well, the Treasury believed that voluntary contributions on the part of business and labor was more consistent with the overall concept of defense bonds, that is, personal sacrifice for the common good. Defense bond advertising thus "rode" on ads placed by marketers in newspapers and magazines, and radio stations donated time for bond promotion spots. Posters promoting defense bonds were placed in buildings in both the public and private sectors. The Treasury's publicity machine was turned on, filling the media with human interest stories of great personal sacrifice related to the selling or purchasing of bonds. The workings of what would become "the greatest mass selling achievement in history" had been put in place.[13]

With this initial promotional campaign, broad awareness of the Treasury's defense bond program was achieved virtually instantaneously. According to Gallup polls, 91 percent of those asked were aware of the program after only one month, and by October 1941, only five months after the campaign's official start and still two months before America's entry in the war, 97 percent of those surveyed had at least heard of defense bonds and stamps. Reaching market saturation levels in such a short period of time was unheard of in the business world. "To my knowledge," a leading advertising executive commented in July, "no promotional campaign, commercial, governmental, or Goebbels', has ever spread its basic message so broadly, so quickly."[14]

Despite broad awareness of the Treasury's new bond program, initial sales of defense bonds were respectable but hardly spectacular. Bond sales in England were, not surprisingly, much higher, having had the dubious advantage of a two-year head start and having been spurred by German blitzkriegs.[15] Lukewarm sales of defense bonds were considered by the press to be a function of the Treasury's dull posters and literature, part of the intentional attempt to avoid the hoopla surrounding the sale of World War I Liberty Bonds. Some, however, criticized the Treasury for not being more aggressive, that hoopla was in fact the American Way:

> Anything worth selling is worth selling with fireworks and whoopla. And all experience in the advertising business proves that the American people have been educated to shy off anything that lacks ballyhoo and showmanship. They love these things. Hen, and they'd have gobbled up bonds as fast as you could have turned 'em out if you hadn't acted as if you was selling ice in Labrador. What was good enough for Woodrow Wilson back in 1917 ought to be good enough for us in 1941.[16]

Other critics viewed Americans' initial ambivalent response to the defense bond campaign as a result of their newfound prosperity:

An announced objective of reducing purchasing power doesn't register very well with folks whose pay envelopes are growing fat after many lean years. Inflation or no, they are enjoying the sensation of spending a few sawbucks.[17]

Opposition to the program from some remaining isolationists, such as Representative Louis Ludlow (D-Indiana) and Representative John Taber (R–New York), did not help the defense bond cause. "What is the necessity of putting on this campaign?" asked Ludlow a couple of weeks into the program. "Is it to get more people interested in the Government?" Taber was particularly critical of the Treasury's spending on its budding promotional campaign. "I do not know but ... we may be ... put[ting] the WPA artists [back] to work to get out a number of these foolish posters," he sneered. "They have 3,000 more of them on the roll than a year ago, with nothing to do."[18]

With the defense bond program working well from a propaganda standpoint but less so in terms of generating revenues, the bombing of Pearl Harbor and the country's entry into the war in December 1941 instantly recast the role of bonds in American society. Bond sales immediately rose, as Americans eagerly looked for ways to strike back at the Axis aggressors. Many actually turned their bonds in for cancellation, so that the government would not have to pay back the investor either the face value of the bond or any interest. More remarkable, the Treasury started to receive outright gifts on an unsolicited basis: cash, securities, jewelry, even gold teeth began to flood in. Forty-two stenographers, in fact, had to be hired by the Treasury just to process the unsolicited contributions. Secretary Morgenthau, speaking at a conference of three hundred bond organizers just a few days after Pearl Harbor, recognized the immediate heightened social significance of bonds: "[Bonds have] helped greatly to crystallize American opinion [and will] give the American people a sense of their own direct and inescapable involvement in this great battle for our way of life."[19]

The bombing of Pearl Harbor and Americans' new enthusiasm for bonds also had a positive effect on the perception of the Treasury's program among the media. "Since the country is united as never before in its history," the *Washington Star* reservedly wrote ten days after the bombing, "the success of this drive may be reasonably expected." The *Saginaw News* was more enthusiastic, extending Roosevelt's idea of partnership in business terms. "Every gift of defense stamps or bonds," the newspaper wrote six days before Christmas 1941, "carries with it a formally subscribed partnership in the greatest business on earth—the defense of the free way of life."[20]

The financial community recognized the gap bonds could fill in the marketplace given the lack of available consumer goods and services, perhaps more so than the Treasury itself. One day after the bond conference the *American Banker* observed:

> During the course of the next dozen months or so, the installment purchasing contracts of millions of American buyers for motor cars, refrigerators and the like will run out, and for most of these buyers there is going to be a period when they will not be able to purchase anything else because of priorities.... Wherefore the idea occurs to us that it would be good practice for every installment buyer to be considered a Defense Bond prospect the day he makes his final payment. The case needs to be put up to him, and pretty strongly, that all or part of the regular monthly payment amounts ought to be put into Defense Bonds with equal monthly regularity.[21]

Others felt that bonds would only hurt the economy, not help it. Laissez-faire capitalists insisted that the marketplace should regulate the supply and demand of goods, not the kind of artificial controls embraced by the Keynesians. "It is fine to give the scriptural tenth to church and charity," wrote the *Chattanooga News Free Press* in January 1942, "but any giving policy that tends to strangle trade and reduce the earning capacity of the people is poor economics." To most in the media, however, investment in bonds was seen as a means to simultaneously fuel the military machine and pave a course toward greater economic stability. For most Americans—both experts and lay people—World War II was seen as a war of production that the United States would inevitably win because of its greater industrial power. Victory was more a matter of time than a possibility. Although Americans felt confident we would not lose the military war, there was a belief that the nation could lose the domestic war of financial security. The parallels between the military war being fought overseas and the financial war being fought at home was made clear to help sell bonds. "The sober ultimate truth is that only our personal savings can now save our civilization," lamented the *Readers Digest* in August 1942.[22]

With the outcome of the war rarely seriously in doubt, however, bonds were presented as and broadly understood to be a loan versus a contribution, their value assured. Bonds were billed as "invisible greenbacks," in every way equivalent to or even better than money. Given this orientation, the future postwar role of bonds proved to be a source of great interest by both the Treasury and the media throughout the duration of the war and the bond program. Popular opinion was that excessive spending would lead not only to wartime inflation but also to postwar depression. Germany in the 1920s was viewed as the worst-case scenario, the most vivid example of a postwar economy out of control. Bonds thus represented not only a means of combating wartime inflation but a promise of postwar economic stability and prosperity. "Small holdings of defense bonds in every home," wrote the *Great Falls (Mont.) Tribune* in January 1942, only one month after America's entry in the war, "represent an accumulation of buying power after the war is over that will stabilize the country and safe-guard our democratic system." This willingness to postpone the fruits of economic prosperity, stemming from Americans' experience in the 1930s, laid the groundwork for the maintenance of a thrift ethos not only during the scarcities of the 1940s but also during the abundant 1950s.[23]

Sales of defense bonds continued strong through the winter of 1942 but began to slump in the spring. The Treasury still did not have a very aggressive marketing campaign, and Americans appeared reluctant to continually invest heavily in bonds on their own behalf. About $6 billion of bonds were sold over the first year of the program, a substantial amount but not nearly enough to cover the costs of the war. Moreover, only a half of the bonds sold to date were Series E, an indication that, as in World War I's Liberty Loan campaign, a disproportionate percentage of big business and the wealthy were taking advantage of the financial incentives offered by the government. It was clear to all that without more effectively reaching the "people," neither the economic objective of fighting inflation nor the ideological objective of uniting a splintered American public would be realized.[24]

Meanwhile, debt was increasing rapidly as expenditures for the war grew, and the administration came under significant pressure to raise more capital. Morgenthau in particular became the target of intense scrutiny, his highly flouted bond program in danger of being labeled a flop. As the national debt hit an all-time high of $17 billion, heads of key government agencies—Marriner Eccles of the Federal Reserve, Harold Smith of the Budget Bureau, and Leon Henderson of the Office of Price Administration—petitioned President Roosevelt for forced savings. Members of the Ways and Means Committee argued that forced savings or a tax increase was necessary, and even many New Deal advisors had serious doubts about the bond program's ability to generate sufficient funds. In a demonstration of his confidence in Morgenthau and "the voluntary way," however, Roosevelt decided to back Morgenthau and the democratic goals of the bond program. As a backup, a compulsory savings plan was prepared to be quickly put in place on July 1, 1942, should the Treasury's bond program continue to falter.[25]

Given another life, the Defense Savings Staff, now the War Savings Staff, took three major steps to more aggressively promote the sale of defense bonds, now called war bonds. First, Secretary Morgenthau set a $1 billion per month quota to begin in July, the amount deemed necessary to fund the war and prevent inflation. The $1 billion per month figure translated to 10 percent of the total national income, which, in turn, translated to 10 percent of each family's income. From then on, bond sales in all 3,070 counties in the United States would be measured against estimates of what the Treasury believed sales should be, putting in motion the use of more high-powered tactics throughout the organization.[26]

Second, the staff redoubled its efforts directed at the payroll savings program, which was proving to be the source of a major portion of total bond sales. The payroll savings plan was based on "salary savings plans" already in place in some businesses, but represented a new idea for most employers. AT&T was the first employer to have adopted such a plan, starting one in the early days of the savings bond program in 1936, but other large companies, such as General Motors and General Electric, enthusiastically supported the plan early in the defense bond program. Such a plan was designed to instill thrift within America's labor force, thrift being a wholesome, redeeming value considered especially scarce among the working class (particularly African Americans), who were believed to have poor savings habits. The plan was also looked to as a means of facilitating good relations between labor and management, another way that bonds could act as a bridge between divided factions.[27]

The Treasury redefined its goal for the payroll savings plan as "90-10," 90 percent company participation, 10 percent of total company payroll. The new official slogan for the bond program became "Let's Make Every Pay Day Bond Day," reflecting the prioritization of the payroll savings plan by the Treasury. By October 1942, twenty-two million Americans, or 22 percent of all adults, had purchased bonds in the Treasury's payroll savings plan, a significant increase over participation rates in the spring. Due largely to greater enrollment in the plan, the much sought after shift from the large investor to the small one was taking place. Sixty-four percent of total bond sales between December 1941 and September 1942 were of the Series E, a good indication that war bonds were indeed becoming the "people's bond." At its peak in the summer of 1944 and spring of 1945, twenty-seven million Americans participated in the payroll savings plan, with an average 76 percent participation in companies offering the plan. Certain individuals, such as farmers, professionals, housewives, and the self-employed, could not participate in the payroll savings plan, although the

Treasury did set up a plan in which regular purchases by such individuals could be made. Secretary Morgenthau, his somewhat dour demeanor now firmly linked to the puritanical value of thrift by his consistent endorsement of the payroll savings plan, became popularly known in the press as "Henry the Morgue."[28]

The third way in which the Treasury acted to more aggressively promote bonds was through the Victory Fund drive, which would turn out to be the first of seven war loans. The Treasury had resisted adopting the "drive" technique, which had been used exclusively in World War I, because it was considered to be contrary to the goal of revenue continuity. Systematic, repeated purchases from current earnings were viewed as superior to drives in fighting inflation. Additionally, sporadic drives were a less efficient means of achieving the Treasury's ideological objectives. Faced with the pressure from Congress, other federal agencies, and the media, however, Morgenthau decided to supplement the ongoing bond program with periodic loan drives to generate more sales. In order to explore the market potential of loan drives, the Treasury tested a bond drive in Vineland, New Jersey, which resulted in an overwhelming rise in incremental bond sales. Given the success of the test drive and the need to bolster sales, drives were integrated within the total bond program. The Victory Fund Committee, an organization independent of the War Savings Staff, was assigned responsibility for the first two drives until it was folded into the latter organization.[29]

With quotas, stepped-up efforts on the payroll savings plan, and periodic drives now providing a steady cash flow to Treasury reserves, the administration turned its attention to meeting the ideological objectives of the bond program. The program's primary mission—to sell the idea of the war to all Americans in order to create a more unified country—was part of President Roosevelt's broader design to ease tensions and divisions on the home front. Roosevelt's vision of how the war could influence popular opinion at home trickled down through his administration, crystallizing the belief that the war presented an opportunity to create social harmony. "By making this a 'people's' war for freedom," two government officials wrote in February 1942, "we can help clear up the alien problem, the negro problem, and the anti-Semitic problem." With specific regard to "the negro problem," Roosevelt's positioning of the war as a fight for freedom was a much more palatable proposition than passing and enforcing antidiscrimination laws, as the latter was viewed as politically suicidal given the president's dependence upon support from southern democrats. Secretary Morgenthau echoed the administration's perspective, seeing bonds as an ideal vehicle to create a more unified America. "When the people really become aflame with the war spirit," he said in May 1943, "all the other problems seem to solve themselves.... The sale of war bonds ... is actually a barometer of the spirit and enthusiasm of the Home Front."[30]

In order to create the image if not the reality of a fully united nation, the Treasury, in cooperation with the Office of War Information and other governmental agencies, used the selling and buying of bonds as a central part of a dedicated propaganda campaign. Soon after the country entered the war, the Defense Savings Staff distributed a pamphlet titled *Our America* featuring photographs of and comments from "real Americans" regarding their reasons for purchasing bonds. The personalized experiences came from a cross-section of individuals, clearly labeled by their occupation or social status: railroad mechanic, rancher, steelworker, flight stewardess, teacher, schoolboy, doctor, farmer, mother, business man, freight car brakeman, and secretary. By presenting the image of America as a patchwork quilt of individuals united through the common activity of buying bonds, the Treasury was attempting to blur the social divisions of class, age, geography, and gender. The Treasury invited readers to forward their own "25-word statement... giving your reason for wanting to own a share in America."[31]

Because of its ideological mission to create greater national unity and social harmony, the Treasury's bond program during World War II demanded an unprecedented effort to reach out to all segments of the population. Bonds were seen as a means to bridge not only the social divisions of class, age, geography, and gender but also those of ethnicity and race. The Treasury devoted special energy to reaching a number of traditionally marginalized groups, such as women, children, white ethnic groups, and African Americans, as inviting these groups to participate in the bond program was perceived by the administration as a nonthreatening means to achieve a more unified, harmonious nation.

Morgenthau recognized early on in the bond program that bridging the country's divisions in order to realize greater national unity relied heavily on the ability to appeal to group affiliations. Because building a national community relied upon many groups joining together for a common cause, the Treasury focused its efforts on the activities of national organizations, forming a National Organizations Division in March 1941, two months before the official start date of the program. Morgenthau was confident that this would be an effective strategy after consulting with Peter Odegard, the expert in public opinion and peer pressure who advised Morgenthau that the psychology of the group held special power over that of the individual. The importance of reaching groups was even outlined in the *Defense Savings Manual* distributed to state and local bond committees:

> Since the [first] World War there has been a great increase in the number, variety, and size of social organizations.... Being of their member's own creation, under his own management and control, made up of like-minded or similarly situated people with common and sympathetic interests, these associations command the confidence of the individual member. Even in the national interest, which transcends the interest of any part, the Treasury intends, whenever possible, to give recognition to these voluntary associations.... In a democratic society, national unity can be achieved, not by force, but by persuasion, not by the liquidation of minority interest groups, but by their incorporation into the framework of the nation.... This sense of taking voluntary part in a national effort is one of the major objectives our present program.[32]

Market segmentation techniques developed between the wars led the National Organization Division to target women with its Women at War program, children with its Schools at War program, and even grandmothers with its Grandmothers' War Bond League. By directing promotional efforts specifically to historically marginalized and disenfranchised groups, such as women, youth, seniors, white ethnics, and blacks, the National Organizations Division was the Treasury's primary avenue to create a more unified society through bonds. Targeting such groups was intended as a means by which the Treasury could "criss-cross" an individual's cluster of associations on both vertical and horizontal axes, a theory suggested by Odegard. Bonds sold in the workplace occurred along a vertical, or hierarchical, axis, Odegard believed, whereas those sold within social settings could be plotted along a horizontal, or peer, axis. The Treasury thus saw in group affiliations the ability to reach the communal dimensions of an individual's identity with the bond message, thereby effectively blanketing all "quadrants" of each American's everyday life. Applying this theory throughout the war, the Treasury emphasized the importance of organizations in the bond program. For its Fifth War Loan drive in June 1944, for example, the Treasury advised county chairmen that "one of the best ways to achieve success is to use established channels where human emotions run strongest—ancestral ties, fraternal affiliations, and service organizations." As national networks of the bourgeoisie, already disposed toward patriotism and community service, such groups provided a vital link between Washington and the "people."[33]

Officials view a Schools at War display at Desmond's, a Los Angeles department store, supporting the Third War Loan. *Left to right:* Robert A. Moulton, chairman, War Finance Committee; George M. Eason, president, Los Angeles City and County School Savings and Loan Association (LACCSSLA); Bluford L. Pinnell, director of display, Desmond's; Avery J. Gray, director of thrift practice instruction, LACCSSLA, and liaison officer, Schools at War Education Section; and Vierling Kersey, superintendent, Los Angeles City Schools, and chairman, Southern California Schools at War Committee. (National Archives)

One of the most interesting efforts to reach a particular market segment was the Treasury's Schools at War program, in which children regularly purchased defense or war stamps. Borrowing from both the thrift stamp program of World War I and school bank plans operating for a generation, the program was aimed at students, teachers, and school administrators. The Treasury worked closely with the Office of Education, which provided mailing lists and advice to the former. The primary purpose of the Schools at War program was not to generate revenue but to give the youth of America a lesson in democracy and citizenship. The program was integrated into the students' educational curricula, in part to have the bond message "trickle-up" to parents and communities. More directly, however, children were viewed as future candidates for the payroll savings plan or the postwar equivalent. Schools at War was thus also an attempt to groom financially secure adults, popularly understood as one of the vital links to national security.[34]

The Schools at War program was officially kicked off on the south steps of the Treasury building in September 1942, with Eleanor Roosevelt in attendance. After a formal ceremony and parade, Liberty Bricks—actual bricks taken from Independence Hall after a renovation—were awarded to schools as prizes for outstanding preliminary participation. The program would eventually distribute more material than any other War Finance agency except the Publicity Division. The Treasury's main strategy was to link the idea of war savings to the full spectrum of primary and secondary school disciplines: mathematics, English, theater, art, and music. Themes central to the bond program—thrift, sacrifice, unity—were weaved into the educational process, blurring the lines between fields of learning and civic duty. Bonds represented a real-life case study potentially relevant to virtually any subject, a way in which nationalism could teach the "3 Rs" and vice versa.[35]

Providers of educational materials to schools capitalized on the emphasis on patriotism during the war by developing curricula using defense stamps as a central theme. A 1942 lesson guide, *Patriotic Plays and Programs,* included plays, songs, and recitations teaching the value of war savings. In one such play, "Helping Your Uncle Sam," defense stamps are used to educate children of the importance of national loyalty over immediate gratification:

> *Doris:* Hello, Clarice and Helen. Where have you been?
> *Helen:* We've been to the post office to buy Defense Stamps.
> *Janet:* Defense Stamps? I remember! Our teacher told us about them.
> *Theodore:* You know, that's the money that is helping our fathers to win the war.
> *Alvin:* Sure enough! I would like to buy some, but I haven't any money.
> *Theodore:* Haven't you bought a single Defense Stamp, Alvin? We have quite a few already!
> *Ann:* Well, it's too late now. We spent all our money on candy.
> *Wilfred:* And gum! That lasts longer.
> *Warren:* If you want to spend money for candy, that's your right. Mother says that Uncle Sam needs every cent to help him win the war.
> *Wilfred:* Maybe we'll buy some bye and bye. Anyhow, we have had a good time today.[36]

In scene 6, Alvin gets a stomachache from having eaten too many sweets and is taught the valuable lesson of country over candy.

Although the primary intent of the Schools at War program was to instill the values of thrift and patriotism, school bond drives did indeed generate funds to help the cause. Sponsorship campaigns, in which children purchased defense or war stamps in order to raise enough funds to "buy" a designated vehicle or piece of military equipment, were at the heart of the program. The school would notify the Treasury of the amount of stamps and bonds sold, and in return the name of the school would often be printed on the "purchased" item. Occasionally, armed forces personnel using the vehicle or equipment would send a letter to the sponsoring school, thanking the children for their contribution to the war effort. The 1943 Buy a Jeep campaign was a particularly popular promotion, with more than ninety thousand Jeeps sponsored by individual schools. The concept was extended to campaigns in which schools sponsored Fairchild Trainers and Flying Fortress bombers and, toward the end of the war, hospital and rehabilitation equipment.[37]

William Tuttle has noted the significant role the Schools at War program played among home-front children, stating that "children felt intimately connected to the war drives." Under pressure from the government, schools, media, and other kids, some children even felt the need to spend their lunch money on war stamps. Forgetting or not having money for war stamps would usually lead to great embarrassment, putting poorer children at a social disadvantage. Kids often believed that not buying a 25-cent stamp would seriously affect America's war machine, an indication of sorts that the Treasury's propaganda campaign was indeed working. By 1944, national bond sales from schools resulted in $510 million worth of war equipment, financing 2,900 airplanes, 33,000 land Jeeps, and 11,600 amphibious Jeeps.[38]

By war's end, about $2 billion of stamps and bonds were sold through the Schools at War program, embodying what one Treasury official called "a payroll savings plan in embryo." The level of support for the program varied widely across the nation, with some opposition voiced by a number of school administrators who believed that through Schools at War the government was playing too large a role in children's education. Roman Catholic parochial schools, on the other hand, were particularly enthusiastic supporters of the program. A college equivalent to the Schools at War program was unsuccessful, a shortage of funds among university students blamed for the program's failure. Beyond the economic issues, however, was the fact that both university professors and students appeared to be generally apathetic toward the Treasury's bond program. "For some reason," an official wrote in retrospect, "college teachers proved less responsive to the defense or war savings program than almost any other professional group.... Meager college response to the Treasury's program was also due to academic preoccupation with the intellectual rather than the practical aspects of citizenship."[39]

The Treasury's objective to reach and use America's youth to buy and sell stamps and bonds did not stop at the Schools at War program. The Treasury again worked with the Office of Education to orchestrate bond campaigns through a variety of youth organizations, which included the Boy Scouts, Girl Scouts, Camp Fire Girls, 4-H Clubs, and Future Farmers of America. As in World War I, the Treasury used newspaper carriers to sell stamps to customers on their routes. Selling a total of 1.7 billion ten-cent stamps, 150,000 carriers from nine hundred newspapers participated over the course of the program. Two campaigns in 1945, one to raise funds to sponsor Water Weasels (M-29 amphibious Jeeps) and another for LCVP landing craft, were especially popular newspaper carrier promotions.[40]

Although women were very much a part of the Treasury's main bond organization, independent women's groups also played a key role in the

Boy Scouts of Baltimore stuffing envelopes for a five-hundred-thousand-letter bond campaign in Maryland during the Third War Loan. (National Archives)

Girl Scouts selling bonds and stamps. (National Archives)

Girl Scouts and girls of the Civilian Defense in San Juan, Puerto Rico, who took part in the house-to-house canvass on Pearl Harbor day 1944. (National Archives)

program. Women's divisions were set up in most states, their mission to sell bonds and the war through existing, often powerful women's organizations. Organizations ranging from the Daughters of the American Revolution to B'nai B'rith adopted the bond program early on, providing mailing lists and distributing Treasury material. One such pamphlet was *We Gals Must Stick Together,* a guide for selling bonds that included a playlet to be performed at meetings, sample speeches, and answers to the most asked questions. Another influential pamphlet was *Mrs. Brown Goes to War,* funded by leading grocery chains, such as A&P, Safeway, Kroger, and Piggly Wiggly. Shipped to grocery store warehouses and put on store shelves just like a can of peas, the pamphlet was available free to consumers. Grocery stores also carried bond promotion in their radio and newspaper advertising, further linking the bond program to food shopping. There is little doubt that the eagerness displayed by supermarkets to help the Treasury reach women went beyond simple patriotism. The bond program was a means of getting women into grocery stores in a very competitive business environment, and a way to establish goodwill among consumers for subsequent fruition.[41]

The Women's Division of St. Louis meets to coordinate efforts for the Second War Loan. (National Archives)

Another interesting connection between the women's bond program and the consumer sphere was the *Home Front Journal,* a newsletter designed for women committee members and important volunteers. The *Home Front Journal* was a joint venture between the Treasury and the *Ladies Home Journal,* the latter offering its expertise in publishing material targeted to women. As *Mrs. Brown Goes to War* offered grocery chains a way to align themselves with a patriotic cause, the *Home Front Journal* was an opportunity for the *Ladies Home Journal* to be associated with the ideologically loaded bond program. Partnerships between the private sector and the Treasury may have been grounded in the common pursuit of winning the war, but companies also considered them good for business, an investment that would pay off in the consumer-driven postwar years.[42]

A wide variety of promotions were conceived by the Treasury and executed by state and local women's bond committees. Women directly sold bonds at many locations, most commonly at booths set up in stores, theaters, and public buildings. Bond promotions led by women often drew upon and reinforced women's traditional gender roles. As Minute Maids and as part of the popular 1943 Molly Pitcher Day promotion, women wore historic costumes to gain attention. Women also led the Outfit the Outfit campaign during the Second War Loan, in which bond rallies were held to raise the necessary funds to feed, dress, and equip a soldier. Bond goals were expressed in terms of the cost for coats, blankets, mess kits, and first-aid pouches for women's "sons, brothers, and husbands." Presenting bonds in terms of feeding, dressing, and equipping a male soldier emphasized women's maternal role as caretakers of the military family. Such representations also likely contributed to the formation of women's contained gender roles in the 1950s.[43]

Women were actively targeted by the Treasury and other government agencies to both sell and buy bonds because of their principal social role on the home front. In support of the Second War Loan, the news bureau of the Office of War Information issued a variety of material to newspapers and magazines to promote the bond drive. One such story was designed to persuade women to purchase war bonds, described by the OWI as a

> story to women's pages on the sense of healthy independence women war workers acquire through the purchase of war bonds, how such purchases give them a feeling of "doing something worthwhile" gained from their war job. Something, too, about the effect of such buying on children's future, preparation for return of men from the fighting fronts, prevention of inflation and loss of jobs after the war.[44]

The OWI's rhetoric summarily captures the caretaker role women were assigned and assumed during the bond program as protectors of the home front and ensurers of their husbands' and children's future. Employment for women during the war was typically positioned in traditionally "feminine" terms, that is, as a means to help bring husbands home and create a secure environment for children. It was ironic that the OWI marketed bonds to women as a means to prevent the "loss of jobs after the war," when many of these jobs belonged to women during the war.[45]

Another gender-specific promotion orchestrated by the Treasury was the war stamp corsage. Made of war stamps instead of flowers, the corsage was used as a table decoration or party favor, an effective device to "domesticate" the bond program, bringing the idea of the war into the home. The Hospital Equipment campaign during the Fourth War Loan was also targeted to and managed by women, designed for organizations whose members did not want to purchase military equipment. Sponsors of a piece of hospital equipment received a citation from the surgeon general, casting women on the home front as surrogate nurses.[46]

The women's bond program was further segmented via the 1943 Bonds for Babies promotion, the Bonds for Brides campaign, and the Grandmothers' War Bond League, launched in 1944. Bonds for Babies was targeted to new parents "and other fond relations," with bond booths set up at maternity hospitals. Additionally, a poster with the headline "For Baby's Future, Buy War Bonds" was distributed to maternity hospitals, prenatal clinics, and infant departments in stores, as well as used as a cover for baby magazines. As support for this promotion, bond committees sent a certificate designed by the Walt Disney Studio to parents of newborns as a sales incentive. With the war being fought to preserve democracy for future generations, babies represented a powerful icon by which the administration could sell bonds and the war.[47]

Bonds for Brides was a promotion in which the Treasury suggested stamps and bonds be given to brides as a shower, wedding, or new home gift. With the assistance of professional home economists, the Treasury offered useful tips to the would-be gift giver. One pamphlet recommended brides be given a bond: "With some little extra such as a cook book which contains money-saving recipes. A sheet of Stamps could be framed. Or the Bond might be hidden away among a box of absolute necessities—soap chips, salt, sugar, soap, a can opener, etc."[48]

Although not an official Treasury program, the Grandmothers' War Bond League allowed grandmothers to be recognized for buying bonds for their grandchildren by recording their bond purchases in a book made available to them. Conceived by Mrs. George C. Marshall, wife of the army's chief of staff and grandmother of three, the league was introduced to the American public by Eleanor Roosevelt during a radio address. More than anything else, the league illustrated the interest in the bond program among particular segments of the population. Virtually all affiliation groups or coalitions either were targeted by the Treasury or stepped up on their own behalf to participate in the most visible demonstration of support for the war.[49]

Another major market for the Treasury were farmers and their families. The Treasury worked closely with the Department of Agriculture to develop a farm bond program, the latter even supplying the former with estimates of farmers' discretionary income during the Seventh War Loan. The Treasury distributed an abundance of bond-related material to rural America, including the pamphlets *Our Good Earth . . . Keep It Ours, The Minute Man Was a Farmer Too,* and for women, *Minute Women in Tobaccoland.* The poster "A Crop that Never Fails" was a particularly common site in small towns. With some help from Hollywood studios, the Treasury produced a number of bond-themed sixteen-millimeter films for rural gatherings, and the American Theater Wing prepared a play about war bonds called *Tomorrow's Harvest.* The Treasury wisely placed ads and applications for bonds in both the Sears Roebuck and Montgomery Ward catalogs, each considered an integral part of farm life. The farm program also featured a number of bond promotions tailored to agriculture and animal raising, such as the Victory Pig campaign. For this promotion, pig farmers, often children, would select a first-class pig from a litter that would ultimately be sold at auction, the proceeds going toward bonds. Pigs and cows were also offered as prizes for the largest buyer at bond rallies, a practice the Treasury discouraged, as meat was considered a scarce commodity.[50]

One of the most important groups contacted by the Treasury early in the bond program was labor, as union cooperation was critical to reaching the millions of blue-collar employees. As America's possible involvement in the war accelerated in 1940, trade unions changed their position of opposing the administration's foreign policy to supporting it. With a pledge of maximum production and no strikes during the war emergency, unions and their members moved significantly closer to the social and political center of the country. Enticed by greater power and benefits and influenced by the cultural mandate of national unity, organized labor reversed its historical class-based stance to adopt what Nelson Lichtenstein has called "consensual politics and social homogeneity."[51]

Consistent with this shift in direction, labor leaders welcomed the Treasury's bond program, believing that the payroll savings plan was not only good for the nation but also good for their members. Government pamphlets such as *Defense Bonds for American Workers* were distributed to a total of fifteen million union members from 150 national and 50,000 local unions. One reason the bond program held special strength within labor was that union members were benefiting from defense plant contracts with highly paid jobs. The Treasury's program even contributed to turning the historical animosity between the AFL and CIO into more of a friendly rivalry during the war years, as the unions competed to determine who could purchase more bonds. Bond drives also provided common ground between labor and management, as the shared effort to raise funds for defense at least postponed some of the conflicts between the two groups. Bonds were thus working exactly as the Treasury envisioned, "solving" domestic problems during the international crisis.[52]

Because their members consisted of the "people," fraternal and civic groups were also recognized as instrumental to the success of the Treasury's bond program. Fifty million Americans from about fifty such groups, including the Elks, the Knights of Columbus, the Kiwanis, and B'nai B'rith, endorsed and actively participated in bond drives. Fraternal and civic groups were seen as important not only because of their huge memberships but also because they represented overlapping sources of potential bond sales. Bond purchases could be made by individual members, by the group as a whole, or by a community through the group's influence. Additionally, members of these groups often worked at companies offering the payroll savings plan, another source of revenue for the Treasury.[53]

Through its populist orientation—having "the people" sell bonds to "the people"—the Treasury was able to fulfill its ideological mission to instill a pluralistic form of national unity in the American consciousness. Unlike other state-building agencies, such as the Office of Price Administration or the Red Cross, the Treasury successfully skirted class and racial divisions by grounding the bond program in democratic rhetoric and policy. Perhaps even more important, war bonds represented an ideal balance between public and private interests, accommodating free enterprise and capitalism within the context of patriotism. Although "sacrifice" was the key discourse of the nation's political economy during the war, as Mark Leff has suggested, bonds offered distinct advantages to the other "sacrifice staples" of wage and price freezes, rationing, and higher taxes. Unlike these other agents, which limited financial gain or consumption—violations of the

American creed of liberty and the pursuit of happiness—bonds were, ultimately, an instrument for prosperity and consumerism. Bonds thus offered a win-win means of sacrificing by helping to win the country's war while investing in one's personal future. Within a climate of "growing privatization of aspirations as the war progressed," bonds offered the unsurpassable dual benefits of idealism and profit. Even during war, the principles of the American Way would determine which government strategies would work and which would fail. Business took full advantage of the opportunity to wed capitalism and patriotism, aligning private interests with nationalism by linking their brand names to appeals for bonds. Through what can be termed "consumer patriotism," class and ideological conflict were largely resolved through the nexus of war bonds, replaced by an "equality of sacrifice" grounded in the postwar promise of abundance for all.[54]

CHAPTER 3

★ ★ ★ The Biggest Selling Campaign in History

From May 1, 1941, to January 3, 1946, the people of the United States loaned the government $185.7 billion, the most money ever raised to fight a war. What motivated eight out of every thirteen Americans to turn their hard cash into securities that took ten years to fully mature and, like all investments, carried some financial risk? What strategies and techniques did the Treasury use to sell bonds to the American people? How and why did bonds emerge as the central rallying point for the war on the home front? Answering such questions leads us to a better understanding of why World War II bonds can be viewed as the most successful consumer product ever sold in history. Given what was being purchased and who was the seller, a case study of the marketing of war bonds adds an important and overlooked chapter to the history of twentieth-century American consumer culture.[1]

The unprecedented success of the World War II bond program was a function of a number of unique, synergistic circumstances that provided the Treasury with what can be considered unfair advantages in the marketplace. First, the Treasury had at its disposal the largest sales force ever gathered—half a million committee volunteers and another five to six million Minute Men who could be and were mobilized during bond drives. Second, it had full access to all media and, with free space and time, an unlimited promotion budget, creating what one Treasury official called the "greatest volume of advertising and publicity ever given to any product or agency." Third, its staff consisted of leaders hand-picked from the worlds of advertising and marketing (including the creator of Elsie the Cow) who donated their services free of charge. The state's enlistment of individuals with business experience was emblematic of the fusion between public interests and private capital during the war. The Treasury's staff and allies drew upon individuals and institutions from a range of political backgrounds, which was consistent with Secretary Morgenthau's decision to approach the sale of bonds as a democratic, pluralistic process.[2]

The Treasury also had access to what was effectively the largest list of potential customers in the world—the names and addresses of all taxpayers in the country. That the Internal Revenue Service shared this list was just one example of the way government agencies worked together for the common goal of winning the war. However, the most significant factor leading to the great success of the bond program resided not in the Treasury's resources but in the market's demand. The American marketplace during the war years was, as one Treasury official described it, experiencing the "highest income in its history with a diminishing supply of goods on which to spend it." Through its marketing of war bonds, the Treasury took full advantage of selling Americans the future while the present was out of stock.[3]

Satisfying the market demand for government securities relied heavily upon the ease of buying them. Businessmen "on loan" to the Treasury recognized that how and where Americans could purchase bonds would be essential to the success of the program. Unlike savings bonds, which had been offered for sale only at post offices, Secretary Morgenthau worked closely with the banking industry to make defense bonds available at banks, more than doubling the number of outlets for consumers and making it easy for them to make bond purchasing part of regular banking activities. The fact that the federal government and private banks worked in concert to sell bonds is significant because it represented one of the major ways in which public and private life coalesced during the war. Selling bonds at banks during World War II contrasted with both the Liberty Loan campaign of World War I and the 1930s savings bond program, an indication of the state's heightened attempt to penetrate as much of the civic arena as possible through bonds. Increasing the number of locations at which to purchase bonds was also consistent with the democratic intent of the Treasury's bond program, and was part of a conscious effort to avoid the elitism associated with the selling of bonds in the previous war. Secretary Morgenthau's vision of bonds as being for the American

Everyman was reflected by his displeasure at seeing a special sales booth open at Rockefeller Plaza in New York. "That's a long way from Fourteenth Street and 23rd," Morgenthau wrote to Harold Graves, his assistant. He continued: "That's the place where they sell the most precious jewelry and it's a high price fur retail [sic] to people on Fifth Avenue.... Those aren't the kind of people I want to reach."[4]

In addition to increasing the number of outlets at which to purchase bonds, the Treasury pursued an aggressive direct-sales campaign to bring bonds to the people. Direct, personal solicitation was found by the Treasury to be its most effective sales technique, with house-to-house (or farm-to-farm) canvassing by both adults and children a common practice. Defense and War Savings Staff volunteers recorded pledges, or "subscriptions," for a purchase of a bond, buyers having to go to an official issuing agent, such as a bank or post office, to make the actual transaction. Volunteers were trained before each bond drive and provided with a sales kit that offered guidelines and tips for campaign strategies and themes. Pledges were reported to county and state committees and measured against quotas assigned by Treasury officials in Washington.

Although technically more promoters than actual salespeople, Treasury volunteers were instrumental to the selling of Series E bonds to smaller, individual investors (Series F and G bonds were sold to banks and large corporate investors directly by regional Federal Reserve banks). Promotional top spin was often combined with direct-sales efforts, as in the Fifth War Loan, when bond salespeople were coined "Bondadiers" and the drive presented as the home-front equivalent to D day. Volunteer salespeople used a variety of creative techniques to sell bonds and stamps. One entrepreneurial woman affixed defense stamps on her body, boarded a train in Miami, and sold the stamps all the way to New York. Buyers chose stamps based on their location on her body.[5]

During bond drives, the Treasury also authorized some businesses and their employees as quasi-official agents for the sale of bonds, as retailers were familiar with handling cash and accounting for sales. Large department stores often issued bonds during drives, and occasionally smaller businesses were allowed to sell bonds directly to their customers. One hundred twenty cigar stores in New York City joined forces to become sales locations for bonds and stamps, for example, as did the Manhattan Tavern Owners' Fourth War Loan Drive Committee when it enlisted the efforts of seventy-five hundred New York City bartenders to sell bonds. Union members also occasionally became authorized bond salespersons, as when Washington, D.C., Teamster milk drivers, icemen, laundry men, and dry cleaner drivers sold bonds on their respective routes for the Third War Loan. Virtually the only profession that had some doubts about the appropriateness of their selling bonds was the clergy, some of whom had misgivings asking congregates in a religious setting to contribute funds for war. Through the enlistment of those in various professions to sell bonds, the private sector was again being engaged to serve objectives established by the state. As a result of this and numerous other joint efforts to sell bonds, it was often difficult to distinguish between public and private life on the home front.[6]

As the infrastructure of the Treasury's sales organization began to take form in the late spring of 1941, the Defense Savings Staff delivered its first line of attack through the traditional avenues of advertising and promotion. The Treasury's fundamental advertising strategy was like that of any marketer introducing a new product—gain maximum publicity at minimum cost. Unlike other marketers, however, the Treasury could realize nearly 100 percent awareness at virtually no cost, using space and time donated by the dominant media of the war years—print, radio, and outdoor—to achieve the maximum number of advertising impressions possible. The total worth of advertising used by the Treasury to sell bonds during the first three years of the campaign was estimated to be a quarter of a billion dollars. Print ads for bonds also "piggybacked" on advertisers' paid placements in newspapers and magazines, providing further exposure in traditional consumer media. The willingness among privately held advertising agencies, media companies, and corporate advertisers to donate space and time to sell bonds was a strong indication of the close alliance between capital and state during the war.[7]

With fifty million radios in use in the early 1940s, the Treasury aggressively promoted bonds via the medium in a variety of ways. The "Treasury Salute" series weaved promotional spots into a variety of musical programs, and the "Treasury Song Parade" ran on 870 stations coast to coast over the Blue Network. Although the program was broadcast to a national audience, listeners could telephone their local station affiliate to purchase bonds. Radio played a vital role in delivering defense bonds' primary selling proposition based in pluralistic democracy. On the "Treasury Hour," a radio show broadcast weekly by CBS starting in July 1941, Secretary Morgenthau made sure the music of artists and composers whose work would be verboten in Nazi Germany was played. Similarly, Morgenthau insisted that a variety of musical forms was represented on the show, again reflective of American pluralism. Jazz, blues, marches, and classics, he knew, appealed to particular segments of the population, and thus should

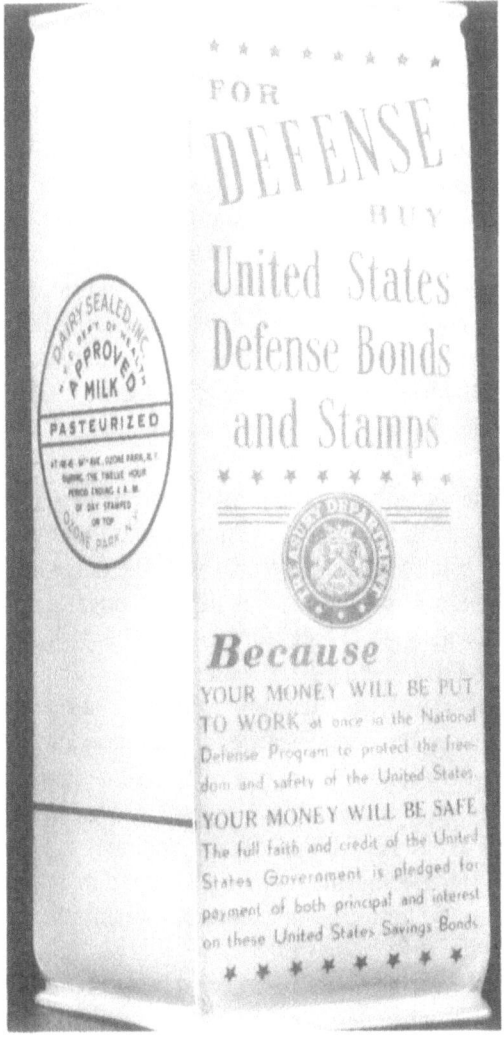

Defense bond advertisement on a milk carton. (National Archives)

be a part of the broadcasts, demonstrating the pluralistic spirit and maximizing the effectiveness of defense bond promotion.[8]

Within outdoor media, billboards and bus and trolley cards carried war bond messages. In addition to traditional media, a wide variety of other collateral material was used to promote bonds during the war, including matchbook covers, menus, milk bottles and collars, greeting cards, theater programs, and inserts placed in bank statements and utility bills. With comic strips one of the leading forms of entertainment in the 1930s and early 1940s, cartoonists integrated pitches for bonds in their stories. The advertising and promotion blitz conducted by the Treasury appeared on all accounts as a marketing campaign for a consumer product with an unlimited budget. "To reach its goal," *Business Week* observed, "the Treasury has organized the biggest selling campaign in history, borrowing all the tricks that are used to move breakfast food and toothpaste."[9]

Perhaps the most important medium of bond promotion, however, at least in terms of presence on the American landscape, was posters. During World War II the Treasury used posters more than all other government agencies combined to promote bonds. As the most visible reminder of the war on the home front, the linguistic and graphic symbols of bond posters, which appeared in virtually all forms of public space, including banks, stores, schools, and factories, are the best way to read the administration's official wartime rhetoric.[10]

War bond promotion in posters revolved around five broad themes, the most common being the most literal, the appeal to Americans to loan the government money in order to supply the armed forces with the necessary equipment and materials to fight a war. Many of this theme's slogans, for example, "Buy that Invasion Bond" (1944) and "Fire Away" (1944), were unabashedly militaristic by today's standards. Popular slogans such as "You Buy 'Em, We'll Fly 'Em" (1942) or "Back the Attack" (1943) suggested a direct connection between the consumer's bond purchase and its application in the field, an effective selling strategy. Providing the fighting forces with adequate gear was also presented as the least Americans at home could do. Slogans such as "A Half-Filled Stamp Album Is Like a Half-Equipped Soldier" (1942) reflected the Treasury's intent to instill a sense of guilt in Americans, even children, who were not investing in the war to maximum levels.[11]

A second major theme in war bond promotion referred to sacrifice. As all Americans were expected to contribute to the war effort to the best of their abilities, buying war bonds was just one of various ways to fight the war at home. The government also urged Americans via aggressive homefront campaigns to conserve materials needed for the war, such as rubber, gasoline, and fats, to salvage scrap metals, to plant Victory gardens by growing one's own vegetables, and to avoid spreading war-related and potentially damaging information. In war bond promotion, sacrifice was typically expressed as merely doing one's fair share. Slogans such as the straightforward "Do Your Part to Win the War" (1942) to the guilt-inducing "Doing All You Can Brother?" (1943) implied that it was the duty of all Americans to contribute to the war effort. The sacrifice theme also lent itself to harder-sell slogans, including those employing anti-Axis imagery. Direct references to the Nazi threat were made in slogans such as "Don't Let That Shadow Touch Them" (1942) and the eerie "Remember Me? I was at Bataan" (1943), spoken by a dead soldier. However expressed, the underlying message of this theme was that any sacrifice Americans could make at home was still far less than the one military personnel were making abroad. While soldiers, sailors, and pilots were risking their lives, one war bond poster suggested to home-front Americans, "All You Need Give is Money."[12]

Another important theme in war bond promotion spoke to a sense of community. National unity—the idea that Americans were joined together for a common purpose—gave larger meaning to the selling of war bonds. Posters as simple as "Let's All Fight" (1942) and "All Together" (1945) to the Christianity-laden "In the Strength of Great Hope We Must Shoulder Our Common Load" (1945) conveyed that Americans were philosophically, even spiritually, engaged in the war effort. A GI waving out of a ship's porthole with the message "Till We Meet Again" (1943) implied a personal connection with those overseas. Offering a sense of scale of the war bond operation, for example, "85 Million Americans Hold War Bonds" (1945), had the corollary effect of assigning guilt to those who had not purchased bonds. Of the selling techniques, appeals through community were the most nationalistic in content and tone. Posters such as "Buy a Share in America" (1941) most clearly articulated Morgenthau's vision of having America buy into the war by buying bonds. Stressing through bond promotion that America was united in its efforts to fight the war also had the effect of labeling alternative views as subversive and counter to national interests.[13]

A fourth common theme in war bond promotion was centered on America's fundamental freedoms. Bonds were portrayed as the literal and figurative price of the Four Freedoms—freedom of speech and worship and from want and fear—which President Roosevelt had firmly linked to national defense in his annual message to Congress in January 1941. Emerging as the tangible expression of these freedoms, bonds were marketed as a small investment and the best guarantee our freedoms would be protected. Freedom was directly expressed in slogans such as "For Freedom Sake Buy War Bonds" (1943), "Save Freedom of Speech, Buy War Bonds" (1943), and "Save Freedom of Worship Each According to the Dictates of His Own Conscience" (1943), and indirectly expressed in slogans such as "Let's Always Be Thankful in America" and "Verboten! You Can't Let This Happen!" Whether directly or indirectly expressed, the message was that freedom was ultimately what we were fighting for and what the war was about. In those terms, the cost of American democracy seemed rather minimal; as one poster slogan stated, "In No Other Land is the Price of Freedom So Small.... It Takes Both War Bonds and War Taxes."[14]

With much wartime propaganda predicated on an optimistic vision of American society, the idea of the future held particular power as a selling point for bonds. Investment in bonds was presented as the key to America's future on a number of levels. In the most literal sense, war bonds represented a financial future, as they appreciated in value until maturity in a decade. For many, bonds held to maturity in the early 1950s would indeed serve as seeds of personal postwar prosperity. A wartime bond purchase grounded in the civic or public sphere was thus intentionally designed to serve private interests after the war. Bonds therefore served as an early indicator of postwar abundance and, in a grander sense, a metaphor for America's emerging status as an economic world power. For more immediate reasons, the administration urged Americans to resist redeeming bonds before full maturity, as suggested by poster slogans such as "Nest Eggs Won't Hatch Unless You Set On Them! Hang On To Your War Bonds" (1944). As well, with most consumer goods unavailable during the war, bonds' appreciating value made them a worthy gift item, as suggested by the Treasury's advice to "Give War Bonds. The Present with a Future" (1943).[15]

A more compelling way to use the concept of the future to sell bonds, however, was to present them not as a financial investment but as an investment in Americans' lives and in the nation itself. In posters such as "For Their Future Buy War Bonds" (1943), "Your Bonds Are a STAKE in the Future" (1943), and "Protect His Future" (1944), bonds were directly or indirectly presented as a way to protect the lives of the ones at most perceived risk—soldiers and children. Emotional appeals such as these drew upon Americans' personal connections to the war, whether they be a relative in the military or family at home. Ultimately, however, bonds represented nothing less than the lifeline of the American Way of Life and the revival of consumer capitalism. Bonds were and are inherently oriented around the future, as they demand temporary sacrifice for subsequent rewards, a metaphor, perhaps, for the Christian Gospel. Although some fears of postwar inflation and depression remained, this orientation toward the future cast the war years with a palpable feeling that prosperity lay ahead. War bonds were thus instrumental in creating the popular perception among many Americans of an emerging society of abundance, perhaps acting in part as a self-fulfilling prophecy.[16]

Posters and billboards such as this one sponsored by Budweiser promised that sacrifice during the war would lead to postwar prosperity. (National Archives)

Another frequent theme seen in war bond promotion, less ideological than practical, was the urging of Americans to join a bond payroll deduction plan. Through this plan, 10 percent of workers' paychecks automatically went towards the purchase of bonds. Payroll deduction was considered key to the success of the war bond program, as it ensured a steady flow of revenue to the Treasury and locked in Americans' commitment to bonds and their involvement for the duration of the war. Fellow employee and supervisor pressure to join such programs clearly played a major factor in the popularity of the payroll deduction plan. Promotion of the plan could be straightforward, as suggested by the poster slogan "You Can't Afford to Miss Either! Buy Bonds Every Payday" (1944), but also lent itself to more high-pressured tactics, as in the 1942 poster message: "It is Goot to Hear Americans are Now Pudding 10% of Der Pay into Bunds! Herman, You Tell Him It Iss Bonds—Not Bunds! For Victory.... Put at Least 10% of Every Pay into War Bonds."[17]

In order to maximize the effectiveness of its advertising and promotional campaign strategies, the Treasury used the advances made in marketing research between the wars. Through the 1920s and 1930s, advertising and marketing were increasingly viewed and practiced less as arts and more as sciences, with both qualitative and quantitative research recognized as the key to understanding the marketplace. Even before the national debut of the program on May 1, 1941, the Treasury tested the effectiveness of various promotional campaigns in six states. Between 1942 and 1945, the Treasury conducted forty research surveys to test advertising and promotional copy, the ultimate aim being to identify the most compelling sales pitches by which to present bonds. This research, commonly referred to as the Likert surveys (named after the project leader), revealed that Americans took the Treasury's occasionally apocalyptic appeals to support the war effort quite literally. Fifty percent of the population, one study showed, believed that the flow of military equipment to the front would stop if people stopped buying bonds, which was, of course, untrue. The Treasury was somewhat surprised by Americans' literal belief of its advertising, an indication that perhaps it underestimated the power of its marketing communications.[18]

The primary purpose of the Likert surveys was, however, to determine why Americans were purchasing bonds, information that could then be channeled back into marketing and advertising plans. Research conducted in 1942 indicated that loyalty motives, for example, helping a family member in the armed forces, topped the reasons for purchasing a bond. These findings offered clear evidence of the strong "bottom-up" appeal of bonds, that people were purchasing bonds for personally defined reasons. Bonds being a "safe investment" was mentioned as the second most important purchasing factor, and patriotism, defined in this study as the desire to preserve the American Way of Life, finished third. Curbing national inflation, the primary financial purpose of the bond program, was nowhere to be found in this study, obviously not a primary consumer concern.[19]

Interestingly, a 1944 pamphlet directed to war bond volunteers for the Fifth War Loan drive cited Americans' reasons to purchase bonds in a somewhat different order. In a section headed "Here's Why They Will Buy," patriotism was listed as the primary motivating factor for bond purchases, defined here as the "natural urge to do [one's] share of helping when there's a war to be won" and the desire to preserve the four freedoms. Second on the administration's list for consumers' reasons to purchase war bonds was the loyalty motive, that is, to support a relative or friend in the service. Third on the list was postwar security, described as "a safe, dependable nest egg to take care of tomorrow," encompassing education, new equipment, household comforts, improvements and luxuries, and old age security.[20]

Although Americans' view of bonds might have shifted in the two years between the 1942 study and the 1944 Fifth War Loan drive, it is more likely that the Treasury was overestimating, intentionally or otherwise, patriotism as a motivating factor for buying bonds. Promoting bonds as serving national rather than personal interests was consistently believed by the administration to be the more compelling selling proposition, despite actual research suggesting otherwise. If indeed bonds were being used to sell the war, rather than vice-versa, claiming patriotism as the first and foremost reason for Americans to buy bonds would be a logical administration strategy. Such evidence also suggests that even in extreme situations of perceived responsibility to one's country, consumers still evaluate purchases in personally defined terms.

Throughout the war the Treasury attempted to present the cost of the war in real, understandable terms. In its initial offering of defense bonds and stamps, in fact, the Treasury translated the cost of bonds and stamps into various pieces of military equipment. According to Treasury promotional material, for example, $18.75, the price of a $25.00 bond, would "purchase" 550 rounds of .30-caliber ammunition for the army, and $75.00 would buy a chronometer watch or nine crew mattresses for the navy. Children were likely excited to learn that their $5.00 stamp would buy two leg splints for the marines. In addition to costing out particular pieces of equipment, the Treasury on occasion estimated the cost of an entire battle in order to justify its continued promotion of bonds. In July 1945, shortly before the end of the war, the Treasury announced that the nation's "investment" in the attack on Iwo Jima was $6.3 billion. With ships costing $5.6 billion and aircraft, supplies, equipment, and personnel costing $700 million, the total amount of this battle alone equaled roughly twice that spent by the navy in World War I. Although such translations were speculative at best, expressing the very abstract costs of the war in tangible terms was instrumental in linking home-front purchases of bonds and stamps to the actual fighting overseas.[21]

In a related sales technique, the Treasury also presented the costs of the war in temporal terms. In September 1943, the Treasury estimated that the purchaser of a one-thousand-dollar bond was funding the entire cost of "America's global war" for four-tenths of a second. Taking some creative license with this alleged fact, Treasury officials suggested that "the buyer may in his imagination pick the split second for which he will be financing the whole war," adding that "this might be the split second when Lae is captured by MacArthur's men, or when Halsey's final salvo finishes the Japanese main fleet, or when Eisenhower's armies drive the last Nazi beyond the Alps." Again, translating the value of bonds into meaningful if aggrandized terms added a sense of scale and urgency to the purchase experience.[22]

Armed with statistics, the Treasury found equally interesting ways to pitch war bonds. Comparing the 1920 purchase price of ten dozen eggs, forty-two pounds of sugar, fifteen pounds of pork chops, and eighty-five pounds of potatoes of $36.71 to the wartime cost of $17.96, the Treasury suggested Americans use the $18.75 "savings" to purchase an extra war bond. In 1942, the Treasury even offered a mathematical formula by which investors could figure out how much of their income should be put into bonds. Starting from one's gross income, the Treasury suggested that after deducting $500 for the wage earner and spouse and $400 for each child or dependent, each American should spend one-quarter of what was left on bonds. It was no coincidence that should every American have actually followed this formula, the Treasury's 1942 goal of $18.5 billion would have been met to the penny.[23]

Rather than having a single strategy or message throughout the war, the Treasury adapted its approach toward selling bonds based on prevailing social conditions on the home front and events overseas. Each of the seven war loans, in fact, had its own dedicated plan, with target audience, selling proposition, and sales technique fluid variables in the Treasury's marketing mix. With the focus of the war shifting from Europe to the Pacific in late 1944, for example, the Treasury reoriented its bond program to reflect Americans' perception of the Japanese as the principal enemy. The psychological warfare being fought in the Far East demanded that the Treasury employ special strategies for the Sixth War Loan. In so doing, the Treasury worked closely with the Office of War Information to prepare a guide for radio broadcasters' bond promotional announcements. The copy platform for the Sixth War Loan was designed "to capitalize on the hostility the American people feel toward the Japanese enemy," with radio copywriters instructed to "select stories of planned brutality" against the Allies in their appeals for bonds.[24]

In the propaganda war against Japan, however, the administration was principally concerned that racist remarks made by broadcasters in the selling of bonds would be heard by all Asian listeners, potentially damaging our relationship with allies China and India and neutral parties Malaysia and Java. The OWI guide advised:

> Any statements on the radio which imply that we are fighting a racial war or which describe the Japanese enemy as "yellow" will be picked up by the

Japanese radio and used to divide our allies from us.... When our radio describes the Japanese as animal-like, or non-human, the Japanese radio is able to twist this description so as to apply to all Asiatics.[25]

To prevent this from occurring, the guide provided a list of terms broadcasters should consider when speaking of the Japanese, divided into two columns, recommended and not recommended:

Not Recommended	Recommended
Slimy	Brutal
Fiendish	Treacherous
Bestial	Cruel
Grinning	Tough
Toothy	Wanton
Monkey-man	Desperate
Jap-rat	Scheming
Yellow	Fanatical
Inhuman	Venomous
Slant-eyes	Ruthless

Also included in the guide were some examples of radio copy considered to be "bad from the standpoint of psychological warfare," with corrections made to the offending copy, for example:

Not Recommended	Recommended
So let's go! The more bonds, the less Japs! We must keep on backing up our fighting men till they have blown every last Son of Heaven to Hades.	So let's go! The more bonds, the shorter the war! We must keep on backing up our fighting men till every last Son of Heaven admits defeat.

Although overseas radio promotion of bonds for the Sixth War Loan served as Allied propaganda, the Treasury and OWI still wanted to sell bonds. As such, the OWI was sure to mention in its guide that "naturally, copy-writers should follow the common-sense rule of avoiding material which will offend or revolt the radio audience."[26]

To generate awareness of the bond program and maintain its momentum, the Treasury executed a wide range of promotions throughout the war. Drawing upon activities and icons associated within popular and consumer

Betty Grable "and her bondbardiers" singing and dancing in the Hollywood movie *The All Star Bond Rally*. Other stars contributing their efforts in the film created for the Seventh War Loan included Bob Hope, Harry James and his Orchestra, Harpo Marx, and Frank Sinatra. (National Archives)

culture—movies, sports, music, literature, theater, and shopping—helped again to shrink the space between private life and the state. Tours that went from city to city to promote and sell bonds created excitement around the program as well as localized national campaigns. Movie star tours were tremendously popular attractions, in which bond purchasers were awarded with an autograph from celebrities such as Lana Turner and Frank Sinatra. Lana Turner, in fact, singlehandedly raised $5.25 million in bonds by selling 105 kisses for $50,000 each. Abbott and Costello's forty-one-city tour was a great success, as was the September 1942 Stars over America tour, in which top actors, including Marlene Dietrich, Humphrey Bogart, Gary Cooper, Clark Gable, Judy Garland, and Cary Grant, made stops at more than 360 communities. The Quiz Kids of radio fame raised millions of dollars in bond purchases on its tour, with no evidence as yet to indicate their shows of this era were fixed. War heroes also toured the country to promote bonds as part of the 1942 American Heroes Day, as did, curiously, Sabu the Elephant Boy, who visited twenty-six cities that same year. Other bond

Biggest Selling Campaign in History

The nation's top singer, Bing Crosby, appeared in the film *The All Star Bond Rally* crooning the new song "Buy a Bond." (National Archives)

promotion tours featured war-related items such as silverware from sunk Pearl Harbor ships, the captured "jewel-studded" baton of Reichmarshall Goering, and a two-man Japanese sub. The original German surrender documents were exhibited as part of the Victory Loan train tour in 1945. These tours were intended to motivate, perhaps incite, Americans to contribute to the war effort. Although the hoopla and gaiety surrounding the touring of Hollywood stars and war artifacts to promote bonds was viewed by some as being in questionable taste, there was no doubt that these tours translated into significantly greater awareness and sales of Treasury bonds.[27]

Endorsements of war bonds by all forms of celebrities could be found in wartime media. In a trade newsletter called *Mailway: News and Ideas on Direct-Mail,* for example, Gypsy Rose Lee, the burlesque queen, gave her own inimitable endorsement in the summer of 1943:

> I wish I could write something very high-minded about War Bonds but my reason for buying them sounds too unpatriotic. With me War Bonds are a solid

Helen Hayes (*center, standing*) and other members of the cast of the film *Harriet Buying Bonds during the Second War Loan*. The bond drive raised money for clothing and equipment for soldiers, hence the soldier on the left holding a shirt and trousers. (National Archives)

Seated in army Jeeps bearing their names, a dozen movie celebrities of the Hollywood Bond Cavalcade get ready to parade through the streets of Washington, D.C., to kick off the Third War Loan. (National Archives)

investment. I'm not doing anyone a favor by buying em. In fact I am gypping the Government only they don't know it. My only worry is that they'll get hep before I can buy more.... It's a schmoozie feeling to know my money is being used to build bombers. Not that I know anything about bombers. All I know is that they run into money. Big money.[28]

Promotion was thus delivered not only in governmental rhetoric but also in many vernaculars.

As part of its total support for the country's war effort, Hollywood went much further to promote the Treasury's bond program. Working with the Treasury's Special Events Section, the Motion Picture Industry's War Activities Committee produced a number of war bond movies, shorts, and trailers, some of which were produced in thirty-five-millimeter format and shown in commercial theaters. Sixteen-millimeter films, carried by some three hundred distributors, were shown in schools, war plants, and a variety of other locations where people gathered.[29] The importance of the showing of bond-related films to the Treasury was made clear by Ted Gamble, national director of the War Finance Division. In May 1944, in support of the Fifth War Loan, Gamble sent a letter addressed to "all 16mm projector owners in America":

> You know that there are few tools more effective for convincing and moving any gathering than the motion picture. The War Finance Division is asking you, as the owner of a 16mm projector, to put it into the service of Uncle Sam for the Fifth War Loan. Lend it, use it to show battlefront films wherever you can: in shop, plant, shipyard, forum, library, union hall, lodge, luncheon club—anywhere people can be assembled to see and hear this message.... You have in your hands one of the most potent weapons to use against the Axis and against inflation. Use it! ... Book your services as a 16 mm. Minute Man in this greatest of all War Loan campaigns.[30]

With each bond drive, the number of films produced and showed increased. For the Fifth War Loan, the Treasury estimated there were twenty-five thousand bond film showings to 10 million people; for the sixth, there were believed to be eighty-seven thousand showings to 23.5 million people. For the Seventh War Loan, Merriman Holtz, sixteen-millimeter consultant for the War Finance Division, announced that showings were expected to hit a new high, and told projector owners that the new films, *Report from the Beachhead, We Said We'd Come Back, It Can't Last,* and *Freedom Comes High,* were available for bond rallies.[31]

Movie theaters held special screenings with the price of admission the purchase of a war bond. Here movie fans buy a bond to see the 1943 film *For Whom the Bell Tolls*. (National Archives)

In addition to complete films, the Treasury also produced a large number of bond-related news clips, which "rode" on newsreels, including a one-minute trailer featuring the payroll savings plan at International Harvester. Perhaps the most famous endorsements for bonds came from Donald Duck and Bugs Bunny, the latter singing Irving Berlin's "Any Bonds Today?" in a promotional cartoon. Bugs Bunny even showed up at the Treasury building in February 1942 and was asked by reporters about his role in the bond program. "I'm in this thing for the duration," said the rabbit.[32]

Athletes and spectators of professional, amateur, and collegiate sports also took part in Treasury bond promotional efforts. In February 1942, President Roosevelt asked all involved in professional baseball, "from executives down to peanut vendors," to contribute to the war effort in a variety of ways. Beyond requesting that 10 percent of professional baseball employees' salaries be paid in defense bonds, he asked that the pro-

A movie theater in Puerto Rico holding a war bond screening of the film *The Thief of Baghdad*. (National Archives)

ceeds of two All-Star games go toward supplying baseball equipment for those in the army and navy. He also insisted on more night games and doubleheaders, free admission to those in the armed forces, and exhibition games between army and navy teams. In addition to agreeing to the 10 percent payroll deduction plan, professional baseball players held a number of high-profile promotions in support of bonds, including Baseball Defense Bond Day in 1941 and a Washington Senators versus Navy All-Stars exhibition game in 1943. Baseball announcers asked for bond pledges on the radio, as when Red Barber raised $100,000 during a single broadcast of a Dodgers versus Giants game. The Baseball War Bond League raised $947 million in bond sales in 1943, and a baseball autographed by both President Roosevelt and Winston Churchill sold for $10,000 in bond sales in September of that year. Participants and viewers of other sports showed similar enthusiasm for the bond program. In 1943, local pugilists fought for bonds in Houston while Jack Dempsey refereed. The Army-Navy football game of 1944 featured a war bond promotion, and the price of admission to the 1944 Ice Capades was a war bond. The proceeds from wagering on pigeon races between Houston and Dallas and on greyhound racing in Oregon went toward bond purchases, and the Bowlers' Victory Legion bowled for bonds for its 1943–44 season.[33]

Music played a large and important part of bond promotion, crossing the lines of many different Treasury activities. As part of the Treasury's Music Project, which operated from 1942 to 1944, a team of Treasury consultants contacted songwriters to compose music and lyrics based around a war bond theme. Berlin's "Any Bonds Today?" emerged as the unofficial theme song for the Treasury's bond program. Sheet music for songs with a war bond theme were very popular among women's clubs, schools, and patriotic organizations. Beside selecting music for bond promotions on radio broadcasts, the Treasury consultants also endorsed school and community Victory Sings, in which children and adults would sing patriotic and fighting songs as part of bond rallies. In conjunction with these songs, the Treasury recommended that Victory Sings include "songs of the people," paying particular attention to the interests of African Americans and white ethnic groups. For African Americans, the consultants suggested "Swing Low Sweet Chariot" and "Go Down, Moses," the latter, according to the Treasury, because of "its intensely meaningful 'Let my people go!'" "If the community is made up of large numbers of Americans of foreign extraction," the bond guide continued, "they might sing some of their folk songs or be represented by groups of folk dancers."[34]

The Treasury's Books and Authors program was one in which writers, artists, literary agents, publishers, and editors collaborated to promote war bonds. The program was managed by the Treasury's Writers War Board, which oversaw the writing of slogans, fillers, posters, and other bond promotional material. Writers also developed short essays about the benefits of investing in bonds, and authors devoted their book jackets to war bond messages. Books and Authors rallies, a literary equivalent to the Treasury's tour of movie stars, were headed by Pearl Buck. She and other writers visited Allentown, Pennsylvania, in February 1943 to kick off the series of rallies, with the price of admission the purchase of a bond. An autographed copy of one of the attending writer's works was typically auctioned off at Books and Authors rallies, which numbered three hundred by March 1944. A related program was the Library War Bond promotion in 1944, in which libraries made available essays on war finance, distributed promotional material, and took applications for war bonds. Twenty states participated in the promotion for the Sixth War Loan.[35]

Community theaters also participated in bond promotions, with George Kaufman chair of the Treasury's committee for the program. Eleven performances of an experimental theatrical project generated $5 million in bond sales, and a number of original war bond plays, including *The Favor* and *To Ease Their Hurt,* were written especially for community theaters. Leading Broadway playwrights and publishers also occasionally waived their copyright fees to allow civic theaters groups to perform hit shows and donate the proceeds to war bonds. In March 1942, the Berkeley (California) Playmakers, a nationally known short-play theater company, offered $125 in defense bonds to the winner of its eighteenth annual one-act play competition. The judges of the competition were writer William Saroyan, film director Irving Pickel, San Francisco drama critic George Warren, and former director the Berkeley Playhouse, Everett Glass. As did many groups in American theater, the company had strong ties to the Communist Party, making the competition of interest to the *Daily Worker,* which reported the story. In 1943, the Women's Section of the War Savings Staff also held a nationwide college playwriting contest, the goal being to produce short plays for community theaters "stressing the human drama behind bond buying." Bonds and community theater intersected in many ways at the amateur level. In 1943, the American Legion of Sapulpa, Oklahoma, produced *Bond-Za-Bustin* (after the popular 1938 Broadway musical *Helzapoppin*) to a packed house, raising $75,000 in bonds and stamps, and in Wellfleet, Massachusetts, a local cast put on a minstrel show as part of a bond rally.[36]

From its collaboration with institutions located within popular culture, it was clear that the Treasury recognized that going into partnership with the private sector was necessary for the bond program's success. As the Roosevelt administration shifted away from its anti–big business stance of the Depression years, the Treasury also tapped into consumer culture, and retailers in particular, to promote the sale of bonds. Selling bonds was a natural fit for retailers, as all elements were already in place to add bonds to their merchandise mix. In addition to the need to build traffic in stores when so much consumer merchandise was simply unavailable, bonds represented a perfect opportunity to build goodwill with customers, which would presumable pay off after the war. All types of local businesses, from small mom-and-pop operations to large companies, found creative ways to sell or promote bonds. The owners of a Donutmobile in New York City, for example, offered free donuts for a two-dollar purchase of stamps, and managers of an ice cream store in Seattle created Minute Man Sundaes, Back the Attack Layer Cakes, and Morgenthau Specials to remind its customers to buy bonds for the Third War Loan. In Kansas City, managers of a laundry service delivered with laundered clothes a card announcing that the Liberty Belles, an organization of bonds sellers, would soon be canvassing the neighborhood. During bond drives, local retailers would also often contribute free products or services to bond purchasers, offering a spaghetti dinner or tickets to a play, concert, or sports event.[37]

Recognizing that making bonds available where consumers ordinarily shopped represented a huge opportunity for incremental sales, the Treasury's War Finance Division devoted an entire section to retail operations. There was, of course, an inherent conflict related to selling bonds within the commercial private sector, as retailers were in the business of selling goods at a profit, not bonds on a pro bono basis. In the spirit of patriotism, however, retailers typically urged consumers to buy bonds first and their merchandise second, again banking that such goodwill would build consumers' loyalty and pay off dividends in the consumer spree after the war. Stores occasionally offered free war bonds with the purchase of an item of significant value. Alberts, for example, a department store in Waterbury, Connecticut, offered shoppers a free twenty-five-dollar bond with three hundred dollars' worth of merchandise. "Here is an ideal opportunity," the store's ad read in January 1942, "to perform a worthwhile patriotic service in supporting your government at no cost to you; and at the same time you will be beautifully furnishing your home (the real pride of every true American) at unprecedented low prices."[38]

The retailer practice of offering free bonds with a large purchase was, however, disapproved of by the government, as was the practice of retailers making bond buyers eligible for scarce consumer goods. Similarly, the Treasury objected to the layaway plan, in which consumers charged a bond and paid off the cost in a number of installments, being applied to government securities. To the administration, offering bonds for sale within the consumer sphere was one thing; tainting them by applying the trappings of commerce was another.[39]

The Treasury, however, could not completely resist employing classic sales promotion techniques, particularly around the holidays. For Christmas of 1942, the Treasury's War Savings Staff developed a special envelope designed to hold a war bond to be given as a holiday present, and for Christmas of 1944, offered a V-Mail gift certificate to friends and relatives of service personnel, redeemable for a war bond. The Treasury also offered a Bond-a-Month Club, although this was designed principally as a surrogate payroll savings plan for non-eligible Americans such as farmers and housewives. The Treasury's borrowing of traditional marketing tactics was yet another way the state looked to the private arena for effective ways to sell bonds.[40]

Because large department stores were often the heart of urban centers during the war, the retail environment was particularly well suited for special bond promotions. July 1942, for example, was labeled Retailers for Victory Month by the War Finance Division, with all retailers asked to set aside a fifteen-minute White Out for Victory period at noon on July 1 to sell only war bonds. For both the Fifth and Sixth War Loans, the Treasury orchestrated a window display contest, in which bonds were awarded as prizes for retailers who constructed the best display using bonds and stamps. Retailers were also largely responsible for the 1943 Shangri-La promotion, in which the proceeds of shoppers' bond sales went toward the purchase of a Shangri-La aircraft carrier intended to bomb Tokyo. Finally, for the Seventh War Loan, the Treasury coordinated the Third Army Plan promotion in which small badges were awarded to retail employees, ranking them from private to general based on bond sales. No other promotion could be more appropriate given the Treasury's use of retailers as a mercenary army in the sale of war bonds to Americans.[41]

The 1943 Four Freedoms War Bond Show, in which Norman Rockwell's paintings and the artist himself toured department stores in various cities, was a tremendously popular event. Rockwell had painted the Four Freedoms after President Roosevelt's speech to Congress, and the February and March issues of the *Saturday Evening Post* made them

A retail display window of G. Fox and Company of Hartford, Connecticut, encouraging shoppers to buy a "Yankee sub bond" during the Third War Loan. (National Archives)

A Savannah, Missouri, retail display window featuring war bonds and stamps as part of an "Axis Easter basket." (National Archives)

famous. Seeing an opportunity, the administration immediately related the idea of the Four Freedoms to that of the Treasury's bond program, stating in a May 1943 Office of War Information fact sheet that "war bonds are a symbol of the Four Freedoms we are fighting for." The magazine and local department stores sponsored the Four Freedoms tour, with the paintings displayed and reproductions offered free to shoppers as an incentive for bond purchases. The Hecht Company, one of the department stores to host the exhibition, used typical retailer language to promote the show: "Here at the Hecht Company, you may not only *see* the originals of famous *Post* illustrations—you may *own* one yourself!" The choice of a department store to exhibit the paintings was perhaps a curious one given the civic nature of the event. A public building might have been more fitting, but a department store was the perfect backdrop for consumers.[42]

An important part of the Treasury's overall promotional program was its publicity or public relations campaign. The Treasury's publicity revolved around three broad themes. The first theme related to instances of bond selling or purchasing considered exceptional because they involved people who were somehow outside the mainstream and thus, ironically, considered most representative of "the people." Such types of people included

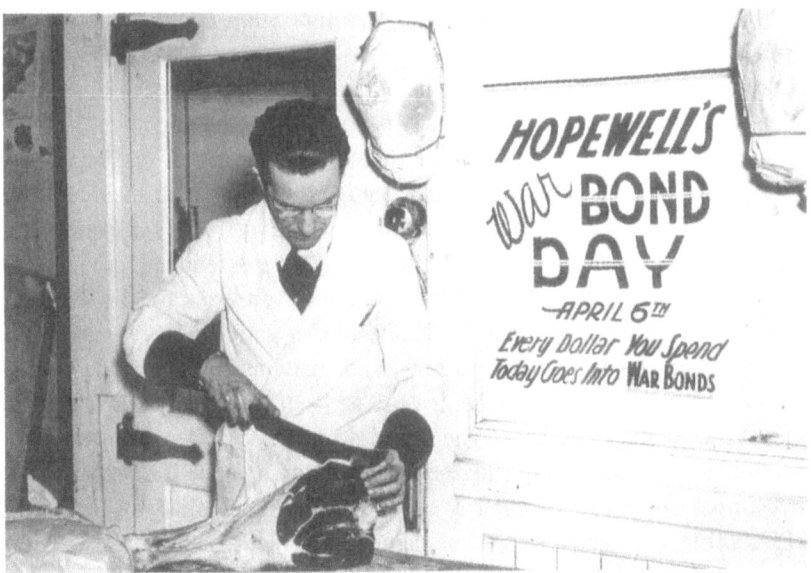

This butcher, like most other merchants and professionals in Hopewell, Virginia, put his entire cash proceeds into bonds on the town's War Bond Day, April 6, 1943. (National Archives)

immigrants, the poor, and prisoners. Prisoners were apparently avid backers of the bond program, a fact the Treasury readily exploited in its public relations campaign. Instances of support among the incarcerated was as strong as evidence as any that all types of Americans, even those who had committed crimes for which they were being punished, stood behind the effort. In February 1942, for example, inmates at the Ohio State Penitentiary invested $6,325.00 in bonds and $1,333.75 in stamps while training for the military in preparation to enter the service when released. Prisons in which inmates were producing equipment and supplies for use in the war were especially strong supporters of the bond program. One hundred twenty such prisons set a $300,000 bond quota for the Third War Loan in 1943. Also for the third loan, twenty-two state penal institutions, including the Women's Reformatory in Shakopee, Minnesota, raised $87,000 in bonds. For this particular rally, prison officials went "bench-to-bench" and "cell-to-cell" to solicit funds, a novel application of the Treasury's canvassing sales technique.[43]

Bond publicity indicated that even those with no apparent personal incentives were purchasing bonds. Alonzo Stevens, a forty-eight-year-old man serving a life sentence at South Carolina State Penitentiary bought $5,000 in bonds, saying, "Eventually, I hope to purchase $15,000 more to bring the war to a successful conclusion as early as possible." The symbol of an individual striving for national freedom despite having no chance for personal freedom was a powerful one within the context of the Treasury's propaganda campaign. Although discouraged, the threat of incarceration was also occasionally used to sell bonds. In January 1942, for example, a superior court judge in Massachusetts sentenced a defendant convicted of arson to purchase $5 worth of defense stamps each week for the duration of the war or face two years in the House of Corrections. The Treasury did not publicize the fact that prostitutes and madams in Hawaii were also "proud participants in war-bond drives," as Beth Bailey and David Farber uncovered in their research. The prostitution trade was a tremendously profitable one in Hawaii during the war, and bonds made for a smart, safe investment for those in such a cash business. One madam who sold $132,000 in war bonds to her colleagues even received a special citation from the unwitting Secretary Morgenthau, giving new meaning to his vision of the securities as the people's investment.[44]

The Treasury made it known that even conscientious objectors to the war found ways to invest in bonds. In July 1942, members of the Quaker, Mennonite, and Brethren faiths were granted their request to the Treasury to purchase securities that would go toward nonmilitary governmental spending, albeit at a lower interest rate. In an interesting contrast to the World War I bond program, in which Quakers and Mennonites were persecuted for not buying bonds because of their religious beliefs, the World War II program was able to accommodate even those who morally objected to the war. Demonstrating such vivid evidence of the breadth of the bond program was another means by which the administration espoused a pluralistic yet united war effort.[45]

The second publicity theme involved extraordinary sacrifice, almost always, again, by "ordinary" Americans. Although major institutional investors—banks, insurance companies, and so on—accounted for a large share of sales of government securities during the war, Secretary Morgenthau's mission to sell the war to the American people relied upon local, anecdotal stories of outstanding personal or community sacrifice. Immediately following Pearl Harbor and America's entry into the war, bonds became seen as a vital way to join the fight on the home front and, more specifically, vent anger toward the Japanese. Two weeks after Pearl Harbor, the First Baptist Church of Sullivan, Indiana, used its church organ fund of $1,083.85 for bonds instead. A city engineer in Portland, Oregon, started a fund in January 1942 for a $500 bond to reward the airman who first "lays an egg on the Jap capital," and the first National Bank of Windom, Minnesota, formed the Mad at Jap Club, the price of membership being the purchase of a bond.[46]

Stories of all forms of sacrifice regarding the purchase of bonds involving individuals, families, communities, even companies became almost routine. An Atlanta alumnus of Georgia Tech singlehandedly raised $1 million for a bomber to be named "the Yellowjacket" after his alma mater's mascot. A Kansas couple purchased bonds with the $12,000 received in life insurance for their son being killed in action in the Philippines. After Meddybemps, Maine (population sixty) became the first town in the country in which all citizens had purchased a bond, the race was on for communities to become "100 percent towns." Despite strikes at both Goodyear and General Tire in October 1942, bond sales continued, and the plants were among the first to reach the 10 percent of total payroll goal. Such stories of personal and group sacrifice were intended to not only strengthen national morale on the home front but also demonstrate to the Axis the country's resolve.[47]

The third type of publicity the Treasury employed was of the unusual or offbeat variety, intended to show the range of support for the bond program. The perception of unity resided not only in evidence of support of the bond program by large institutions but in the local and particular as well. Agriculture often served as a prime source for such material, as in the case of Victory Pig Clubs, in which the pick of a litter was designated by a child to be raised and then publicly auctioned off for bond subscriptions. A pig named King Neptune, for example, sold for $5 million in bond subscriptions, which, an agricultural specialist in the Treasury was quick to report, was "not the prize Duroc boar which also brought in $5 million when 'hogtioned' by the National Breeders Association in Memphis, Tennessee." In 1942, Robert P. Moorman, an eighteen-year-old 4-H Club member from Rose Hill, South Dakota, sold his state fair prize-winning Hereford calf to Armour and Company for $525 and promptly invested the money in war bonds. In another typical agricultural story, 4-H members picked seven million pounds of "bondberries," that is, blackberries used to purchase war bonds. War Savings Staffs in rural states worked closely with agriculture-based organizations to publicize the Treasury program among farmers and farmers-to-be. In early 1943, the Future Farmers of America held a writing contest on the theme "Why Farmers Should Buy War Bonds" in all southern California schools teaching vocational agriculture. The best essays were submitted to local and state bond committees for use in subsequent publicity efforts.[48]

Political figures, eager to display their patriotism, often jumped into the bond fray, sometimes in unorthodox ways. In January 1942, for example, Senator O'Daniel of Texas suggested that Americans voluntarily abstain from alcohol and direct the savings toward the purchase of bonds. Although he offered figures showing that implementation of such a plan would cause the Treasury's coffers to virtually overflow, Keynesian theory prevailed. Elected officials found bonds to be an opportune way to offer compromise within political debates. In the debate over whether defense workers should receive overtime wages, Senator Prentiss M. Brown (D-Michigan) proposed that overtime be paid in bonds versus cash. (Morgenthau opposed this idea, saying that such a mandatory payment of bonds would "pretty well kill the voluntary plan.") It was also not unusual for bond-promoting politicians to display the sort of regional pride and competitive spirit usually reserved for sports contests. For the Third War Loan in September 1943, Governor Dwight Griswold of Nebraska proposed a bond sales contest to forty-seven other state governors, wagering a corn-fed hog against any other item of similar value. Planning to win the bet, Governor Griswold invited the ninety-three county War Finance chairs to a lavish dinner to include Michigan beans, Minnesota butter, Kansas turkey, Arkansas beef, Idaho potatoes, and Colorado buffalo.[49]

Children and students also often served as the protagonists in human interest stories related to bond buying and selling. In Los Angeles, for example, it was reported that eleven-year-old Charles Gallenkamp had taught his dachshund to lick war stamps, a feat that enabled Charles to sell hundreds of dollars worth of securities. In 1942, an Italian language club in a Hartford, Connecticut, high school purchased a one-hundred-dollar bond to be awarded upon maturity to a deserving member of the school's class of 1952. The Treasury was no doubt eager to report a rare instance of collegial support for the bond program, when graduates of Vassar College wore war stamp corsages at their commencement ceremony. Such stories involving unusual circumstances among "usual" people were designed to serve as clear signals of the democratic, pluralistic nature of the bond program and, thus, of American society as a whole.[50]

As the war drew to a close in 1945, the Treasury reoriented the bond program to reflect the shift in both military scope overseas and the cultural climate at home. For the Seventh War Loan in May 1945, the Treasury began the transition from wartime military spending to postwar consumer savings. "Now it is time," said Secretary Morgenthau, "for us to get back to serious business—to the business of taming and civilizing the Japanese in the East and to the business of helping to rebuild civilization in the West."

The Treasury's foremost concern now was immediate redemption of securities by a large number of bond holders. This possibility was considered a threat to both the short-term financial interests of the federal government and the long-term financial interests of the American people. The actual redemption rate of bonds to date were actually lower than the Treasury had anticipated, with only one in four bond holders having redeemed one or more bonds. Of those who had redeemed bonds before their ten-year maturity date, half cited "emergency expenses" as the reason. As part of the attempt to encourage Americans to hang onto their bonds, considered an important step toward realizing the promise of postwar abundance and prosperity, recognized figures outside the immediate periphery of the Treasury began to play a larger role in bond promotion. "The war savings pool," declared Supreme Court Justice William O. Douglas for the Seventh War Loan, "can become an instrument to guarantee for tomorrow both security and opportunity."[51]

By August 1945, the war over and Harry S Truman as president, Secretary Morgenthau had resigned his post, succeeded by former congressman and judge Fred M. Vinson. Bonds were now Victory Bonds, with the Victory Loan the final war-related drive. The Treasury had already fully shifted its approach to reflect the emerging peacetime economy, viewing a savings program as a primary means to achieve the postwar obsession with national security. "Millions of our citizens have learned the value of thrift," said Secretary Vinson. "National stability will be advanced by having our national obligations held by the greatest possible number of citizens." The unofficial audit of the bond program revealed that Americans had purchased eighty-five million defense, war, and Victory bonds, which, in addition to institutional investing, accounted to $185.7 billion of war-related government issues. By the spring of 1946, the postwar savings plan was laid out in detail, with U.S. savings bonds presented as an ideal way to fight postwar inflation, spread the national debt, and encourage personal thrift. Supported by the new bond slogan "You Backed the Attack, Now Back Your Future," the Treasury was prepared to lead postwar American society into the promised land of boundless growth and unlimited opportunity.[52]

PART TWO

★ ★ ★ **War Bonds and Labor, Class, and Ethnicity**

CHAPTER 4

★ ★ ★ **On This We Are United**

If World War II was to truly become a people's war, the Roosevelt administration recognized early on that America's class divisions and hostilities would have to be lessened. National unity was dependent upon not only "solving" the country's racial, ethnic, and religious "problems" but also developing a greater tolerance of others' economic and social status. Confronting the sensitive issue of class was a potentially risky but necessary step the administration would have to take to present a stronger front to its enemies. The Treasury's bond program was an ideal vehicle with which to bring together people of different socioeconomic backgrounds and deliver propagandist ideology blurring the lines of class.

For the Treasury, one of the principle paths to achieving the administration's goal of national harmony resided in effectively reaching the working class and, specifically, labor. Via its defense bond campaign, Secretary Morgenthau and other Treasury officials saw an opportunity to overcome the class-based distrust and tension that lingered after a decade of economic unrest. Tapping into the traditionally strong patriotic sentiment held by the working class through bonds was viewed a means to give them a personal, economically grounded stake in the war. By selling shares in America to workers, animosity toward fellow citizens and institutions—particularly management and the government itself—would be deflated. Through the common discourse of sacrifice now for later rewards, the country's labor force would prove to invest in bonds in order to serve both their national and personal best interests.

The war itself would, in fact, revive labor, which had been reeling since the "Roosevelt recession" of late 1937 and 1938. The economic downturn had severely slowed production, employment, and union organizing between 1938 and 1940. Despite the potential economic incentives of the war buildup, for the most part labor leaders remained isolationist through 1939 and early 1940. This was largely a function of unions' post–World War I experience, when the fear of depression created a highly unstable environment for labor. Labor's working class, however, were much more likely to be prointervention, as Jewish and ethnic Americans sympathized with their peoples' fates in Eastern Europe. By 1941, most of labor supported intervention in Europe to defeat fascism and defend American progressive democracy. The war became, in labor's view, a "liberal crusade" on a world stage, a fight to preserve and spread the same type of principles it espoused at home.[1]

Because of these very principles—brotherhood, democracy in action, and so on—unions gained a certain degree of social status during the war. Labor used the circulating rhetoric of enlightenment ideology to its advantage, making clear the parallels between their own pursuit of freedoms and the nation's. On a more fundamental level, however, labor made gains through the economic partnership with its new ally, the federal government. By choosing to contract for war production with private capital, the Roosevelt administration was reliant upon unions and their members to deliver the necessary materials for war. In exchange for defense contracts, the government expected labor to contribute to the war on various levels. Outside of maximum production through no strikes or slowdowns, the Roosevelt administration counted heavily upon labor for a large revenue stream from bonds. The Treasury devoted an entire section within its National Organizations Division, headed by James B. Houghteling, to gain labor's support for the bond program. The dedicated effort paid off, as the labor community responded to the Treasury's program with more bond sales than any other single group in the nation.[2]

The Treasury's bond program was in fact one of a number of parallel mechanisms designed to ease labor conflict leading up to and during the war. As did bond rallies, the focus on production helped resolve labor's ideological stance toward capital and the state, which had wavered through the New Deal. Through what Charles S. Maier termed "the politics of productivity," labor offered pledges of maximum production and no strikes in exchange for the employment and wage benefits resulting from large defense contracts. Rather than through class antagonisms, union strength resided in acquiescing to pressure to join the economic partnership between big business and the federal government. As is the arena of production, bonds offered labor an opportunity to join the emerging consensus predicated on "the twin blessings of patriotism and economic prosperity."[3]

Despite union members' tremendous support for the war through Treasury bonds, labor's collective power diminished over the course of World War II. The restoration of capital during the war would ultimately prove to supersede union gains as the Roosevelt administration looked to big business to lead the path toward social democracy. The staple pursuits of labor—collective bargaining, right to strike clauses, and so on—were increasingly defeated as capital was relied upon to stabilize the American economy and deliver the promised fruits of consumption. The consensus among government, labor, and business that emerged during the war significantly weakened the "class-based construction of Americanism" in place through the 1930s. Inequalities between capital and labor (like racial, ethnic, and religious bigotries) were no longer "natural" but, rather, chinks in the American armor that threatened national security.[4]

To consolidate its power, labor became more centralized and bureaucratic as the war progressed, taking on some of the organizational trappings of its consensus cousins, big government and big business. As the business community pursued what Elizabeth Fones-Wolf called "an aggressive campaign to recast the political economy of America," New Deal liberalism and labor each suffered. By 1944, the nation's economic and political landscape became decidedly more conservative, setting the stage for a strong anti-union sentiment. As labor shifted from assertion to accommodation during World War II, it gradually positioned itself as a fundamental part of the inevitable postwar consensus built on a political economy of military preparedness.[5]

Defense production, beginning in earnest in 1940, doubled the number of union members and increased labor's economic strength. The culture of labor changed dramatically during World War II, as many more women, African Americans, teenagers, and farmers took jobs in defense plants. These new workers perceived unions as essentially "irrelevant" because of the high wages they were earning. Among labor leaders, however, wages and working conditions remained important issues, with the real possibility that management and the government would take advantage of union support for the war. Many union members were confronted with a dilemma that pitted their national loyalty against their traditional working-class consciousness, that is, how to negotiate "abstract patriotism" against the "daily struggle" that was part and parcel of labor's mission.[6]

One of the major ways labor found a balance between national and class identities was through the buying and selling of bonds. Insight into the dynamics between war bonds and unions and their members can be found in the pages of the three major labor newspapers, the *CIO News*, the *Daily Worker*, and *Labor Action*. The labor press regularly carried news about bonds, with the exception of *Labor Action*, which ran few articles about them, and then only ones that were somehow critical of the program. Although the *CIO News* ignored the program through 1941, the newspaper consistently devoted to space to bond stories after Pearl Harbor and frequently published Treasury press releases. Both the *CIO News* and the *Daily Worker* carried bond advertising. In February 1942, for example, the *CIO News* ran a bond ad featuring an illustration of Abraham Lincoln. Borrowing Lincoln's words, the caption read "Buy Bonds for Victory so that 'Government of the people, by the people, for the people, shall not perish from the Earth.'" Rather than focusing on other aspects of the bond program, such as financial incentives for the nation or individuals, the newspaper expressed through bond advertising a message consistent with its own ideology.[7]

Corporations also sponsored bond advertising in labor newspapers to build goodwill among its union workers. In December 1942, for example, International Business Machines took out a full-page ad in the *CIO News*, titled "The Glory of Democracy," which urged the purchase of war bonds.[8] Bond ads often featured an illustration of defense work in progress, linking two methods of sacrifice, war finance and war production. In a November 1944 Dow Chemical bond ad, "The Chemistry of Hope," Uncle Sam was portrayed working in a defense plant.[9] In bond advertising directed to labor, analogies were typically drawn between workers on the home front and workers overseas, that is, the armed forces. Studebaker, a consistent advertiser in the *CIO News*, ran such a bond ad in June 1945 as the war neared its end. The ad foreshadowed a common theme in postwar America, easing the transition of the armed forces back to civilian life:

> We can all make it easier—mentally as well as physically—for our men and women in uniform, if we prove to them now, with Extra War Bonds, that we're with them every step of the last hard miles that lie ahead.... It's our golden opportunity to show our valiant, hard-hitting fighters that we're really worthy of what they're doing for us.[10]

Bond drives were an important way labor contributed to the war effort, but unions took part in a variety of other causes. Union members, like many Americans, participated in Red Cross blood drives, gathered commodities in scrap and salvage drives, and grew vegetables in victory gardens. Other agencies soliciting for union members' money were the Community Chest War Fund and CIO War Relief, the latter asking Detroit auto workers to give one hour of pay per month. Through its multiple efforts, labor's presence and prestige grew on a local, community level. Where before the war management typically worked with social service agencies (and workers were simply "shaken down" for contributions), large unions such as the AFL and CIO gained direct access to such agencies during the war.[11]

Because they often served as the most central public demonstrations of support for the nation, bond rallies were occasionally the source of labor conflict. In February 1942, for example, CIO workers picketed a bond rally at the Statler Hotel in St. Louis to protest what they believed was an underrepresentation of labor on Defense Savings Committees. The picketers, members of the United Catery Workers and Statler Hotel employees, also happened to be on strike. Union members claimed that Tom Dysert, president of the St. Louis Chamber of Commerce, had deliberately chosen the hotel in order to weaken the union's position. "Although some CIO leaders had been among the most boisterous supporters of Defense Savings," a reporter at the scene noted, strikers said they would not be "buffaloed by 'patriotic' mumbo-jumbo." The union suspended the purchase of a $750 bond, but not without some ambivalence. "A few of the CIO leaders were confused and torn between their natural class militancy and their supposed obligation to the government," the reporter for *Labor Action* wrote, a testament to the shifting in the American political economy from conflict- to consensus-based. Although the politics of the strike complicated the issues, the local's concern about underrepresentation was clearly not a red herring, echoed by CIO president Philip Murray two months later at the landmark meeting among the nation's "Big Three" unions. While pledging his union's commitment to the payroll savings plan, Murray urged that labor "be given a greater voice in the participation and administration" of the Treasury's bond program. This desire for greater representation on bond committees mirrored the AFL's and CIO's pursuit of a larger role across government agencies, particularly the Office of Production Management (OPM), later the War Production Board (WPB).[12]

Industries with a vested interest in the management of the bond program also on occasion voiced their protest against administrative policy. After hearing of the government's intent to obtain advertising space and time for bonds free of charge, newspaper publishers made their opinion known that they should receive revenue for bond ads. In March 1942, led by *Editor & Publisher*, a newspaper trade magazine, one hundred publishers protested the free advertising plan, claiming that advertising space was "as much as an instrument of war as steel, or copper, or rubber, or cotton, and should be paid for as such." Interestingly, in reporting the story, the *CIO News* distanced itself from other newspapers, making it clear that the labor press would accept the government's request for free advertising space for bonds. The fact that the labor press was more willing than more commercial publishers to align with government policy was perhaps indicative of some remaining resentment on the part of business toward an administration perceived as hostile to private interests.[13]

Another instance of politics within the newspaper industry was played out through the ideological dynamics of bonds. On March 20, 1942, the generally right-wing *Chicago Tribune* published a letter from a reader who saw the Treasury's bond program as one more case of wasteful New Deal spending. Comparing bonds to a New Deal program dedicated to a better understanding of "musical science," the reader declared (under a heading of "Notice to Boondogglers") that "the government does not need any help from me to buy bonds or stamps... and this is notice I am not buying any until these conditions [administrative spending on unnecessary projects] are remedied." Simply for publishing the letter, the *Chicago Tribune* was editorially attacked by other newspapers, perhaps most vociferously by Conrad Komorowski, a writer for the decidedly progressive *Daily Worker*. "His [the letter writer's] position is but the logical continuation of the *Tribune*'s copperhead course, which incited such treason," wrote Komorowski.[14]

The Treasury's relatively brief consideration of forced savings in the fall of 1942—after the surge of bond buying in the first half of the year—touched a nerve within the more oppositional segment of the labor community. In September, Henry Judd, a writer for the radical union newspaper *Labor Action*, voiced his protest of the 10 percent forced savings proposal, addressing his remarks to Secretary Morgenthau. Ten percent was, Judd wrote, "an awful lot to ask, Mr. Secretary, particularly when these same workers read about the fancy earnings of Mr. Boss.... Reports about big corporations buying blocks of bonds for $50,000, etc. only cause a big laugh, for everyone knows about their profits from government contracts." Judd had a valid point, his observations a fair reflection of the sentiment among a portion of the working class. Judd spoke directly to the issue of class revolving around bonds, declaring that "the masses of people . . . know, feel and see that the financial burden of the war is being placed on their shoulders. Does this induce them to buy more or less bonds, Mr. Secretary?" Judd concluded by suggesting to Morgenthau that the Treasury "save the Hollywood glamour boys and girls for Hollywood."[15]

Although labor and management were usually united behind the bond effort, sparks flew sporadically, particularly early in the program, before firm corporate policies were set with regard to campaigning. In January 1942, for example, members of the Federation of Architects, Engineers, Chemists and Technicians set out to put up a Treasury poster promoting the sale of bonds and stamps. After seeing the poster, with the headline "See Your Shop Steward," management at the Shell Development Company objected strongly to its presence. "Permission to post such a slogan," said the *CIO News*, "might constitute recognition of the union—from which Shell Development recoils in horror." In a similar incident two months later at Bethlehem Steel, a Brooklyn shipyard, management refused workers' request to adopt the payroll savings plan and denied the union permission to solicit purchases among members in the shipyard. Local 13 of the International Union of Marine and Shipworkers of America had planned a $100,000 drive through payroll deduction with the membership, according to the union's secretary, Leo Handler, "patriotically behind the proposal." The struggle for power between labor and management during the war thus occasionally intersected with the bond program, as factions lobbied over who determined the right to buy and sell bonds on company grounds on company time.[16]

Despite these sporadic instances of conflict and class militancy, bond drives typically functioned as a site of consensus and unity among labor, management, and the government. Recognizing the importance of labor to the success of the bond program, the Treasury actively sought out union leaders to work alongside administration officials. In May of 1942, for example, the Treasury appointed Milton Murray, president of the American Newspaper Guild, a consultant to the War Savings Staff. Murray's job was not only to assist the press section by providing news material regarding bonds, but also to call upon the sixteen thousand guild members in eighty-six locals to appoint campaign committee chairs. The new partnership between labor and the Roosevelt administration was bidirectional, with leaders of large unions often in direct contact with elected officials in Washington. Such was the case also in May 1942, when R. J. Thomas, president of the United Automobile Workers, wrote to Representative Andrew May, chairman of the House Military Affairs Committee. Thomas suggested that the government buy everyone in the armed forces one twenty-five-dollar bond every month as part of the increased compensation package proposed in Congress. The idea stalled, but was indicative of the more open lines of communication between labor and the government during the war.[17]

As with the nation as a whole, labor immediately responded to the bombing of Pearl Harbor and America's entry to the war by stepping up bond purchases. A week after the bombing, the *CIO News* urged its readers to participate in the program. "As union members we can take immediate practical steps to fulfill [our] obligation," an editorial read. "We can arrange that defense savings stamps be sold in our union offices along with dues stamps." The Amalgamated Clothing Workers in New York City quickly moved to allot 10 percent of weekly wages to bonds, and Local 227 of the CIO Oil Workers International Union in Houston raised $6,000 for bonds. The sinking of ships and killing of fellow union members at Pearl Harbor struck a particular chord with labor. Three weeks after the bombing, CIO Automobile Workers set a goal of $50 million in bonds to build a battleship to replace the USS *Arizona*, which was sunk. "The son of a UAW-CIO member went down on the Arizona," UAW-CIO president R. J. Thomas wrote in a letter to Secretary Morgenthau. "We are answering that dastardly act by purchasing these bonds." A month later, the Aluminum Workers of America pledged to raise $6 million in bonds to build a submarine in memory of George G. Leslie, a member killed at Pearl Harbor. In March 1942, five different CIO unions adopted a payroll savings plan to replace sunk ships. Union leaders wrote to Secretary of the Navy Frank Knox of their Bonds Float Ships campaign to raise enough money to build a battleship, a small aircraft carrier, a light cruiser, a submarine, and ten merchant cargo vessels.[18]

Individual union members often displayed what could be considered extreme support for the Treasury's bond program. Soon after Pearl Harbor, Clayton C. Harter of Massillon, Ohio, bought four $1,000 bonds with money received in back pay resulting from the settlement of the "Little Steel" strike of 1937. Harter was one of thousands of workers unfairly discharged from Republic Steel who received a cash settlement after the Labor Board awarded members $1.5 million. In October 1942, members of Local 2141 of the United Steelworkers at the American Steel and Wire Company in New Haven, Connecticut, applied most of their retroactive wages won in a settlement to buy $21,675 in bonds. With few consumer goods available, bonds were a sensible way to invest such cash windfalls. For some union members, a personal attachment to relatives overseas was the basis for going beyond the normal call of patriotic duty. In March 1944, for example, Mrs. Anna Rossetti, a CIO member at the Westinghouse Electric and Manufacturing Company plant in East Pittsburgh, designated all her pay toward the purchase of war bonds. A member of Local 601, the United Electric, Radio, and Machine Workers, Rossetti had a husband in the military (Ralph, also a CIO member), a paratrooper brother, and a brother-in-law in the Marine Corps.[19]

Locals and entire union memberships occasionally showed extreme support for the nation through bonds. In January 1942, five thousand United Automobile Workers held a defense bond rally despite being temporarily laid off as their plant was retooled to produce military equipment. In April of that year, five locals of the Industrial Union of Marine and Shipbuilding Workers representing forty thousand workers in Baltimore led a bond drive of $1.5 million, the cost of building one of their "Liberty" ships. The workers intended to name the ship the *Philip Murray* to "memorialize labor's contribution and all-out effort to win the war." Late in the war, March 1945, Packard Local 190 in Detroit presented a $500 bond to Diana Wigle, the two-year-old daughter of a UAW member killed in action. "In his [Lt. Wigle, who was posthumously awarded the Congressional Medal of Honor] memory," said Ted Bankowski, educational director of the union, "we want to give his daughter this bond to help insure the fine education he would want her to have."[20]

Support for the bond program was typically strongest when campaigns were somehow linked to the goods or services union members produced or provided. In June of 1942, for example, CIO barbers in Brooklyn sold bonds and stamps while they cut hair and offered shaves. "Ours is a service trade, nevertheless our work is most essential," said P. C. Di Neri, secretary treasurer of the CIO National Committee of Barbers and Beauty Culturists. "We are cultivating human neatness and beauty," he added. "The personal appearance has a strong bearing for the maintenance of the morale of each individual." For the Third War Loan drive in September 1943, the Amalgamated Clothing Workers led a Clothe the Army campaign, setting a goal of $2.5 million in bond purchases per month. Almost all U.S. Army clothing was made by CIO workers, and ACWA officials were determined to keep the American soldier the "best-dressed in the world." Meeting the union's goal would raise the necessary money in bonds to clothe the entire army, estimated at $110.01 per soldier. The next month in Milwaukee, the United Steelworkers of America and management at the Heil Company jointly set out to purchase enough war bonds to put a Garand M-1 rifle, a weapon the company manufactured, in the hands of every Heil employee in the armed forces.[21]

Women's labor groups often led their own bond campaigns, as when the women's auxiliaries of the CIO, AFL, and Railroad Brotherhood held a joint bond rally in April 1942 in New York City. The occasion served as the first time women of the three unions met on an official basis and presented an opportunity for labor to publicly place national interests ahead of any particular union's. "We trade women recognize only three letters of the alphabet," announced Betty Hawley Donnelly, vice president of the New York State Federation of Labor, "and those letters are not AFL or CIO—those letters are U.S.A." Added Beatrice Abramson, president of the Greater New York Council of CIO Auxiliaries: "We know what fascism means—death to the trade unions, degradation of women, the dark ages. Part of the job of defeating fascism is the regular, systematic saving of our pennies and nickels and dimes."[22] Even the *Daily Worker* recognized the threat Nazism and fascism posed to women and the role that bonds could play in winning the war. In a March 1942 editorial, Clara Bodian urged union and progressive women to support the Treasury's program:

> There is a big job for American working-class women to do in buying and selling defense bonds and stamps to strengthen our war effort.... We women in the trade unions and the auxiliaries, in the churches and lodges and fraternal groups, must do our share to answer this great need.... Women's rights as human beings and as citizens—our very right to organize into trade unions and auxiliaries and the rest—are at stake.... We women in labor and progressive groups can show the way.... Let us organize our campaign in the real American way, selling defense bonds and stamps at all meetings, luncheons, house parties, educational forums and other gatherings, selling them from booths in our own and our husbands' meeting halls. Yes, let's even cut down on movies and beauty treatments if we must.[23]

Other progressives were equally enthusiastic about the administration's bond program. George Kristalsky, a leading Michigan communist running as the Progressive candidate for the Hamtramck City Council, sold $3,050 in bonds at a March 1942 rally at the International Workers Order. (Backed by labor, Kristalsky finished eighth in a field of fifty-eight, won the party nomination, but lost in the general election.) The ability for the Treasury to enlist communist endorsement demonstrated the virtually universal appeal that bonds offered during the war. Because of the Nazis' philosophical grounding in totalitarianism, even those who were in peacetime ideologically opposed to both mainstream politics and corporate capitalism found government securities to be an acceptable, even attractive, means to fight our foreign enemies.[24]

Through the common ground of patriotism combined with financial self-interest, war bonds also operated a site for unity among different labor organizations. Unions that had displayed competitive antagonisms toward one another in the 1930s put aside their differences during the war, bonds acting as a primary rallying point. Two months before women's auxiliary groups from the AFL, CIO, and Railroad Brotherhood met for the first time, men from these same unions joined efforts for a bond drive. For Labor Defense Bond Week in February 1942, these unions engaged in a friendly competition to sell and buy bonds. With George Meany, national secretary-treasurer of the AFL at his side, Allen S. Haywood, national director of the organizations for the CIO, emphasized the important for labor unity. "On this we are united," said Haywood. "Our country is in danger. Everything we have hoped for is in danger. The AFL, CIO, and the Brotherhood are behind MacArthur. We have got to fight the appeased. This is a people's war." Two years later, leaders from these same unions met again to promote bonds on a national radio broadcast sponsored by the Treasury. Secretary-Treasurer James B. Carey, quoting CIO president Philip Murray, recognized labor's unique and vital role in the war: "It is up to us [labor] to supply the weapons the soldiers and sailors need, to make them and pay for them. Organized labor knew, long before any other group of the population, that fascism was a deadly enemy of freedom, the deadly enemy of labor unions, of political and economic democracy, of religion, of the security of the home itself." The CIO alone had raised an estimated $1.25 to $1.5 billion in bonds in 1943, but Carey pledged that it would do even better in 1944.[25]

The ability for bonds to bring together people and organizations by deflating special or competing interests was perhaps best expressed through the formation of joint labor-management bond committees. Just as major unions had never found a reason to formally sit down together and work toward a common goal until World War II bond campaigns, labor and management struck up unprecedented alliances to sell and buy bonds. In August 1942, American Federation of Hosiery Workers set up a bond committee made up of members from both labor and management, a rare partnership between traditionally rivaling factions. Upon hearing of the committee, Secretary Morgenthau was delighted, as it was exactly that kind of partnership he believed was necessary to both win the war and solidify America's economic footing. Morgenthau publicly praised the hosiery bond campaign, declaring he was "especially pleased because [it] is an undertaking which is based on the work of a joint committee on which management and labor are equally represented." Union president McKeown went further, seeing the parallels between such a committee and labor's very mission: "The joint labor-management effort follows the basic tenet of democracy. Dictatorship is the enemy of democracy and of the trade union movement which can function only in the free air of democracy."[26]

That same month, labor and management joined together for the first nationwide bond campaign. Charged with the pun-filled campaign slogan "Banded Together to Bond-Bard the Axis," the United Rubber Workers formed a labor-management committee with executives from General Tire, Firestone, Goodrich, and Goodyear. Morgenthau again took notice, saying that "we at the Treasury Department are regarding this joint labor-management War Bond drive in your industry with unusually keen interest." The campaign to enlist 100 percent participation in the 10 percent payroll deduction plan was, according to labor, management, and Treasury officials, "100 percent successful." After the drive, Morgenthau made the connection between the joint effort and the larger implications, saying that "this spirit that all of you have shown is strong assurance that we can overcome whatever obstacle may lie before us." A little more than a year later, a study commissioned by *Labor-Management News,* a propagandist publication of the government-sponsored War Production Drive, found that both production and bond sales were indeed higher in industries with joint labor-management committees. Reviewing eighteen industries employing more than eight million workers, the study reported that sixteen of the thirty-four corporations that led the nation in payroll savings plan bond purchases had such committees. The study offered firm, quantitative evidence to validate Treasury consultant Peter Odegard's theory that the psychological appeals of belonging and a shared sense of purpose would result in higher bond sales.[27]

When it could, labor's working class was also eager to compare its share of bond sales to those of the wealthy. In March 1943, using Treasury figures, the CIO published an "Economic Outlook" that indicated workers were increasing purchases of war bonds "while the rich [were] cutting down on their purchases." This perhaps overstated finding was based on the huge increase in 1942 purchases of bonds with $25, $50, and $100 maturity values. During 1942 the number of bond purchasers rose from seven hundred thousand to twenty-five million, with total maturity value of bonds sold rising from $5 to $370 million. In this same year, however, sales from $500 maturity value bonds declined from $400,000 to $250,000, with a similar trend in the $1,000 class. Although the CIO may have leaped beyond the numbers in its conclusion, the important point was and is the class-based construction of meaning gleaned from the data.

William Chenard (*right*) taking a break from his job as a battleship linoleum maker to buy a bond from his supervisor, John McDonald, in a New Jersey defense plant. (National Archives)

Often resentful of the large profits the industrial elite appeared to be making from large government contracts, labor and, more broadly, the working class, often took the opportunity to highlight its outstanding contribution to the war effort.[28]

For both patriotic and political reasons, union leaders also publicly promoted labor's record of bond purchases. CIO president Philip Murray was, with the possible exception of his counterpart AFL president William Green, the most vocal supporter of labor's contribution to the Treasury's bond program. Because of their power to influence huge numbers of Americans, Murray and Green were often asked by Secretary Morgenthau to kick off bond drives on national radio broadcasts. On such a broadcast in April 1943 to announce the Second War Loan drive, Murray announced that more than four-fifths of all industrial workers in the country were buying bonds regularly. By July of that year, a study conducted by researchers at Princeton University showed that "union members [were] buying far more War Bonds than other people in the same income group." The study found that 90 percent of union members—practically all beneath the fiftieth percentile in income—were buying bonds, whereas just 60 percent of non-

Celebrities occasionally visited defense plants to promote bonds. Here Annabella, a French American singer, makes an appeal for bonds to employees of Bell Aircraft in Marietta, Georgia. (National Archives)

union members beneath the fiftieth percentile were buying them. The payroll savings plan, which systematically converted 10 percent of workers' salaries into bonds, was of course the principal reason for the disparity.[29]

Although labor as a whole accounted for a huge percentage of bond sales, some unions obviously participated more than others, with those whose members were benefiting from well-paying jobs through large defense contracts at the top of the list. Only a year into the program, members of the United Automobile Workers had already purchased $50 million in bonds, with leaders pledging another $50 million over the next year. Secretary Morgenthau saw the UAW's past results and future promise as "renewed proofs that American labor is back of [sic] war effort heart and soul." It was not unusual for unions benefiting from sizable defense contracts to convert much of their own financial assets into Series F and G bonds. By May 1944, the Amalgamated Clothing Workers of America, one of the nation's largest unions with 325,000 members, had put 75 percent of its holdings into United States and Canadian war bonds.[30]

Aware of the enormous contributions labor was making to its bond program, the Treasury developed promotional materials dedicated to further exploiting the opportunity. Throughout the war, the Treasury's Film Section targeted labor groups with movie shorts featuring union bond drives and military equipment in action. In December 1942, for example, the Treasury distributed to public movie houses in steel-producing cities the film *Steel Bond Drive Nears 100% Goal.* The tactic was a direct attempt to achieve a 10 percent salary, 100 percent participation payroll savings plan within the country's entire steel industry. By November 1944, there were eleven different war bond films made available to labor in support of the Sixth War Loan drive. Five were produced by the Navy Department (sixteen millimeter, running time ten to twenty-one minutes), six by the War Department (two-minute trailers). Featuring "vivid war action and stories of the home front," the films were designed to be shown at union meetings and other labor affairs. For the Seventh War Loan, the Treasury made available to unions *Story of a Transport,* a sixteen-millimeter film shot by Coast Guard photographers. The film traced the unusual history of a transport ship, the *Wakefield,* which was formerly the luxury liner *Manhattan.* After being bombed at Singapore by the Japanese, the liner was refitted to carry troops. Such a story, weaving a narrative of the destruction of an icon of the rich reborn to help GIs fight the war, was surely thought to stir the working class at home.[31]

Also for both patriotic and political reasons, Secretary Morgenthau looked for opportunities to reward labor for its generosity and had little difficulty finding them. In February 1942, Morgenthau presented blue-and-white defense bond flags to two CIO-organized firms (with big military contracts), Chrysler Tank and Great Lakes Steel. These were the first defense plants to realize 90 percent participation in the payroll savings plan, and Morgenthau was eager to present them as models of cooperation during the war emergency. "What you have done in subscribing to the plan is a credit to both management and labor," he announced as he presented the flags. Morgenthau was so confident in the ability of labor to raise huge amounts of revenue through bonds that he doubled the limit organizations were allowed to purchase. After July 1, 1942, organizations could purchase up to $100,000 in Series F and G bonds in a calendar year, twice the previous amount set by the Treasury. Their cash holdings suddenly rather sizable, large unions had led the request for the increase to ensure the safety of liquid assets. July 4 of the year was thus celebrated by many labor groups by substantial bond purchases. Although accurate figures were not available, the *CIO News* reported that the "majority of the nation's international unions and hundreds of the 60,000 local unions with substantial treasuries" invested to the maximum limit.[32]

Secretary Morgenthau seized every opportunity to publicly praise labor's support of bonds, recognizing the chance to bring government and labor closer together. In November 1942, in a press conference exclusively for labor papers, Morgenthau shared that "the Treasury normally looks to the financial community for backing, but I have always said that the most consistent and most helpful backing I get comes from organized labor." Outside of the somewhat obvious puffery, a reason for holding the rare press conference was to defuse widespread rumors that lower-income groups, that is, the working class, were cashing in bonds after sixty days. Morgenthau denied the rumor, saying that total redemptions had been "trivial." Treasury figures released in March 1943 confirmed Morgenthau's statement, with only 2.2 percent of $100 or lower maturity value bonds redeemed through 1942.[33]

James H. Houghteling, whose title by January 1944 read director of labor relations of the War Finance Division, was equally praiseworthy of labor's support of the bond program. In his own statement to the press, Houghteling claimed that "there is no single group of citizens in this country more whole-heartedly in favor of the Treasury's War Bond program than the officers and individual members of organized labor." Houghteling also noted the high percentage of union members in the armed services, linking unions' effort on the home front to that overseas. By November of that year, the Treasury was armed with some truly impressive if not amazing statistics regarding labor's financial contribution to the government's coffers. Houghteling was able to report that from November 1941 to date, union members had purchased somewhere between $10 and $12 billion in bonds—one-third of all bonds sold by the Treasury! Most defense plants had met or surpassed their bond quotas, indicating a clear connection between government contracts and high bond sales. This piece of research is further evidence that patriotism or nationalism is heightened when individual or group interests are simultaneously served.[34]

As the war drew to a close, labor leaders continued their support of the Treasury's bond program, seeing union members' holdings of government securities as also important in the postwar period. In May 1945, CIO president Philip Murray made a personal plea for the union's members to hang onto their bonds and to continue purchasing them:

> I urge all loyal CIO members to maintain and increase their War Bond purchases. It is important that as the boys begin streaming back from Europe—as they will shortly—and later coming back from the Pacific, they find a

maximum number of War Bonds piled up to await their return and to help the difficult change over to a peacetime basis.[35]

As did many others anticipating an unstable economic period as industry converted back to the production of consumer goods, Murray believed that financial security resided in a nest egg of war bonds.

Finally, in Detroit in December 1942, three thousand members of the American Slav Congress held a dual bond and blood drive in a confluence of labor and ethnic support for the country. Leo Krzycki, head of the congress and vice president of the Amalgamated Clothing Workers of America, joined Michigan governor Van Wagoner and civic leaders to "rededicate themselves to the war effort on the anniversary of Pearl Harbor." With a high percentage of ethnic Americans union members, the intersection of labor and ethnic identities within the locus of bonds was not a rare event during the war. This introduction to the role of ethnic Americans in bond drives leads to another examination of how members of defined communities explored and expressed their group identity within the context of wartime patriotism.[36]

CHAPTER 5

★ ★ ★ **Consent of the Governed**

For the Fourth War Loan in February 1944, Albert Einstein donated the original copies of his theory of relativity and new theory of mathematics manuscripts to the Treasury. The documents, valued at $100,000, were publicly auctioned for bond subscriptions, ultimately raising $11 million in bond purchases. Earlier in the war in New Orleans, Giuseppe Lupo, a deaf cobbler, purchased a $100 bond with money he was saving to buy an earphone. After the story was circulated, a woman donated an earphone to Lupo. These acts of personal generosity, and the public response they drew, were viewed by Treasury officials as perfect examples of immigrants' loyalty to their adopted country. To the administration, ethnic Americans' support of the government's bond program was firsthand evidence that the war being fought overseas was indeed a "people's war for freedom."[1]

The circulation of stories reporting outstanding support of the bond program among members of white ethnic groups was part of a large, dedicated effort to motivate first- and second-generation Americans to purchase bonds and, ultimately, create a more united national community through their sale. Although the administration was clumsy in its references to ethnic groups, calling them alternatively "united nationalities," "citizens of foreign ancestry," and "foreign origin groups," the war's grounding in unity through pluralism was ideally designed for appeals to ethnic communities. White ethnic groups had proved to be vigorous supporters of World War I Liberty Loan drives, eager and, occasionally, pressured to display their patriotism in a time when immigration was threatening or at least redefining Anglo-Saxon American identity. Because World War II bond drives (and the war itself) were grounded in a pluralistic version of democracy, however, there was a greater understanding and acceptance of the idea that Americans could be ideologically united yet retain their distinct ethnic identity. Rather than attempt to coerce or force immigrants to become "100 percent American," that is, to adopt the cultural codes of the dominant Anglo society, the Roosevelt administration believed that loyalty was more likely to come from "consent of the governed"—ethnic groups' voluntary desire to belong to a national community.[2]

Bond drives among ethnic Americans thus became "Kallenesque," in the spirit of Horace M. Kallen's original theory of cultural pluralism. In 1924, Kallen envisioned an "American nation in which ... people would find it possible both to declare their loyalty to America and remain true to their ancestral culture." The nation, according to the theory, would consist of autonomous ethnic communities with their own cultural codes while remaining loyal to the federal government. It was not until World War II, however, that Kallen's idea of multiculturalism became validated, as ethnic and racial prejudice became associated with Nazi racism. Cultural pluralism became the defining character of American democracy, an alternative to the prescribing of Anglo-American language and customs for ethnics. Bond drives would prove to combine the folk traditions of ethnic subcultures with concepts of private capital, creating a powerful fusion of personal, communal, and national interests.[3]

With tolerance of cultural difference considered by the Roosevelt administration to be a demonstration of American strength, ethnic groups were also perceived as an asset in fighting the war. According to the 1945 government pamphlet *Foreign Nationality Groups in the United States,* for example, the administration's positioning the war as a "struggle of ideas" was considered a particularly effective platform by which to motivate a cross-section of the American people. "Ideas, rather than race or nationalism, have guided American history," the pamphlet declared, which "gives emphasis anew to our unity in basic principle." Beyond the ideological component, however, ethnic groups were also viewed as an asset by the government because they were believed to be capable of affecting morale in their native homelands. The Office of War Information considered ethnic Americans to be a positive resource, a "powerful weapon" able "to influence opinion and events in their native countries abroad." Wartime agencies such as the Coordinator of Information and the Office of Facts and Figures distributed propaganda material to the foreign-language press in hopes that such information would trickle into both Allied and Axis countries in Europe. Rather than attempt to extinguish ethnicity, then, an idea that had failed in Wilson's "100 percent Americanism" programs of World War I, many in the Roosevelt administration viewed ethnicity as something that could help win the war. Bonds campaigns thus represented an ideal opportunity for the administration to exploit ethnicity in order to raise revenue, publicly embrace America's inherent pluralism, and use as foreign propaganda.[4]

Instead of being blind to or attempting to erase ethnic identity, then, the Treasury seized Americans' ties to their ancestral homeland as a marketing opportunity. Because bond drives could accommodate ethnic identity within the context of patriotic support for the United States, bonds were perceived by the administration as a means by which ethnic Americans could reconcile potential ambivalence regarding their national loyalty. The bond sales records of a wide range of groups, including the Society of Mayflower Descendants, the China Society of America, the Ancient Order of Hibernians, and the Sons of Pericles, were used as prime evidence of the broad support for America's war effort. War bonds became a symbol of the American freedom to preserve and celebrate one's ethnicity, as suggested by the Treasury's observation that "citizens of foreign origin came to America to enjoy the blessings of freedom, and they can be depended upon to help preserve our common liberties by fighting for them—and buying Bonds."[5]

While encouraging local ethnic community leaders to orchestrate bond drives, the Treasury occasionally could not resist offering its own expert advice. "Give these people a goal to reach among their friends," the administration instructed local ethnic leaders, "[and] suggest special pageants—they respond to color and drama built around memories of the motherland." In addition to recommending that ethnic Americans hold bond drives in traditional costume, the Treasury also believed that food could help boost bond sales at rallies. "Food of the different nationalities can be utilized to great advantage," the Treasury's publication, *Minute Man*, advised in May 1943. Going further, the Treasury suggested that "many older women in the [nationality] groups can play an active part in the war effort by preparing pastries, breads, and other dishes that can be taken out and sold at War Saving rallies for War Stamps."[6]

The Treasury's efforts to sell bonds to ethnic Americans operated at the national, state, and local levels. As it did in World War I, the Treasury printed and distributed posters for bonds in various foreign languages. A 1943 poster, for example, with the headline "For Your Future," featuring an illustration of the Statue of Liberty with a glowing torch, was printed in Czech, Greek, Italian, and Polish. Notables of European origin represented the Treasury in personal appearances, such as when Marlene Dietrich sold bonds to German-born workers at the Gruen Watch Company in Cincinnati. At the local or community level, state War Finance Committees were assigned responsibility for helping to coordinate ethnic group bond rallies, particularly during war loan drives. Ethnic Americans were recruited to solicit for bond pledges in their own communities, often encouraged to speak in their or their ancestors' native language as they performed house-to-house canvasses.[7]

The Treasury recognized the importance of ethnic groups very early on in the bond program. Within the first months of the defense bond operation, Secretary Morgenthau enlisted the efforts of a number of recognizably liberal European refugees to promote defense bonds on the radio. Einstein, Thomas Mann, and Louis Adamic were among those who participated in radio broadcasts delivered in twenty-two foreign languages over 162 stations to reach immigrant groups. Ignace Jan Paderewski, a pianist and former minister of Poland, Emil Ludwig, author and native of Germany, and Hendrik Van Loon, a Dutch journalist and author, also took part in the Treasury's "America Preferred" radio series directed at ethnic Americans, which was broadcast over the Mutual Network.[8]

The Treasury worked with other agencies, such as the Office of Emergency Management (OEM), in coordinating bond promotions to ethnic Americans on the radio. There was high demand for bond promotional announcements among managers of foreign-language stations, as evidenced by their vigorous complaints to the OEM for more spots. Seeing the opportunity that "some special foreign language programs would pay big dividends," Lew Frank Jr., the president of the OEM, suggested that the Treasury redub its "Treasury Star Parade" music broadcasts with foreign-language announcements promoting war bonds. "This," Frank wrote in a December 1943 memo, "should be done in as many of the following languages as the budget will permit," after which was listed:

Italian	49 stations
Spanish	46 stations
Polish	45 stations
Yiddish	16 stations
French	12 stations

Greek	18 stations
German	10 stations
Czech	9 stations
Slovak	10 stations
Hungarian	17 stations

Providing these dubbed broadcasts, Frank believed, "would do a great deal to pacify the belligerent foreign language program managers."[9]

The Treasury actively recruited notable personalities as spokespersons to promote bonds to ethnic Americans. More so than in the general bond program, famous "ethnically defined" Americans represented visible symbols of success and, often, attainment of the American dream. These spokespeople also often differed from their counterparts in the mainstream bond program by their association with "high" culture or intelligentsia. Whereas most personalities from the main program were drawn from popular culture (popular music, movies, and sports), ethnic personalities such as Adamic, Mann, and Einstein were more likely to be leaders in the arts and sciences. Arturo Toscanini was perhaps the Treasury's leading figure in the promotion of bonds to ethnic Americans, conducting three concerts with the National Broadcasting Company Symphony Orchestra for the Defense Savings Program from January to April 1942. "It is fitting," Secretary Morgenthau said at the launch of this program, "that Mr. Toscanini should be helping so actively in the campaign for the sale of Defense Bonds and Stamps since he was one of the first to recognize the evils of Fascism and has fought them consistently with great courage." Morgenthau was referring to Toscanini's refusal to play the Italian Blackshirts national hymn, "Giovanezza," in 1931, and his decision a few year later to not conduct the Wagner festival at Beyreuth, which was under Nazi sponsorship.[10]

Others in the classical music world volunteered their services to promote bonds to particular ethnic communities. In 1943, the Metropolitan Opera Company of Chicago performed special concerts for both a Hungarian American audience and a Lithuanian American audience, each of which raised one hundred thousand dollars in bond pledges. Because classical music was still in the 1940s the popular music of many ethnic groups and recalled European homelands, it served as an emotionally powerful device by which to reap bond sales.[11]

In the months leading up to Pearl Harbor, various foreign notables were asked by the Treasury to convince Americans—particularly those of recent immigration—of the country's stake in the war. Even the relatives of foreign notables were occasionally asked to endorse bonds to the American people. In June 1941, Eva Curie, daughter of the French scientist Marie Curie, made a nationwide petition for the purchase of defense bonds on the CBS radio network. Her speech was later transcribed and distributed to state War Finance Committees. Investing in bonds, Curie maintained, was Americans' best opportunity to save their own country while helping to save Britain and rescue her native France. Even isolationists could hear the urgency in pleas from foreigners such as Curie, and be persuaded to convert some of their earnings into defense bonds:

> I know very little about financial matters, but it seems to me very obvious that, in time of danger, to invest your money in the free country where you live is the only reasonable gamble you can make with Destiny. You are all passengers on a ship. If the ship were sunk, you would lose everything. You are asked to keep afloat the vessel which carries your own lives.[12]

Occasionally, the Treasury worked with other government agencies to broadcast bond drives to foreign countries on shortwave radio as a propaganda tool. In 1942, for example, the Treasury worked with the Office of Coordination of Inter-American Affairs to broadcast a Spanish-American War Bond Committee rally to South America. The rally, held in a Latin American neighborhood of New York City, featured prominent Latin American speakers and entertainers.[13]

In addition to radio, the Treasury used a wide variety of promotional print material to reach ethnic Americans and influence opinion abroad. By August 1942, the War Savings Staff had produced promotional material for war bonds in the same twenty-two languages designed for radio broadcasts. The range of languages indicate the breadth of partnerships the administration desired to form with ethnic groups: Czech, Danish, English, Finnish, French, German, Greek, Hungarian, Italian, Lithuanian, Norwegian, Polish, Portuguese, Romanian, Russian, Serbo-Croatian, Slovak, Slovene, Spanish, Swedish, Ukrainian, and Yiddish. Brochures, pamphlets, and posters were distributed primarily to foreign-language newspapers, which then offered them to groups or individuals. State administrators could also order promotional material targeting ethnic groups directly from the War Savings Staff.[14]

Parallel with the production and release of promotional material for bonds, the Treasury's News Bureau led an active public relations campaign directed to ethnic Americans. The campaign consisted of distributing to the foreign-language press stories relating to the general bond program as well as those with a particular "ethnic" angle. Stories released the week of December 10, 1944, for example, included both general bond propaganda, for example, "Loses Leg for Country: Sells Bonds From Wheel Chair," and clearly ethnically oriented reports, for example, "Intensified Bond Drives Among Nationality Groups." To promote bonds to Euro-Americans via the press, the Treasury even looked to ethnic officials within the administration. M. S. Szymczak, a member of the Federal Reserve's Board of Governors, was recruited in November 1942 to write an article in the *Minute Man*. Titled "Faith and Freedom," the article was timed with the 450th anniversary of the "discovery" of America by Christopher Columbus.[15]

Although ethnic American and foreign notables lent a certain legitimacy and status to the Treasury's bond program, it was ordinary people who best represented Secretary Morgenthau's vision of the program as democracy in action. The theme repeated most often by Morgenthau and other Treasury officials—bonds as "the people's" investment—came alive through the stories of ethnic Americans such as Steve Vasilokos, "the White House peanut vendor." A 1943 War Savings Staff radio announcement reported that Vasilokos, a naturalized American citizen, was selected as "the Common Peoples' Man of the Year" at a Greek American war bond rally. While operating his peanut stand near the White House, Vasilokos sold thousands of dollars worth of war stamps and bonds through subscriptions or pledges. Like most promotional techniques directed to ethnic Americans, the radio announcement made the key link believed to be crucial to eliciting their support, that between America and one's native homeland: "Steve has heard from his friends in Greece, been told what it means to attempt to fight the Nazi invaders without enough planes and tanks and bullets. So Steve wants to sell more Bonds, to buy more weapons for American fighting men."[16] Greek Americans were such strong supporters of the bond program that the American Hellenic Educational Progressive Association (AHEPA), their largest fraternal organization, was made an issuing agent for its $50-million campaign in 1943. This was an unusual measure, as the Treasury naturally guarded the actual distribution and sale of government securities closely, primarily limiting them to banks and post offices. Making AHEPA an official agent of bonds was a sign of confidence and trust in the Greek community, likely leading to greater sales.[17]

Americans who, because of their ancestral heritage, had a special stake in an Allied victory served as particularly effective spokespeople for the Treasury's bond program. For Jewish Americans, whose religion often superseded ethnicity as operative identity, bonds represented a means to fight Nazi anti-Semitism and deflate the belief that Jews were responsible for the war. Jewish organizations immediately and eagerly embraced the bond program, as when both the Order of Sons of Zion and the Jewish Postal Workers of America bought a $10,000 bond within the first two weeks of the bond program. Jewish women's groups, such as the Women's Supreme Council of B'Nai Brith and the National Ladies Auxiliary of Jewish War Veterans, were very active in bond campaigns. The efforts of particular individuals, such as Jewish immigrant Jake Ulevitz of Milwaukee, were cited by the Treasury as the kind of sacrifice other Americans should be making. As the leading bond salesperson for the B'nai Brith, the national Jewish fraternal organization, Ulevitz had sold $4 million worth of bonds in the Second War Loan and was in the midst of matching that figure for the Third War Loan. Ulevitz's very presence in the United States was presented by the Treasury as a form of debt, with selling and purchasing bonds ways to pay off that debt. Ulevitz credited his professional success as "an insurance man" to opportunities found only in America, believing that his record of bond sales represented "something paid off for everything I owe." The presentation of bonds as defender and instrument of the American dream was made even more compelling when told through the stories of Americans such as Jake Ulevitz, whose lives would have been in great jeopardy in their homeland.[18]

Jewish Americans purchased war bonds in extraordinary amounts and ways. In February 1943, Julius Klorfein pledged $1 million in bonds in exchange for the right to acquire the "Love in Bloom" violin once owned and played by Jack Benny. The pledge was made at a bond rally in the "bargain basement" of the Gimbel Brothers department store in New York, with Danny Kaye serving as auctioneer and master of ceremonies. Klorfein, the president of Garcia Grande Cigars, was a Russian immigrant active in Jewish charities. His wife, a member of the American Women's Volunteer Service and a hostess at the Stage Door Canteen and Merchant Seaman's Club, bought $175,000 worth of bonds at the rally in support of the Klorfeins' son, Arthur, a boatswain's mate first class in the Coast Guard. Also present at the rally were Billy Rose, the theatrical producer, who pledged a bond purchase of $100,000 for a letter written by George Washington, and an anonymous man who also pledged $100,000 for a Bible once belonging to Thomas Jefferson. Speeches were made by both of the Gimbel brothers, Bernard and Frederick, the former calling the bond rally "the world's greatest bargain sale." In response to Adolph Hitler, who

The B'nai Brith war bond booth in Pittsburgh. (National Archives)

once said, "A department store is a monument to a decadent society," Bernard Gimbel stated, "All I can say is that this is the best answer of democracy to Hitler." The total amount raised at this one bond rally was $2,775,925.[19]

Both German Americans and Italian Americans also held a complex but exceptionally supportive stance toward investing in bonds. Because of their ancestry, individuals of these ethnic groups were more likely to be considered possible spies and saboteurs, and subject to arrest or relocation. Although some Italian and German Americans surely retained some ambivalence regarding their national and ethnic loyalties, the vast majority looked to bonds as an ideal opportunity to voluntarily and publicly demonstrate their support for the Allies. In one such rally in 1943, $100,000 in bonds were raised at a bazaar sponsored by the German-American Conference Relief Fund. The drive was an effort of the New York City German-American War Bond Committee, one of a number of local

German American bond organizations throughout the country. Such organizations offered German Americans a formal means of proving their patriotism while retaining their proud heritage when it was held in low regard.[20]

Italian Americans, too, were attracted to bond drives because of the ability to simultaneously express ethnic heritage and national loyalty. In part to show members' unequivocal support for the United States, Italian clubs across the country consistently invested the bulk of their organizational funds in bonds. The Italian Club of Tampa, for example, dedicated all its available resources to bonds three weeks after the bombing of Pearl Harbor. In 1942, Italian Americans of San Francisco celebrated North Beach Victory Day in Washington Square, with actor Leo Carillo headlining the program. Italian Americans' response to Italy's surrender to the Allies in 1943 was clear evidence that action overseas often had a direct effect on war bond sales. Italy's surrender coincided nicely with the Treasury's Third War Loan, as Italian Americans across the country, according to a press release, "welcom[ed] the opportunity to declare themselves on the side of the United Nations, and to support the war, and shorten it, if possible, by the one means in their power, the power of their dollars."[21]

Italian Americans' investment in Third War Loan bonds was indeed exceptional. In New York, Generoso Pope, head of the Third War Loan committee in the state, felt "confident [Italian Americans] would double if not triple their previous purchase of war bonds." Pope's prediction was realized, a single Italian American banquet reportedly bringing in $1.4 million in pledges in just twenty minutes. In Massachusetts, Italian Americans were reported to be standing in line outside banks, waiting to buy bonds, immediately after news of the surrender. In Washington, D.C., Italian Americans were apparently as fervent, with "practically every Italian club meeting turn[ing] into a bond selling drive." "Italian Americans have appeared at banks with their bankbooks in hand," a press release reported, "and have placed all their saving in bonds." Finally, in Philadelphia, Donato De Grossa, a sixty-three-year-old Italian-born American who had shined the shoes of federal judges for more than fifty years, celebrated Italy's surrender by purchasing a $1,000 bond. The strong response among Italian Americans to the bond program was attributed by the Treasury to their desire to help restore democracy in Italy by both supporting U.S. soldiers and assisting government agencies to distribute necessary food, clothing, and medical care. This dual motivation—to help both fellow Americans and those of a shared heritage—will be seen as analogous to African Americans' striving for a Double V, victory over enemies abroad and home. In both ethnic and racial terms, then, owning bonds was viewed as a means of forming identity based on nationalism and common cultural background.[22]

Asian Americans' response to the Treasury's program represented some of the most interesting sites of bond consumerism. Because of the risks associated with being mistaken for Japanese Americans, Chinese Americans had a particular interest in public displays of patriotism and national loyalty. This may have been a factor for Joe Shoong, an operator of a chain of stores in San Francisco, who purchased one hundred thousand dollars' worth of war bonds as part of a half-million-dollar drive in the city's Chinatown district. The local bond committee targeted Chinatown's twenty thousand people by setting up payroll savings plans in stores such as Shoong's, the goal being, again, "100 percent–10 percent."[23]

Chinese American women were also actively involved in the buying and selling of war bonds. In Seattle, the Chinese Women's Group was selected Organization of the Week by the women's division of the county's War Finance Committee. The group earned the award by selling twenty-six thousand dollars in bonds in less than four days for the Sixth War Loan. The range of other women's groups in Seattle that had also been commended for their bond selling achievements is an indication of the breadth and power of the Treasury's bond program. The Chinese Women's Group had been selected over groups such as the Washington State Bataan Relief Organization; the Hatasu Temple, Daughters of the Nile; the Junior League; the Seattle Sorosis Club; the Insurance Women's Club of Seattle; the University Post, American Legion Auxiliary; the Bethlehem Shrine, Order of the White Shrine of Jerusalem; the Hotel Greeters Auxiliary; the Waitresses' Union; the Seattle Garden Club; the Russian Sewing Circle; the Colonial Dames; the Beatrice Fisken Chapter, Daughters of the British Empire; and the American Women's Voluntary Services.[24]

Other Asian American groups in Seattle, such as the Filipinos, were highly active during the Sixth War Loan. For the drive, Seattle Filipinos sponsored a Victory Bond wagon, which included both native Filipino dancing and music from a ten-piece Coast Guard band. The goal of this drive was the purchase of an eighteen-foot nose section of a B-29 Superfortress bomber, which was prominently displayed on the bond wagon. As the names of some of the above women's groups suggested, the overlap between ethnic and fraternal groups was significant in many communities such as Seattle, with bond drives acting as common ground between the two during the war. As further evidence, master of ceremonies for the Filipino bond program was Joseph Jainga, grand master of the grand order Eyes of the Philippines, a Filipino fraternal group. Members of two women's' fraternal organizations, the Filipino Community Women's Society and the Burgos Lodge Women's Auxiliary, also took part in the drive.[25]

East Indian Americans, many of them residing in southern California, were considered by the Treasury to be "completely anti-Axis." On Indian Independence Day in 1943, Indian Americans held a rally in Pershing Square in Los Angeles, raising $150,000 in bond sales. R. Lal Singh, editor of *India News* and a member of the Indian National Congress, served as master of ceremonies of the rally. Singh also sold bonds to members of the southern California Indian community, including Murad Sonkur, a representative of the United Automobile Workers Union, Local 904MCIO. The rally was a truly international affair, Indian Americans deciding to include in the performances a Scottish bagpiper, an Australian singer, a West African drummer, a Trinidadian Calypso singer, and a Chinese actress.[26]

Perhaps even more indicative of the breadth of the bond program were occasions in which Japanese Americans took part. Prior to the Pearl Harbor bombing and subsequent interring of many Japanese American citizens, members of the Japanese Grocers Association of Portland, Oregon, made a substantial investment in defense bonds. It is ironic, if not tragic, that many of these same buyers of bonds would soon be perceived and treated as enemies of the United States. Even after Pearl Harbor, however, Americans of Japanese descent participated in bond drives. In March 1942 in Honolulu, the *Nippu Jiji,* a newspaper whose readers consisted largely of Hawaiians of Japanese heritage, sponsored a war slogan contest. Designed to "stimulate interest in American war aims," the newspaper received approximately five hundred entries and awarded bonds and stamps for the "best slogans expressing war aims or objectives for which Americans are fighting." First prize (a fifty-dollar bond) went to Hawaiian Defense Savings Staff employee Richard K. Matsuda for his submission, "That Democracy Shall Not Die." Second prize (a twenty-five-dollar bond) went to Kay Kashiwaeda for her entry, "The Man Who Relaxes Helps the Axis." Other slogans to which the judges awarded honorable mention provide interesting insight into popular Japanese American sentiment following the bombing of their home by the Japanese three months earlier:

"Buy Defense Bonds and Get the Nippons" (George Moriguchi)
"We're in It, We'll Win It" (Tomiye Azama)
"Unity Through Words but Victory Through Work" (Masaru Koike)

Sally C. Tsujimoto, selling war bonds during the Third War Loan while working in the War Relocation Bureau in Washington, D.C. Tsujimoto's husband, Private George M. Tsujimoto, served in the 442d Japanese American Combat Team at Camp Shelby, Mississippi. (National Archives)

"Onward to Victory for Democracy" (George Takashi Ito)
"Less Words and More Action in Everything We Do" (Yukie Uyeda)
"Burn on You Victory Beacon, We'll Bring Home the Bacon" (Lester Tomikiyo)
"Serve America First, Last, and Best" (Harry Shiraiski)
"Work, Watch, and Win" (R. Okubo)
"Let's Work, Build, and Fight for American Liberty" (Fred Yamaoka)
"A Bond a Day Will Keep the Bombs Away" (Richard K. Matsuda, again)
"We Stand United, Prepared, and Willing" (George Izumi)
"Our Shoulders to the Wheel Until Victory is Ours" (Yoshito Inouye)
"For Liberty We Stand. For Humanity We March" (Reynold Tanijo)
"The Axis Started It. Let's Finish It." (Stanley Morimoto)[27]

Consent of the Governed

The Sato family of Parkdale, Oregon, sign pledges for bonds. (National Archives)

Although personal accounts and novels such as John Okada's *No-No Boy* attest to the ambivalence many Japanese Americans felt regarding the direction of their loyalty, this admittedly biased sample indicates strong support for the United States among Hawaiian Japanese Americans. Again demonstrating moral and financial support for the United States, Hawaiian Japanese American workers of the Makalopa Project of the Pacific Naval Contractors purchased thirty-seven hundred dollars in defense bonds from the Hawaiian state committee administration.[28]

Other ethnic groups in Hawaii enthusiastically supported the United States through bond drives. Months before the bombing of Pearl Harbor, members of the Puerto Rican Civic Association of Hawaii recognized their territory as a key strategic military position. Describing the Hawaiian Islands as "the eastern-most defense outpost of the nation in the Pacific," the group decided to use its building fund for bonds. The resolution to purchase defense bonds foreshadowed events to be:

> We who came from Puerto Rico, which is now being transformed into the "Gibraltar of the Caribbean," because of the current world crisis, realize perhaps better than most people how necessary it is for American citizens to invest in Defense Savings Bonds in order to guard the freedoms and liberties

Colonel Olimpio Diaz (*center*), chairman of the Sixth War Loan drive in San Juan, Puerto Rico, J. Rodriguez Pou, vice chairman of the drive (*right*), and volunteers at the opening of the war bond booth in Plaza Baldorioty, San Juan. (National Archives)

which we enjoy under the Stars and Stripes. Virtually all of the 800 members of our association are earning exceptionally higher wages these days because of the current defense preparations in Hawaii, but we realize that these so-called good times will not last forever and that there is perhaps a day of reckoning due when these defense works are completed.

Consequently, in addition to investing our association's building fund money in Series F Bonds, the individual members of our association have pledged themselves to purchase Series E Bonds to the limit of their financial ability.[29]

A dedicated effort to reach Native Americans was also part of the Treasury's bond program. Native Americans across the United States responded enthusiastically to bond drives, although their status as a nation within a nation led to complex legal situations. Whereas the Office of Indian Affairs in Juneau, Alaska, was applauded for its purchase of $110,646 in bonds, the Klamath Indians of Oregon were confronted with legislation banning the investment of tribal funds. The Klamaths had already bought $235,000 worth of bonds on an individual basis, but had to petition Congress in order to invest an additional $150,000 in tribal money.

Corporal Ismael Ramirez (*right*), Coast Artillery of San Germain, Puerto Rico, buys $30.5 million in Seventh War Loan bonds with a Puerto Rican government check from Ted Gamble (*center*), War Finance Committee director, while Sgt. Tom Purcell of the Military Police humorously serves as an armed escort. At maturity after the war, the bonds were to be invested in schools, hospitals, roads, and other public improvements. (National Archives)

Similarly, Seminoles in Oklahoma had to petition for the release of $50,000 in tribal funds in order to purchase bonds immediately following the bombing of Pearl Harbor. Making a case for the tribe in an editorial, the *Toledo Blade* argued that "these red men not only forgive, but volunteer substantial support to the Great White Father."[30]

Native American children, such as those of the Polk County, Texas, reservation, also participated in bond rallies. In Phoenix in September 1943, Native Americans from a dozen tribes performed native ceremonies and dances at a bond rally at the Phoenix Indian School. Like that of Japanese Americans, the dynamics surrounding the national loyalty of Native Americans during World War II are especially complex, as documented in nonfictional accounts and in novels such as Leslie Marmon Silko's *Ceremony*. William Tuttle has observed that Native Americans' support for the war varied widely by tribe, and that the war both revived

Members of the Klamath tribe line up to buy bonds. At the time this photograph was taken, 420 members of the 1,400-member tribe had already purchased $229,725 in defense bonds. (National Archives)

and disrupted traditional social customs. Other scholars, such as Eric Hobsbawm and George Lipsitz, have noted how ethnic groups preserve traditional expressions of their culture by adapting them to current needs. Because of the unique set of issues involved, Native Americans' investment in war bonds warrants further study, as it can undoubtedly contribute key insights related to our understanding of Native American patriotism during World War II.[31]

A host of other ethnic or nationality groups took part in bond rallies, mixing the cultural codes of their ancestral homelands with those of the United States. Bond drives became occasions for communal celebrations of ethnically defined rituals, opportunities to display patriotism within the context of ethnic heritage and vice versa. Bond drives gave ethnicity-based social occasions a special spark, an added incentive for members to serve both community and nation. The range of bond drives within the Polish American community illustrates the central role bonds played for ethnic groups on the home front. In Cambridge, Massachusetts, for example, the Women's War Savings Committee included a bond drive as part of its rather tony "Polish tea" program, and across town, Polish Americans of

Janian Federkiewicz of the Polish Alliance Society of Boston selling a bond to a navy officer in the Copley Hotel in Boston during the Third War Loan. (National Archives)

East Cambridge, a working-class neighborhood, purchased bonds at St. Hedwig's Polish Church. Under the direction of the church's priest, Reverend John Dziok, parishioners dressed as Minute Maids sold bonds and stamps to congregates every Sunday, averaging four thousand dollars a month in sales. With bond drives pulling from all segments of a particular ethnic community, bonds may have contributed to lessening perceived socioeconomic differences. In ethnic communities, bonds thus appeared to act, as the administration intended, as a means of creating pluralistic unity by cutting across class lines.[32]

Polish Americans across the country supported bond drives in a variety of ways. In Buffalo, New York, Polish Americans led a Buy a Bomber campaign in early 1943, more than doubling their quota of $175,000 with sales of $485,000. Polish Americans of Milwaukee held a bond drive in a traditional Polish setting as part of a Defense Day Parade in September 1941. "The young ladies ... wore striking colorful Polish peasant costumes which created a great deal of interest throughout the program," noted one observer. In 1943, 73 Polish Women's Club members of Southbridge, Massachusetts, dressed in traditional costume, served a dinner with food they had donated to 150 bond buyers. The diversity of the settings within the Polish American community alone suggests the depth to which bond drives and, by inference, national loyalty, were woven into the fabric of ethnic subcultures during World War II. Virtually any occasion could be recast as an opportunity to demonstrate communal pride in both national and ethnic identity.[33]

Based on bond drives held by a variety of ethnic communities, it was clear that federal laws governing the investment of communal funds pertained only to Native Americans. Scottish American communities in various parts of the country, for example, actively invested collective funds in government securities. In 1941 the Scottish Clans of St. Louis bought twenty-five thousand dollars' worth of defense bonds at a local bank with Alexander Kennedy, the Clans' deputy royal chief, dressed in full Scottish regalia. In December 1944, members of the Scottish American community of Seattle took part in the aforementioned Victory Bond Wagon, as the Washington Scottish Pipe Band marched downtown to "pipe for war bond sales." The *Seattle Times* urged that "Seattle folk who hanker for the skirl and drone of the bagpipes" attend the program in support of the Sixth War Loan. The band, composed of Scottish natives or descendants, was the official band of the Washington State Guard and had received commendations from both military and civic leaders. For these Seattle Scots, as for most ethnic communities, bond rallies were just one way to contribute toward winning the war. Two members of their band, in fact, had been killed in action during the war, and the remaining members had dedicated themselves to "furthering the war effort in every way possible."[34]

In early 1943, Mexican Americans in Denver held an American-Spanish Victory Bond drive although, a reporter noted, there were "no wealthy people in this group, and all the purchases of War Bonds were made in addition to the money invested in the pay-roll savings plan." As part of the drive, the film *Les Emigrantes,* with dialogue in Spanish, was shown to members of a sold-out audience who had each, as admission, purchased a bond with a value of at least twenty-five dollars. More than twenty-five hundred dollars in war stamps were sold at the drive's concluding rally, with native Mexican music and dances part of the event. The mayor of Denver was present, and State Administrator Ralph Nicholas appeared in a sombrero. At the rally, two Mexican serapes, or woolen ponchos, were donated and auctioned off after being displayed at the May Company department store. One of the serapes featured the image of President Roosevelt, the other the likeness of George Washington. Rather than take away from the "Americanness" of the drive, the inclusion of Mexican language, music, dance, and clothing seems to have added a sense of cultural energy. Bond drives such as these expanded the boundaries of national identity, redefining what was and what could be considered American during the war.[35]

Ethnic Americans with political, social, and religious affiliations often combined bond drives with their organizations' activities. In July 1941, just two months into the bond program, for example, the Lithuanian Citizens Political Club of Hartford, Connecticut, had already purchased the second of two $10,000 defense bonds. Also in 1941, defense bonds were awarded as prizes at the annual United Swedish Societies Festival in Portland, Oregon. In 1943, the Toledo War Committee of the United Hungarian Churches and Societies of Toledo (Ohio) sold $113,725 of bonds in less than two months. Americans of Mediterranean and Middle Eastern descent, such as the Greek Duration Bond Salesmen of Virginia and the Palmerian Society (young Syrian Americans) of Cabell County, West Virginia, also integrated bond drives into organizational programs. Another group of Middle Eastern heritage, the Syrian Lebanese Society of South Carolina, organized a citywide bond drive in Columbia in 1943, with a bond purchase the ticket of admission to the drive's dance and rally.[36]

Bond rallies among ethnic Americans became particularly festive occasions when timed with "nationality days," that is, anniversaries of noteworthy events in the history of other nations. The Treasury was well aware of the opportunity nationality days presented, advising state organizers to time bond drives with them because they had "strong emotional appeal." In September 1942, for example, Portuguese Americans celebrated the four hundredth anniversary of the discovery of California by the Portuguese explorer Cabrilho in 1542 with a war bond banquet in Oakland. That same month, Italian Americans in New York City timed a bond drive with Columbus Day, raising $3.5 million in bond sales, and Polish Americans of the city celebrated Pulaski Day with a bond rally in Central Park, generating more than $50,000 in sales. Bond rallies were organized not only around nationality days but tied to virtually any event that could elicit pride in the homelands of ethnic Americans. In San Francisco, the Lafayette Club and other French societies in the Bay Area celebrated the arrival of French war vessels in early 1943 with a bond rally and auction, raising $530,000 in bond sales. At the auction, six pairs of hard-to-find nylon stockings brought in $10,000, and a painting of a

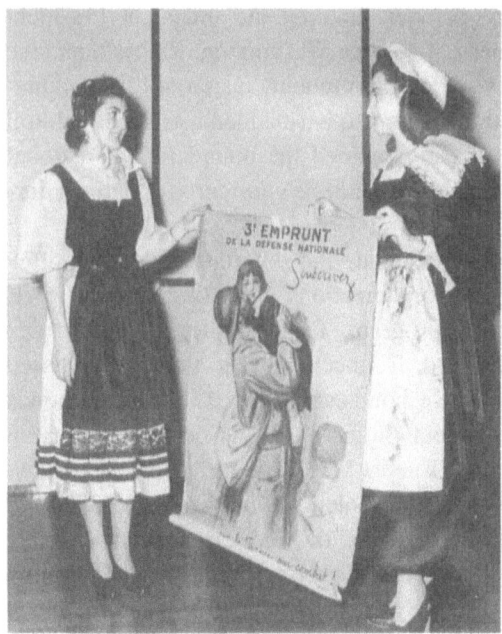

French Americans at a French war stamp tea held at the Cambridge Boat Club, Cambridge, Massachusetts. Sponsored by the Cambridge Women's War Savings Committee, this was the last in a series of foreign group teas promoting the sale of war bonds and stamps. (National Archives)

Native American, completed by an inmate of San Quentin prison, was sold for $27,000 in bonds.[37]

An extremely compelling site of bond buying revolved around I Am an American Day on May 16, 1943, proclaimed by President Roosevelt and organized by the War Savings Staff's Foreign Origin Section. In anticipation of the day, for some weeks preceding it a host of ethnic groups set up booths in many of the nation's downtown areas to sell bonds, holding special programs such as "Vote for Bond Queen" and "Hang Hitler" to boost sales. American Slovaks of Allegheny County, Pennsylvania, raised $315,000 during their I Am an American Day bond drive, enough to buy a bomber christened the *American Slovak*. On the day itself, ethnic Americans "merge[d] their nationalisms in a great demonstration of American unity" via all-nation pageants, playlets, and community sings performed in native costumes. Bond drives were also introduced into "Americanization schools" across the country designed to familiarize "new Americans or about-to-be Americans" with national habits and customs. Pitches for bonds were woven into the naturalization ceremony itself on I Am an American Day, with immigrants taking the oath of citizenship and then offering to buy a war bond to show support for their freshly adopted country.[38]

Consent of the Governed

Slovak War Mothers at the opening of the $6-million Slovak American War Bond Drive in Whiting, Indiana, on August 30, 1943. (National Archives)

No single city exemplified pluralistic support for the bond program more than Pittsburgh. In June 1942, Mrs. Clifford Heinz, chair of the women's activities group for the Allegheny County War Savings Committee, invited Mrs. Francis P. Tarnapowicz to join the committee's speaker bureau. Tarnapowicz, a Polish American well known in the Pittsburgh ethnic community, conceived the idea to establish special booths at which nationality groups could promote and sell bonds and stamps, primarily to those of their own ethnicity. As chair of the local nationality group committee, she helped set up eight such war bond booths in the city, four of them Polish, one Czechoslovakian, one Serbian, one Lithuanian, and one Chinese. The four Polish booths were named after cities or recognized Polish individuals: Warsaw, Paderewski, Gory, and Polonia. Open for business every weekday from 11:00 A.M. to 6:00 P.M., the booths were managed and staffed entirely by women.[39]

The dedication for each nationality war bond booth was a special occasion, filled with the national or regional customs of ethnic Americans' homelands. One Treasury reporter described opening day dedications and rallies as "colorful events with booth attendants and others in native costume, speeches in native tongue as well as in English, a drum and bugle

The opening of the Paderewski war bond booth in Pittsburgh in July 1942. (National Archives)

corps or other musical organization, and the emotional excitement which one expects of foreign extraction groups."[40] At the dedication of the Serbian booth, three girls in native costume sang the nationalistic "Chetnik Song," prompting one in attendance to buy a $1,000 bond. At the opening of the Chinese booth in the city's Chinatown area, Chinese American children were enlisted to sing "God Bless America," which reportedly brought tears to the eyes of many of those in attendance. Four hundred children sang the Polish hymn "Polish Still Lives" at the dedication of the Gory booth in a predominantly Polish neighborhood of the city. The rally was held near the community's Catholic church, with the church's priest playing a visible role in the program. Pittsburgh's nationality war bond booths were typically located near neighborhood churches, with the cooperation of local priests actively sought in order to promote booth activities to congregates.[41]

Bond organizers in Pittsburgh capitalized on the success of the nationality booth idea, expanding their number to more than a dozen by March 1943. Two more booths were added to the Polish contingent, one named Lidice, the other Wilhelmina. The French booth was dedicated on January

Clara Marculaitis at the dedication of the Lithuanian war bond booth in Pittsburgh. As a Lithuanian girl during World War I, Marculaitis dug trenches first for Germany and then for Russia as her homeland changed hands. (National Archives)

15, with French Americans auctioning off dolls, perfume, handkerchiefs, and French cakes, earning $5,600 in war bond sales. "They sang French songs and spoke in French," reported an observer at the scene. Although war bond booths typically operated independently, ethnic communities occasionally joined together to work toward a larger goal. In less than a month in early 1943, nationality groups of Pittsburgh pooled their booths' sales of $1 million, enough money to buy two bombers, the *City of Pittsburgh* and the *City of Allegheny County*. At a victory tea rally at the Hotel William Penn, representatives christened a model of a bomber with water drawn from the city's three rivers.[42]

The citizenship and sacrifice associated with the purchase of bonds by Pittsburgh's nationality booths characterized that made by many other ethnically defined groups in America during the war. First- or second-generation Americans felt a special obligation to back the attack through bonds, to demonstrate loyalty to the United States while also celebrating their own cul-

Serbian Americans at the opening of the Serbian war bond booth in Pittsburgh. The women sang the "Chetnik Song," the anthem of Serbian guerrillas, and are holding a picture of Serbian general Braza Mihailovick. (National Archives)

tural heritage. The Treasury recognized that the war's being fought in Europe made white ethnic Americans prime candidates for buying bonds. America was positioned in government propaganda as a savior nation, with the purchase of bonds ethnic Americans' best way to help free their native lands from Axis aggression. Although the Treasury consciously attempted and succeeded in persuading white ethnic Americans to show support for the United States by buying bonds, it purposely avoided undue pressure and coercive tactics. Even at a time when Anglo-Americanism was considered the ideal, the Liberty Loan program of World War I had shown that such efforts would backfire against the administration. The Treasury astutely understood that the most effective way to gain the loyalty of "foreign-origin" groups was to allow, even encourage them to proclaim their ethnicity at bond rallies. The Treasury's bond program is prime evidence that these two spheres of loyalty are by no means mutually exclusive, that national and ethnic identity can not only coexist but also be synergistic in expression.

The Chinese war bond booth in Pittsburgh. (National Archives)

White ethnic Americans' broad and enthusiastic support of the Treasury's campaign suggests that the administration's goal to create unity through pluralism was indeed achieved, at least in bond drives. The cultural symbols of many different ethnic groups were fused with the symbols of national identity, effectively expanding the parameters of "Americanness." The nation's dominant Anglo-American identity, already weakened during the Depression, further eroded during the war due to pluralistic activities such as bond drives. As Euro-, Asian, and Middle Eastern Americans independently and collectively expressed their ethnicity through bonds, the country's awareness as a multicultural nation grew in both imagined and real terms. War bonds acted as a vehicle of authentic cultural pluralism, an agent of diversity rarely matched in American history.

The dedication of the Russian war bond booth at Diamond and Market Streets in Pittsburgh on November 14, 1942. Pledges totaled $268,150. (National Archives)

At the dedication of the Lebanese war bond booth on November 21, 1942, "it rained but the rally went on," according to Mrs. Tarnowicz. Pledges added up to $72,100. (National Archives)

Lebanese Americans sang and played native instruments at the opening of their war bond booth in Pittsburgh. (National Archives)

The dedication of the Syrian war bond booth on December 3, 1942, was held in a high school on Pittsburgh's Fifth Avenue. Baklava was auctioned off for pledges, which amounted to $86,400. (National Archives)

Americans of various ethnicities dedicate the Victory Nationality Booth in Homestead, Pennsylvania, a suburb of Pittsburgh. The rally raised $57,000 in bond sales. (National Archives)

The "Nationality" Women in Defense float promoting war bond booths in Pittsburgh. (National Archives)

Representatives of different war bond booths celebrate their success at the victory tea rally at the Hotel William Penn. (National Archives)

PART THREE

★ ★ ★ **African Americans and World War II Bonds**

CHAPTER 6

★ ★ ★ William Pickens and the Inter-Racial Section

Just as gaining support of the Treasury program among white ethnic groups was viewed by the administration as an example of democracy in action, selling bonds to African Americans was considered a vital step toward achieving national unity. As the Defense Savings Program was being readied for rollout in March 1941, James L. Houghteling, director of the Treasury's National Organizations Division, called William Pickens, field director of the NAACP. Houghteling asked Pickens to join the Treasury staff to go "about the business of selling the idea of buying bonds and supporting the present war effort" by heading the division's Inter-Racial Section. The administration believed that a concerted effort to reach the nation's thirteen million African Americans was necessary to fulfill the ideological objectives assigned to the Treasury's bond program. Consistent with the administration's hiring "experts" as a means of scientifically managing the war, William Pickens was hand-picked to lead the section because he was considered uniquely qualified to sell the idea of the war to African Americans, and motivate them to take action by purchasing bonds. A press release announcing his appointment emphasized that Pickens "speaks the language, thinks the thoughts, lives the lives of his own people.... Because he knows and understands them, Negroes believe in him."[1]

Pickens's renowned ability to effectively communicate with blacks was developed over a thirty-five-year career of teaching, lecturing, and admin-

William Pickens. (National Archives)

istrating. A child of a former slave, Pickens achieved academic success as a youth in Little Rock, Arkansas, and went on to Yale University, graduating Phi Beta Kappa. His view of the world shaped by Jim Crow, Pickens was eager to compete with whites on the relatively even playing field of academia. He began his teaching career at Talledega College in Alabama in 1904 and took the position of vice president at Morgan College (now Morgan State University) in Baltimore in 1918. In his writings and lectures, Pickens sided with W. E. B. Du Bois in the ideological debate between Du Bois and the more conservative Booker T. Washington, arguing for full equality for African Americans as early as 1906. In 1910, Pickens became a founding member of the Niagara movement, the precursor to the NAACP. Although consistently controversial as a social critic, Pickens's outstanding speaking and fund raising skills brought him to the NAACP full time in 1919. As assistant director of branches, Pickens worked under James Weldon Johnson, field secretary of the organization, and later, Walter White. While with the NAACP for twenty years, Pickens also served as contributing editor of the Associated Negro Press.[2]

Through his tenure with the NAACP between the world wars, Pickens clashed with the organization's leaders on a number of key issues. Pickens was critical of the Garvey movement and generally sympathetic to Communists, each stance in opposition to official NAACP position. Also unlike his colleagues, Pickens was a vocal critic of President Roosevelt and the New Deal, believing the government to be a dictatorship with fascist overtones. Pickens subscribed to a socialist democracy with a planned economy, and supported Upton Sinclair's bid for California governor in 1934 and Wendell Willkie in the 1940 presidential election. As America prepared for war in 1940, however, Pickens and the NAACP reversed their roles. Walter White opposed Roosevelt's foreign policy, whereas Pickens had supported intervention since 1938. In his biography of the man, Sheldon Avery notes that Pickens was openly critical of Adolph Hitler since 1934, aware of the threat the German leader posed to both blacks and Jews. In order to present a united front, Pickens believed African Americans should temporarily ease their fight for full civil rights, similar to what they did during World War I. This difference in view would prove to forever alienate Pickens from the NAACP and the African American protest movement.[3]

To Treasury officials, however, Pickens appeared to be an ideal candidate to spearhead the administration's effort to target bonds to blacks through the Inter-Racial Section. Besides being politically aligned with current Roosevelt domestic and foreign policy, Pickens had personal connections with key figures of the black bourgeoisie across the country. When asked for a recommendation for the position by Houghteling, both Walter White and Judge William H. Hastie, head legal counsel to the NAACP, not surprisingly, suggested Pickens. Although the African American press was critical of the NAACP's allowing (perhaps encouraging) him to leave the organization, Pickens himself was eager to accept the one-year position (with the option of renewal). In addition to being rid of the organizational politics, Pickens saw the job as an ideal opportunity to be directly engaged in the fight against Nazism. The annual salary of fifty-six hundred dollars—twice what he was making at the NAACP—made the decision to accept a fairly easy one.[4]

The Treasury was particularly attracted to Pickens because of his proven ability to translate intellectual or ideological thought into common language. Additionally, although Pickens had positions of power within the black community, his motivation to take the post was perceived as being free from direct political overtones: "When he speaks to [African Americans] of the part they can play in the Defense program, they will listen to him without the suspicious fear lest they be 'taken in' by a smooth speaking, self-seeking smart politician," the Treasury announced. The administration's confidence in Pickens was so great, in fact, that Pickens became the first black official to be appointed by the Treasury in twenty-five years, when Republican administrations regularly named African Americans to the position of register.[5]

Pickens was chosen also for his appeal to liberal whites. He was a popular figure among whites involved in organizations dedicated to racial harmony and brotherhood, and the Treasury believed that he could convert other whites to subscribe these attitudes within a climate more tolerant of difference. "Negroes in Oklahoma and Arkansas are clamoring for him," Pickens's press release read,

> and it is certain that white people will be present at their meetings.... If, at meetings sponsored by this important branch of Government, a Negro speaker can touch and inspire the hearts of white Americans it will certainly change their racial attitudes. And the very knowledge that whites are changing, that they are giving their eager attention to a Negro spokesman, will soften the bitterness of a jim-crowed people.[6]

The Inter-Racial Section was part of the Defense Saving Staff's National Organizations Division, which was created to direct bond programs to particular segments of the population. Although some Treasury officials suggested it be called the Negro Organization Section, Houghteling determined "the Inter-Racial section is better and in all points satisfactory," as the chosen name implied the cooperation and harmony the administration was trying to achieve, at least symbolically. As with the Treasury's special effort to reach women, the Inter-Racial Section was designed to work in concert with, rather than independently from, the general bond program.[7]

With the Inter-Racial Section, the administration had a concerted, dedicated program to promote war bonds to blacks. It was imperative that the administration sell the "idea of the war" to African Americans, as it was clearly blacks who held the key to making pluralistic democracy a viable narrative of nationalism during the war. Although the black mainstream was demonstrating strong support for the war on a number of levels including the purchase of bonds, the glaring contradictions between the nation's democratic ideals and its institutional racism remained. Further leveraging African Americans' patriotism and lessening their opposition to administration policy was considered vital not only to maintain harmony during the current crisis but also because of the implications for the postwar period. In many ways, the wartime tension between African Americans' racial and national identities would foreshadow their heightened ambivalence of the postwar years, when African Americans emerged as the country's most vocal dissenters.

Through the promotion of bonds, the Inter-Racial Section was thus intended to help solve what was commonly referred to in administrative circles as "the negro problem." Whereas white America was generally united during the war years—the embodiment of the liberal consensus save for some persistent ethnic tensions—OWI polls revealed that African Americans were ambivalent toward the war effort. The research indicated that, as John Morton Blum has observed, blacks were "fundamentally patriotic but also frustrated, pessimistic, cynical, and insecure." Although loyal, African Americans believed that claims of the war being fought for true democracy fell short of reality, and that any fight for freedom was not on their behalf. African Americans' attitudes toward the war reflected the complex relationship between their national and racial identities. Unlike white Americans, many black Americans had mixed and multivalent feelings relating to the war, a function of their historical marginalization. For example, many blacks viewed government propaganda about the defense of democracy with deserved skepticism. From an African American perspective, the war's selling points of freedom, liberty, and preservation of the American Way of Life did not have the same credibility as to most whites. Additionally, while African Americans' hatred of Germany was indisputable, many blacks held a certain degree of empathy with the Japanese, since they were another people of color. Still, blacks' enlistment in the army and navy was above 60 percent of their per capita quota, despite the military's segregation and refusal to admit them to the Air Corps or marines.[8]

In addition to the more mainstream segment of African Americans who were ambivalent to the administration's "idea of the war," a thriving black subculture wanted absolutely no part of what they saw as a "white man's war." Robin Kelley has written how the teenage Malcolm Little (Malcolm X) and others found empowerment in the underground subculture of the black working class during the war, an alternative site of African American radical politics. Through the semiotic codes or "style politics" of the zoot suit, bebop music, jive language, and innovative dance, Malcolm and his peers articulated the undeniable racial tensions in urban America. Rejecting both white patriotism and the values of the black bourgeoisie, black hipsters actively evaded the draft and operated outside the boundaries of the dominant hegemonic culture. Through their "subversive refusal to be subservient," zoot suiters did not subscribe to the Double V ideology because, as Dizzy Gillespie put it, they could "never even remember having met a German." Other blacks, identifying with another people of color, actually supported the enemy, forming pro-Japanese clubs. For these radical groups of African Americans, there was only one enemy and it was the one at home. Within the existing racist climate of home-front America, no appeals made by the administration could be strong enough to persuade them to support the war, much less buy war bonds.[9]

Effectively forced to take some action, the OWI and other government agencies took on the unenviable mission to enlist African Americans' support while staying within the boundaries of the country's ingrained racial inequities. The core of the administration's attempts to solicit blacks' support resided less in demonstrating the realities of democracy in America than in providing a case for its potential. Recognizing that the United States being color blind was a losing argument, administrative officials, including William Pickens, pointed to the ideals of the American enlightenment, contrasting them with the racist philosophies embedded in Axis fascism and totalitarianism. As Koppes and Black have noted in their analysis of representations of African Americans in wartime movies, the OWI believed that gaining blacks' unequivocal support of the war relied upon their positive portrayal in society. This policy, a vivid example of what Blum has called President Roosevelt's "necessitarian" approach to domestic tensions during the war, made full use of the myth and symbol imagery that was becoming the chief ideological currency of the consensus. Rather than fulfill democratic ideals by granting African Americans full civil rights, never a real possibility at the time given the institutional racism in the United States and focus on the international crisis, the government, according to Blum, "consciously substituted propaganda for black rights." From one perspective, then, the Inter-Racial Section led by Pickens was one more weapon in the administration's home front war to win blacks' support while staying within the confines of 1940s racial dynamics.[10]

Beginning with only Pickens and a single clerical assistant in May of 1941, the Inter-Racial Section added another executive, Jesse O. Thomas (previously field secretary of the National Urban League), and two additional clerks later in the year. In February 1942, with America's entry into the war accelerating the bond program, two additional salaried executives were added to the Inter-Racial Section to administer African American programs in the field. Nell Hunter, previously a staff member of the National Youth Administration, was named in charge of women's activities, and John Whitten was appointed as head of fraternal and labor bond drives. Hunter and Whitten were added to the Inter-Racial Section's staff as it became clear that Pickens's hectic travel schedule could not accommodate additional speaking engagements at bond rallies. In addition, having such specialists on the staff afforded the section access to and expertise in groups considered key to generating war bond sales. Hunter attended national and regional meetings of fraternal auxiliaries, labor union auxiliaries, federated clubs, business and professional women's groups, church meetings, sororities, and the National Council of Negro Women, which alone had a membership of eight hundred thousand. Eleanor Roosevelt had a personal interest in the National Council of Negro Women and was an active participant in bond programs sponsored by the NCNW, which was conveniently headquartered in Washington.[11]

Whitten's primary assignment was to meet with industry employees and employers across the country, focusing on states with a high density of African American workers. Whitten met with black workers on the job, in their homes, and at union meetings to persuade employees to set aside a portion of their earnings for war bonds. Labor deserved special emphasis because of the growing number of blacks working in defense plants by 1943; more than 210,000 African Americans, in fact, were members of the CIO alone in that year. As with the general bond program, the key to success in African American labor bond drives resided in achieving a high percentage of systematic deductions through the payroll savings plan.[12]

In the field, fifteen African American community or business leaders volunteered their time to the War Finance Committee for one dollar a year to coordinate bond sales in nineteen states and the District of Columbia. These representatives focused their efforts on areas of the country with large numbers of blacks. African American subcommittees were also established in states with large black populations, a move that generally went smoothly in the North but was met with some resistance in the South. The Treasury's solution in the latter's case was to name presidents of black colleges as chairs of African American state War Finance subcommittees, as these individuals commanded a certain degree of respect even within the Jim Crow climate. The net result of this organizational design was somewhat ironic; in northern states such as New York and Illinois, African

American subcommittees operated essentially as an independent unit, whereas in the South they worked on a more integrated basis.[13]

The Inter-Racial Section's fundamental strategy in selling bonds relied less on promotional material than on personal appeals supported by a well-orchestrated public relations program through the print media. (Outside a very few posters that featured African Americans and were clearly designed for a black audience, the Inter-Racial Section shared the same promotional material as the general bond program. Given the Treasury's attention to detail, this was very likely a conscious decision, part of Secretary Morgenthau's mission to make the bond program a democratic, unifying force.) The Inter-Racial Section focused its efforts and resources at weekly black newspapers, which supported the bond program through editorials, stories, and reprinting of the section's press releases, often including a portion of a recent speech made by Pickens or another staff member. There were 108 African American newspapers during the war, 7 with a circulation of twenty thousand or more.[14] The section's "Negro Press list" consisted of 240 black journalists and another 100 "special people." Weekly newspapers regularly sent material produced by the Inter-Racial Section included:

Baltimore Afro-American
Black Dispatch (Oklahoma City)
California Eagle
Chicago Bee
Chicago Defender
Cleveland Call and Post
Houston Informer
Kansas City Call
Los Angeles Sentinel
Louisiana Weekly
Louisville Defender
Miami Whip
Nashville Globe and Independent
New York Age
New York Amsterdam Star News
Norfolk Journal and Guide
New York People's Voice
Philadelphia Tribune
Pittsburgh Courier
St. Louis Argus[15]

The one African American daily, the *Atlanta World,* was a particularly enthusiastic supporter of the bond program, leading Pickens to write in 1944, "Its editors have seen eye to eye with the executives of the section of the Treasury devoted mainly to pushing the sale of war bonds among the readers of that paper." Winning space in the black press depended heavily on good relations with the Associated Negro Press, which "consistently sent our [the Inter-Racial Section's] material to many scores of Negro papers all over the country, and in that way has helped our publicity immensely." The national organization of African American newspapers, the Negro Newspaper Publishers' Association, was as well a strong supporter of the section's aims. "In the final push to complete victory," said John Sengstacke, president of the association at a meeting late in the war, "the Negro press marches as a phalanx to put over the Seventh War Loan." In attendance, Pickens urged the black press to continue to motivate African Americans toward action: "Tell your readers that through purchases of War Bonds they guarantee the future existence of America and themselves—without the former, the latter will be of no avail."[16]

In June 1944, Ted Poston of the Office of Emergency Management emphasized the importance of providing news releases to African American newspapers to promote and sell bonds:

> The Third and Fourth War Loan Drives were two of the most successful campaigns conducted in the Negro press by the News Bureau, OWI.... These campaigns were successful because Treasury had the foresight to accept our suggestion and employ a full time Negro newspaper man for the direction of each campaign. This man worked closely with the Interracial Section of the Treasury's War Finance Division and was able to get daily and lively reports from all parts of the country, which they released immediately to the Negro newspapers. This is quite necessary since 99% of the material issued by the Treasury to the daily newspapers is of no interest at all to the Negro press.[17]

It was clear to Poston and other administration officials that a special, concerted effort was required to effectively reach the black community with war bond information. Public relations directed to a black audience occasionally overlapped with the general bond program, but for the most part reflected activities exclusively relating to African Americans. This was, of course, consistent with the paradoxical nature of the Inter-Racial Section itself, a government agency predicated upon a belief in togetherness while operating within a structure of separateness.

Beyond devoting space to Inter-Racial Section news releases and reporting bond activities, the black press often offered editorials regarding the opportunity war bonds represented. The *Southern Frontier*, a monthly published by the Commission on Interracial Cooperation based in Atlanta, for example, offered this optimistic view of how war bonds could lead to both African American economic independence and racial harmony:

> [Because of their investment in war bonds], the 13,000,000 Negroes of the United States will have a back log of money which should be of rare value in developing their own racial enterprises.... Economic *dependence* robs an individual of *independence* in practically every field of endeavor.... Inter-Racial good will between Negro and white peoples of the United States might grow and spread after the war in proportion to the number of Negroes who have a financial interest in the Government and the extent of that stake.[18]

African American newspapers such as the *Southern Frontier* would also reprint articles from other newspapers, black and general, it found consistent with its own position on matters of race or war bonds. The *Southern Frontier* found this editorial from the *Dunn Dispatch* worthy of reprinting, despite its rather paternalistic tone:

> The report of the work done in the United War Fund Drive by the members of the Negro race in our community is significant, not only for the amount raised, but for many other reasons.... One highly significant fact of this and other campaigns is the sense of responsibility which both the people and their leaders are showing. More and more it is apparent that the Negro in America is fast growing up where he can and will take his rightful place as a responsible citizen in a free democracy.[19]

African Americans' journalistic support for the bond program was not limited to the popular press. More high-brow publications, such as the *Negro Quarterly* and the *Brown American*, included war bond advertisements, either reprinted from Treasury materials or in original "Little Magazine" style.[20] Perhaps the most significant contribution made by black publications to the Inter-Racial Section's objectives, however, was the *Pittsburgh Courier*'s creation of the Double V campaign in February 1942. Standing for Double Victory—victory over enemies abroad and at home—the campaign succinctly and compellingly captured the complex, ambivalent attitudes many African Americans held toward the war. The *Pittsburgh Courier* went so far as to use a graphic treatment of the Double V campaign on its stationary.[21]

Although the majority of African Americans recognized that the struggle for equal rights would be in some ways slowed by the war, the Double

Edgar T. Rouzeau (*left*), of the Fourth War Loan Desk of the Office of War Information, conferring with Arthur Sylvester, managing editor of the *Newark Evening News* and head of the Press Volunteers in the bond campaign. Rouzeau, who had recently returned as a war correspondent for the *Pittsburgh Courier*, handled publicity for the Negro press in cooperation with the OWI. (National Archives)

V was recognized as a means to make the links between fascism abroad and segregation at home clearer. Robert L. Vann, editor of the *Pittsburgh Courier*, drew the connection between the fight overseas and the one for blacks at home two months before the official start of the Double V campaign: "We call upon the President and Congress to declare war on Japan and against racial prejudice in our country, certainly we should be strong enough to whip both of them," he wrote on December 13, 1941. For moderate blacks, the Double V was a channel or safety valve to vent anger at persistent racial discrimination during the war, whereas for the black elite, it represented a means of aligning with the administration's goals while pursuing the fight for equal rights. Although the Double V was unilaterally seen as too radical in the South (even among progressives) and too conservative by leaders such as A. Philip Randolph, it represented the middle ground blacks were seeking. The African American "masses" recognized that the opportunity to continue fighting the war at home relied on first winning the war abroad, a war against an enemy far more racist than most Americans. The popularity of the Double V explained how many blacks could show strong support for the war but define the postwar implications in terms quite different from those used by whites.[22]

Perceived by too many whites as terms for conditional loyalty, however, including the Roosevelt administration, the Double V was destined to be a short-lived campaign. President Roosevelt himself assigned Attorney General Francis Biddle to quiet black newspapers' "subversive language," such as that being used by the *Pittsburgh Courier*. Under pressure (i.e., visits from the FBI), the *Courier* cut the space devoted to the campaign in half from April to August 1942. Although the movement was essentially over by the end of the year, the Double V continued to manifest itself in other avenues into the postwar civil rights era. Through its publication the *Crisis*, the NAACP also reaffirmed the Double V message in its own wording, an indication of the theme's power and broad support: "If Hitler wins, every single right we now possess and for which we have struggled here in America for three centuries will be instantaneously wiped out. If the Allies win, we shall at least have the right to continue fighting for a share of democracy for ourselves."[23]

After determining that the Inter-Racial Section's basic promotional strategy to sell bonds to African Americans would involve personal speaking engagements in concert with an aggressive public relations campaign, William Pickens's next task was to determine to which groups the program should be targeted. With deep roots in and connections to the NAACP and black colleges, Pickens knew that the most effective and efficient strategy was to tap into the existing network of local, regional, and national black institutions and organizations. "For three months," Pickens said in August 1941, "I have been gathering into the Treasury lists of Negro organizations in various communities." Working through the solid African American infrastructure of schools, business leagues, churches, fraternal societies, civic organizations, and community councils offered the greatest chance to gain black support for the war by lending legitimacy to appeals, localizing the national program in individual communities, and offering economies of scale. Perhaps most important, however, these institutions and organizations bridged the gap between a largely disenfranchised African American population and the power bloc, and thus served as models for blacks aspiring to share in the American dream. As the power bloc constituency of the African American community, these organizations' members would be most likely to align with the consensus ideology and contribute to a trickle-down effect toward those blacks who held more resistant and conflicting views. It was thus the "black bourgeoisie" who held the key to selling the war and bonds to the African American community at large through their influence as leaders at the local level.[24]

As a former college professor and dean, Pickens understood the importance of having the African American academy support the administration's goals. Pickens and Thomas visited most black colleges and universities in the early months of the Inter-Racial Section's existence, rebutting isolationists' and pacifists' arguments and persuading administrators and faculty to support the war effort. With the exception of a few intellectuals who refused to accept the "idea of the war," such as then Howard University law student Pauli Murray, the African American academy wholeheartedly endorsed the administration's objectives and bond program. As Pickens wrote in 1944, "Most of these schools are headed by patriotic and far-seeing Negro men and women and they took hold of the stamp-buying, bond-buying program with alacrity and zeal." The strong support for the Treasury's bond program shown by the African American academy contradicted that within mainstream universities and colleges, as students and professors of the latter were notoriously poor supporters of the program. This disparity indicates the significance the bond program held for the black bourgeoisie, who recognized the value of bonds as a means of climbing the socioeconomic ladder.[25]

The Inter-Racial Section's influence within the educational arena accelerated in late December 1941, spurred by Pearl Harbor and the United States' entry into the war. It was then, for example, when the faculty of Tuskegee Institute unanimously endorsed a payroll allotment plan for defense bonds and stamps after a visit by Staff Assistant Thomas. Dr. Frederick Douglas Patterson, president of Tuskegee and chairman of the Negro Division of the Alabama Defense Savings Committee, "expressed hope that Tuskegee's example [would] be followed by other educational institutions," illustrating how targeting the black elite would cause a ripple or trickle-down effect, multiplying the power of the section's power.[26]

Supervisors of Jeanes Teachers in Alabama, Mississippi, and Louisiana also passed resolutions that same month to support the sale of bonds and stamps, again in response to an address by Jesse Thomas. In his address, Thomas set the stage by retelling the story of Anna T. Jeanes, a wealthy white Philadelphian "of old Quaker stock" who in the early years of the century dedicated the interest of $1 million in principal to cover the salaries and expenses of "well trained young colored women" devoted to "improving the educational status of Negroes in the rural areas of the southern states." Here again a trickle-down strategy was employed by Thomas by targeting community leaders with significant influence:

> As you Jeanes Supervisors visit schools from day to day and hold meetings with the teachers in the counties over which you have official jurisdiction, you can serve your Government in a very successful manner if you will become the medium through which your schools may be reached.[27]

Much later in the war, Charles McLean, another member of the Inter-Racial Section staff, would visit twenty teacher colleges across the South on behalf of the Schools at War program. McLean's mission was to make "first-hand contact ... with persons who are directly responsible for the promotion of war bond activities among the Negro school children of the nation." Selling staff, faculty, and students across all levels of the African American educational strata represented an important dimension of the Inter-Racial Section's activities, proportionately greater in fact than the Treasury's mainstream Schools at War effort. In July 1942, Pickens wrote in the *Crisis* that all African American universities and colleges and most of the hundreds of black high schools had a Schools at War program in place, a much higher percentage than in the program as a whole.[28]

The Inter-Racial Section also focused on the business arena in order to tap into the infrastructure of the black bourgeoisie. Business leaders, particularly in insurance and banking, as well as Negro business leagues became a prime target audience for the Inter-Racial Section. For Pickens, the Negro business community was an obvious target because it served as a shining example of the promise of American democracy. "The life of the Negro Business League and the progress of Negro business men for the last forty years," he told the league in August 1941, "these are an index of the true character of this democratic country." Business leaders deserved particular attention because of their ability to understand and pass on why bonds represented such an important economic opportunity for African Americans. "It is you and your comrades," he told the same audience, "who can bring to the attention of colored people and all people the manifold meaning of the program of the United States Treasury to unite American citizens in defense savings; for the good of the investor, his fellow countrymen and his country's future."[29]

Pickens was equally attracted to the business arena because of the metaphor it provided for America itself. Pickens saw free-market capitalism as emblematic of America's democratic principals, the underlying basis for equal opportunity. Leaders within the African American business community, Pickens believed, would recognize the value of war bonds not only for their country but for themselves. As he wrote in 1944, "[African American] business institutions and social clubs have deposited the money saved in their treasuries and have publicized the program among their members, not only for patriotic reasons but in order to better the basis of their organizational strength in the post war period which lies just ahead."[30] Prominent African American business leaders themselves spoke of the dual benefit that war bonds could provide investors. In a statement issued through the Treasury's War Finance Committee, for example, C. C. Spaulding, president of the North Carolina Mutual Life Insurance Company, reiterated Pickens's pitch for bonds:

> The American people, and most especially the Negroes, have shown commendable loyalty and foresight by the manner in which they have cooperated with the Government in each of the six war loan drives.... Let us continue to show our patriotism in a practical way, and benefit personally at the same time.[31]

Within the African American business community, then, we see clear signs of the Double V in action. African Americans were supporting the war through the purchase of bonds not only to defeat the enemies abroad but also to achieve socioeconomic progress for themselves, thereby defeating enemies at home who would otherwise stand in their way. In his appeal to black business executives in his article in the *Crisis,* Pickens stressed that national loyalty was not the only reason to invest in bonds. "Most ... people love their country," Pickens wrote, "but one does not have to love the other fellow in order to take advantage of a good business offer that comes through that other." From such evidence, the ways in which the Double V played out in bond drives indicate that within African Americans' definition of patriotism during World War II was a strong awareness of racial identity and difference, and that the opportunity for social and economic advancement represented one of the truest tests of America's democratic principles.[32]

In addition to educational institutions and business organizations, religious groups represented the third major audience the Inter-Racial Section targeted in its mission to sell the war and bonds to African Americans. The two largest black churches, the National Baptist Church and the Negro Methodist Church, not only boosted the spirits and morale of African American soldiers and their families during the war but also endorsed war bonds and actively sponsored bond drives. Baptist and Methodist ministers recommended war bonds from their pulpits "without quibble and ... without apologies," Pickens wrote in 1942. Pickens noted the contribution made by Negro churches, suggesting that the church clearly recognized that war bonds represented a unique means of economic advancement for African Americans: "Great church conventions and conferences of all denominations have welcomed the presentation of patriotic messages and addresses by leaders of the Inter-Racial Section and have urged upon their membership the purchase of the war securities, both as a patriotic act and as a sound investment."[33]

With the church such a presence in many African Americans' lives, Pickens not surprisingly made war bond appeals along religious lines. Just as some members of our American democracy were not very democratic, Pickens argued, some members of Christian churches were not very Christian. If one would not abandon his or her faith because of some suspect congregation members, why should one lose faith in America because of a few bad apples? The church was still the church of all its members, both good and delinquent, and America was still the country of all its citizens, both tolerant and prejudiced. By using such analogies to which audiences could personally relate, Pickens effectively overcame the many obstacles inherent to selling a war to some dissatisfied customers.[34]

The urban black bourgeoisie was not the only group of African Americans the Treasury targeted its bond program, however. Having been a "gentleman farmer," Secretary of the Treasury Morgenthau intended to fulfill the democratic mission assigned to bonds by reaching out to rural communities and farmers through dedicated programs and local canvassing. Over the course of the war the Treasury, and the Inter-Racial Section specifically, devoted extra attention to promoting bonds to those in rural areas, as initial bond drives in these regions fell short of expectations. Part of the Treasury's rationale for targeting rural Americans was the fact that farmers were experiencing increased earnings but military production made investment in new agricultural machinery and equipment impossible. "Dangerous dollars" could be taken out of farmers' pockets and loaned to the government for the current emergency. To Pickens, the fact that Treasury bonds offered the same interest rate and security for "Henry Ford or any black farmer of the lower counties of Georgia" illustrated the democracy of war savings.[35]

Although huge numbers of blacks moved to northern cities during the Great Migration, the 1940 census showed that 38 percent of the country's African Americans still lived on farms in sixteen southern states. With a total count of some 681,790 black farmers, the Treasury developed a program to give African Americans in rural areas their own personal stake in the war. In October 1942, Jessie O. Thomas recruited nine special Treasury deputies to sell bonds and stamps to African American farmers and rural groups in nine Southern states. The deputies were recruited from agricultural faculties of Negro land grant colleges and brought to Washington for training. As these nine African Americans received instruction in the art of selling from Pickens, Houghteling, and others, five more deputies were being sought to pitch bonds to black farmers in their respective state.[36]

Pickens's and his staff's itineraries consisted of a dizzying blur of train rides across the country to fulfill Morgenthau's vision of selling the war by selling bonds. In 1943, when formal records for the section began to be kept, the Inter-Racial Section staff attended 370 meetings, at which 354,182 people were estimated to be present. In 1944, the section spent 706 days in 258 cities, made 174 addresses, and attended 714 rallies, conferences, or meetings at which 267,812 people were estimated to be present. As a spokesperson for the administration, Pickens's mission was to defuse potentially threatening separatist ideologies among blacks and instill an ideology that aligned with the interests of the power bloc consensus. Behind his and his staff's appeals for bond purchases was the indirect appeal for African Americans to subscribe to the administration's call for national unity. Government endorsed forms of separatism, such as segregation policies, which were clearly in conflict with the tenets of a pluralistic democracy, would be downplayed by Pickens as the imperfections of a society that had not yet realized its full potential. Pickens would concede the flaws of practiced American democracy, instead focusing its possibilities, something he often referred to as the "Star of Democracy." The core of Pickens's ideology was the firm belief that America had and was continuing to make steady progress toward "the great ideal of Democracy laid down in our fundamental law."[37]

Pickens was one of the administration's loudest voices pledging an egalitarian pluralistic society, and African Americans took his message seriously, believing their patriotism earned them equal rights. Pickens aligned with other black leaders who believed full recognition of blacks' civil rights was more likely to be achieved through economic power rather than through social protest. He steered away, however, from more radical interpretations of African American economic independence such as a "black economy" or "black capitalism" as such separatist views were in opposition to the administration's call for national unity and harmony. Thus, despite the country's record of inconsistency toward fulfilling its constitutional framework with regard to treatment of blacks, America's mythic symbols of democracy and individual liberty remained the major selling points in the promotion of war bonds to the African American community. By shifting the focus to the promise of democracy and the potential of the unique American experiment, Pickens deflected much of the potential criticism. For blacks, appeals based in democratic values would hold a particular resonance, not only because they contrasted so dramatically with Nazi racism, but because of the inspiration of hope. "We are going to hang together in this country," Pickens wrote in April 1942, "over racial lines, religious lines, economic lines, political-party lines, and all other lines. When we face a foreign foe, we are all AMERICANS!"[38]

Although populist New Deal ideology was now recast as what was good for corporate America was good for the American people, presenting bonds as in the interests of the smaller investor still had special meaning to an audience whose members were largely on the bottom rung of the economic ladder. Pickens's rhetoric was heavily steeped in the anti–big business sentiment of the New Deal, as when he told the National Baptist Convention, "The government wants the people and their own organizations, rather than the big money interests, to get the security, and the good interest on these investments." While the Everyman theme was central to selling war bonds to all Americans, Pickens emphasized why bonds were a particularly good investment for African Americans. "It seems that our Government might have had a disadvantaged minority, like the Negro, when they planned these bonds," he told an Atlanta audience in July 1941. "No loan shark or cunning creditor can come between the simplest citizen and his Government and get that citizen's money. Neither the gambling syndicate nor the numbers king has a chance, so long as the United States Government holds that money." Presenting the government as a paternalistic guardian of money that otherwise might be lost to predators was an interesting selling strategy the Treasury Department did not use for a predominantly white audience. Pickens was astutely positioning federal securities as a safe haven in which African Americans could invest extra cash, as both legitimate (i.e., banks) and illegitimate alternatives often cheated blacks.[39]

As pitched to African Americans, considered by the administration to have poor thrift habits and to be generally financially irresponsible, the Puritan ethic of saving now for future financial security offered particular salience and shaped the ways in which the Treasury targeted bonds to blacks. This was clearly evident in the plans for the Second War Loan, when the Office of War Information scheduled, in its own words, a feature story to the Negro Press, taking off from the fact that Booker T. Washington was a sort of Benjamin Franklin of thrift when few Negroes understood much of the importance of saving, how he saved, what he had to say about thrift (it's in his book), and what he did with the money he saved. Tie in, simply, with bond-buying as end-product of thrift.[40]

For the general public, bonds were positioned as an investment for future consumerism, but for blacks, they represented opportunity for social and economic advancement. Bonds were positioned as a unique opportunity for blacks to gain a foothold in the emerging abundant and prosperous society, and thus operated as a carrot for improved socioeconomic status, the principal means to greater equality:

> I hope that the colored people of Rochester will stand way up front in buying bonds during the Third War Loan. It is not only an honorable and patriotic thing, but it is a shrewd matter of business for the colored people of the United States to have as much of their money as possible in the hands of the Government, especially in the period following the war.[41]

Often turning this theme upside down in standard advertising fashion, Pickens stressed that without buying war bonds, "colored people ... would be further toward the rear end of the line than they are going to be when this war is over."[42]

Perhaps Pickens's most compelling argument for blacks to join the cause was to stress how long African Americans had been in the New World, and their long history in defending America in all its wars. John Schaar suggests that the core of patriotism is a love for one's "homeplace," and in this sense it was vital that Pickens convince African Americans that their homeplace was indeed America. "Our Afro-Americans started coming here in 1619, twelve years after the Whites came to stay," Pickens reminded audiences across the country. "Averaging the groups," he continued, "the oldest American man, next to the American Indian, is the American Negro." The corollary to establishing this nation as African Americans' homeplace was emphasizing the past, present, and future role of the Negro in American democracy and national defense. "The Negro also helped to create and always defend this nation; he was a soldier with George Washington," Pickens argued. "This is the Negro's country in the realist sense and the one he must defend, in order to defend his own future and his posterity." Whereas bond pitches to white audiences occasionally addressed Americans rallying around previous crises, Pickens relied heavily upon this "homeland" theme in order to appeal to African Americans' patriotic values grounded in an historical sense of place.[43]

Pickens conveyed a similar message to Peter Odegard, the consultant hired by Secretary Morgenthau to formulate the war bond marketing strategy. In a May 1944 memo to Odegard, presented as a treatise in typical Pickens style under the title "The American Negro and His Country in War," Pickens cast war bond purchases by blacks as the latest of a long line of demonstrations of patriotism to their country:

> When we started our "Defense Savings" program in May, 1941, ... the colored people had been so often told in words, and so emphatically told by acts and treatments, that they were aliens in America.... [But it is] not his complaints against America, but his loyalty and devotion for generations [which] distinguish him. He has exceeded honest expectations in war and peace, in work and patience. For two hundred years in all our national and international crises, he has been at first an enigma, at last an element of confidence; at first, emotional and complaining; at last, devoted and achieving.... The American Negro is Negroid—but is far more *American* and *human*.[44]

Although he was clearly an outspoken advocate for his race, Pickens believed that the universal, mythic qualities of Americanness superseded those associated with being black. Pickens's priority of country over color would make him appear too conciliatory to the administration by black nationalists and ultimately weaken his standing even among such moderate groups as his former employer, the NAACP.

By vilifying Nazi rhetoric and actions against people of color, Pickens vividly illustrated the special interest African Americans should have for the Allies to win the war, even before the United States' entry. Pickens neatly deflected criticism from black leaders who viewed the war as "a white man's war" by comparing Nazi's view of blacks to that held by most Americans. Containment was the answer for blacks to ultimately achieve democracy in America: "The smaller element of fascism can be made to triumph here if it is backed up by fascism in the rest of the organized world. Hitler fascism does not allow minority people the status of citizens, and, believe it or not, does not allow Negro people the status of human beings." Pickens's retort to those who drew parallels between Nazi fascism and American racism was to suggest that it was necessary to, again, contain the latter, that allowing fascism to flourish abroad would only fuel it internally: "We do have fascist-minded individuals in our own country; but the best way to keep them down is to keep the foreign fascist out. We need have no illusions; the colored people of the United States have more interest in this question of fascism than has any other race in our country."[45]

Pickens's belief in a perfect, idyllic form of democracy was aligned with the main themes of "myth and symbol" ideology, to which most key figures in the war and postwar years subscribed. His rhetoric emphasized the superiority of commonality over difference, and the threat oppositional forms of separatism posed to America and its special democratic mission. Pickens's language and imagery in selling war bonds is filled with transcendental, sacred references to American democracy most eloquently expressed by writers and intellectuals of America's nineteenth-century "Enlightenment," particularly Whitman and Thoreau. By creating the popular image of American democracy as an unsullied star in the distance to which we must advance, Pickens skirted the gross historical and contemporary persecution of African Americans. "Although it is the mightiest and the most advanced democracy in the world today," Pickens told a Memphis audience in August 1941, "it has not caught up with the star on which its founders first gazed." No mention was made, of course, of America's founding fathers' ownership of black slaves or the exclusion of blacks from all forms of civil liberties, including citizenship itself, when gazing at the star of democracy.[46]

With his grounding in myth and symbol ideology, Pickens looked to the Constitution for the American ideal, untainted by a few bad apples. Although in fact it was, as Garry Wills points out in his examination of Lincoln's Gettysburg Address, the Declaration of Independence that called all men equal, not the Constitution (which was tolerant of slavery), Pickens saw the Constitution as African Americans' best weapon to achieve their Double V. "There are enemies of democracy within our democracy," Pickens told an Indianapolis audience, "but our Constitution and custom give us a fair way to fight this enemy within. If the more terrible enemy from without should triumph over us, we cannot have the legal right to fight, for we will have no protecting Constitution." By drawing upon the sacred symbol of the Constitution in his speeches to African Americans, Pickens positioned war bonds not as the necessary financial means to fight a war, but in much more noble terms, specifically a unique opportunity to make strides toward true equality. This strategy of selling bonds as a means to win the war abroad in order to have the chance to win the one at home was obviously not employed for a white audience, for whom there was only one war and one potential victory.[47]

Pickens saw the United States as a singular organism, its people the cells of the body. Some of the cells were darker, a larger number paler, but all were operating to keep the body republic alive. Cells working against each other, that is, a nation divided by race, would weaken the organism, making it susceptible to outside forces. Rather than a fragmented site of divided interests and racial oppression, then, Pickens saw America as an extended community, its unity threatened by an outside enemy: "What a church or a club or a family it will be," Pickens gushed, "when Hitler has been defeated and the boys come home and the factories slow up, if that church or club or family has all or a majority of its members with savings in the United States Treasury!" Purchasing bonds was thus not just an individual act but a communal one as well, offered to all Americans and designed to benefit all Americans. Pickens often elaborated on his family metaphor, suggesting that as was the case with most families, the American family was "imperfect." As he proposed in his "few-bad-apples-in-the-church" argument, as one would not abandon his or her family because it was imperfect or had some imperfect members, it would be foolish or illogical for blacks to divorce themselves from their national family. He extended this metaphor by noting that as children, his sister Annie was his rival within the family but ally outside the family, implying that when faced with a foreign, more dangerous foe, even white rivals should become close allies.[48]

Despite the obvious contradictions between America's claims to democracy and its treatment of African Americans, the Inter-Racial Section's efforts to promote war bonds through such powerful symbols as community motivated many African Americans to support the war. In his *Imagined Communities,* Benedict Anderson aptly describes how the concept of community can make marginalized groups venerate the symbol of a nation and fight on its behalf:

> [A nation] is imagined as a *community,* because, regardless of the actual inequality and exploitation that may prevail in each, the nation is always conceived as a deep, horizontal comradeship. Ultimately it is this fraternity that makes it possible, over the past two centuries, for so many millions of people, not so much to kill, as willingly to die for such limited imaginings.[49]

Recognizing African Americans' legitimate desire to be full members of the imagined American community, the Inter-Racial Section weaved a dream of justice into war bond promotion, stirring blacks' national loyalty and effectively drawing upon their human and financial resources.

Although William Pickens's appeals for racial equality and democracy in action were well received by audiences both black and white, he was not completely immune to criticism or controversy. Aligning himself so closely with the Roosevelt administration's policies left Pickens open to attacks by African American organizations that held more oppositional views as well as by certain anti-Roosevelt factions. In 1942, Pickens became a persona non grata to the NAACP, following his praising of the all–African American Tuskegee air squadron. Pickens accommodated the idea of segregated training camps and military units, believing that such "domestic struggles should not be abandoned, but should be tempered and [re]directed." Pickens saw the Tuskegee squadron, which went on to combat in Italy with other groups of black pilots, as the latest example of African Americans' historical defense of their homeland, a proud display of patriotism. The NAACP, however, believed that because the squadron was not integrated, it illustrated at best "separate but equal" status for blacks, and was therefore unacceptable. This difference in opinion proved to be the last straw in the official relationship between Pickens and the NAACP, and Pickens's position was terminated by the organization in June 1942. Despite the break, Pickens continued to work with various members of the NAACP, with the bond program one of the few areas in which both parties saw eye to eye.[50]

The greatest criticism regarding Pickens during the war, however, came not from the NAACP but from white conservatives. In February 1943, Congressman Martin Dies (D-Texas), chair of the House Special Committee to Investigate Un-American Activities (HUAC), included William Pickens on a list of thirty "bureaucratic totalitarians" who were undeserving to be on the government payroll. Dies accused Pickens of being a Communist, although the FBI had previously cleared him of such charges. Dies's underlying motivation for this and other investigations of liberals was his desire to undermine what he perceived as persistent New Deal bureaucracy. After the House voted 163 to 111 to cut funding for Pickens, Houghteling and Graves came to Pickens's defense and the matter was resolved by the Treasury internally. Dies, on the other hand, went on to defeat in the 1944 congressional elections.[51]

Despite such attacks from the Left and Right, however, Pickens retained broad support from the white and black mainstream throughout the war years. An editorial published in the *Richmond Times-Dispatch* responding to the House's action titled "Why Crucify Pickens?" summarily captured general sentiment regarding William Pickens: "He is giving valuable service to the cause of better and more harmonious race relations in this country in these critical times. Moreover, he is urging upon the Negroes wholehearted support of the war, is traveling all over the United States addressing Negro rallies in the interest of the bond campaign ... and he is a force for sanity and restraint in a sometimes tense situation between whites and blacks."[52]

James Houghteling, Pickens's boss, echoed these thoughts in December 1943 in a letter to Sidney Osborn, the governor of Arizona. After a visit by Pickens to Arizona, Governor Osborn sent a letter to Secretary Morgenthau, praising Pickens. Houghteling wrote back to Osborn, saying that Dr. Pickens was "a man of remarkable gifts and of sound common sense, who is greatly respected by white people and colored people alike, [and] has been instrumental in persuading the colored population to save money and to buy many million dollars of War Bonds." "This is a fine thing," Houghteling continued, "not only for the future of the Negro race in this country but also for the future of good racial relations."[53]

Although at times shaky, a function of the pressure associated with the highly visible and occasionally controversial bond program, the relationship between Pickens and Houghteling was mutually respectful. Toward the end of the war, with the bond program a clear success and Allied victory in the wings, Pickens sent Houghteling a note thanking him for choosing him for the job and summing up his experience as director:

> In all the positions [I have] held (including the NAACP), the American people have always been *my people*, and I have never been anything less than an American. Some minds cannot distinguish between fighting the faults of one's fellowmen and the evils of one's country, and fighting one's fellowmen or one's country. But the difference is true and important. The colored Americans' participation in the War and in War Finance has been good work not only for their country but also for their race. In spite of some cunning demagoguery from within and some bitter opposition from without, they have lived up to their traditional attitude toward their country in its hour of greatest danger.[54]

Some months later, Houghteling would send a note back to Pickens, praising Pickens's efforts and achievements:

> I want to take this occasion to assure you that you have not only my complete confidence in the work which you are doing, but also my sincere admiration and affection. I am convinced that no one else could have accomplished the tremendously beneficial results which you have obtained in bringing the patriotic and constructive message of United States Savings Bonds to the entire colored population of this country. You have shown superb patience and Christian fortitude in facing and overcoming many obstacles. We have been sailing uncharted seas and have had all the difficulties of pioneers.[55]

The shared feelings between William Pickens and administration officials did not stop at the Treasury's doors. Pickens was a devout supporter and friend of both Franklin and Eleanor Roosevelt, given to spontaneous outbursts of praise for them. After listening to Roosevelt's March 1, 1945, report on the Yalta Conference, Pickens could not resist sharing his enthusiasm with Houghteling:

> He [Roosevelt] is one of the greatest Presidents of the United States. Some day, say 50 years from now, posterity, including the descendants of those who now fight and malign him, will build to him one of our greatest monuments.... I am proud to have been one of his contemporaries and to have thought well of him and his great aims.[56]

With exactly such a monument being completed for him, fifty years after his writing, Pickens showed remarkable foresight of the legacy Roosevelt would leave upon the American people.

After the war, William Pickens would face difficulties in returning to work outside the public arena. Because of his serving as a spokesperson for the administration over the full course of World War II, Pickens found himself alienated from groups that had opposed government policies toward African Americans. His loyalty and dedication to public service firmly cemented, however, Pickens stayed on with the Treasury until retiring in December 1950, promoting the purchase of United States Savings Bonds among blacks. With the principal selling points of savings bonds centered on planning for a rainy day, Pickens continued to emphasize the value of thrift for people of color. To William Pickens, government bonds still offered African Americans the economic means of achieving a personal and communal victory, a unique opportunity for blacks to work toward full racial equality and civil rights.

CHAPTER 7

★ ★ ★ **The NAACP and War Bonds**

In June 1942, the NAACP protested an act of racial discrimination against one of its members by asking African Americans to renew their pledge to purchase war bonds. Throughout the war, the NAACP's official magazine, the *Crisis,* included advertisements for bonds alongside editorials and articles calling for an end to Jim Crow and blacks' "separate but equal" status. Why and how did the NAACP view the purchase of government bonds as consistent with the fight for full equality? The role of war bonds within the NAACP provides a unique window into the development of the civil rights movement and offers interesting insights related to the relationship between national and racial identity.

Although scholars such as Harvard Sitkoff have long held that it was the 1943 riots that sparked the civil rights movement, historians continue to push back its beginnings. Korstead and Lichtenstein, for example, have argued that the civil rights era began during the country's mobilization for defense as African Americans became more urban and proletariat. As blacks became vital to the military-industrial economy and racism became equated with Nazism, a climate more tolerant of black activism developed. With strong ties to the Democratic Party, the CIO was a key catalyst for this cultural shift. Union rights and civil rights were linked through the circulating American ideals of democracy and liberty, and African American identity recast as a major constituent of the working class.[1]

Recognizing the opportunity to point out the contradictions between the nation's ideals and its practices, black leaders became more aggressive. A. Philip Randolph's proposed March on Washington in July 1941 and the subsequent passage of Executive Order 8802, creating the Committee on Fair Employment Practices (FEPC), gave African Americans more legal ammunition to fight racist conditions in the workplace. Although winning the war overshadowed domestic issues such as "the Negro problem," race came to the forefront of America's consciousness. Michael K. Honey has observed that the war both "heightened racial confrontation" and "increased interracial cooperation," resulting in conflict in the short term but ultimately leading to desegregation and the end of Jim Crow. The emphasis on national unity during the war also worked to blacks' advantage with, according to Korstead and Lichtenstein, the "patriotic egalitarianism of the government's wartime propaganda" one of the key factors in the creation of a "rights consciousness" for many African Americans.[2]

As the core of the emerging black bourgeoisie, the NAACP played a major role in spearheading the pursuit of equal rights as the country prepared for and fought the war. Membership in the organization grew nine times from 1940 to 1946 as African Americans' "rights consciousness" spread. In 1940, the NAACP remained divided in Roosevelt's domestic and foreign policies, those opposed because of the administration's failure to pass an antilynching bill. After Pearl Harbor, however, the NAACP became fully interventionist while upholding a "two front" policy: unqualified national loyalty alongside the pursuit of full equal rights. Although many whites, including administration leaders, viewed these two fronts as essentially mutually exclusive, the NAACP believed that patriotism could accommodate protest and vice versa.[3]

At the center of this intersection of patriotism and protest during World War II were government bonds. For the NAACP and African Americans at large, purchasing war bonds became part of the fight for civil rights from within the system. As the black protest movement shifted to the courts from the streets over the course of the war, bonds were a means of gaining social and economic power through official, institutional channels. Like labor, which saw in bonds an opportunity to demonstrate national loyalty and simultaneously fight for the rights of the working class, the NAACP invested heavily in bonds to support both country and race. Secretary Walter White and Assistant Secretary Roy Wilkins of the NAACP emerged as central figures in the Treasury's effort to sell not only bonds to African Americans but also, in William Pickens's words, to "sell them the United States of America."[4]

Pickens and his colleagues at the Defense Savings Staff recognized the importance of the NAACP to the success of the Inter-Racial Section very early on. In May 1941, the first month of the bond program, Lorimer D. Milton, staff advisor for the Defense Savings Staff, asked Wilkins if Pickens could address the NAACP at their thirty-second annual conference to be held in Houston in June. Wilkins agreed to put Pickens on the agenda, but allotted him only ten to fifteen minutes, the same amount of time as other government officials who were speaking at the conference. Despite his twenty years of service to the NAACP, Pickens would receive no preferential treatment from the organization, a fact no doubt related to the strained relationship between Pickens and his former employer. Milton himself was at the Treasury only because of a recommendation by NAACP leaders. A month after Houghteling called Pickens to join the Treasury, Harold Graves asked White and William Hastie to recommend candidates to staff the Inter-Racial Section, specifically to "suggest three or four persons who would be most helpful in bringing . . . bonds to the attention of Negroes." White asked Milton, an executive of the Citizens Trust bank in Atlanta, to visit with Treasury officials, and Milton joined the Defense Savings Staff in May.[5]

The lingering tensions between Pickens and NAACP leaders were made clear a few months later. In an article announcing Pickens's appointment to the Treasury, the *Survey Graphic* had recently stated that he was "in charge of the Negro division for the sale of defense bonds." Pickens reacted vehemently to the misstatement and blamed the NAACP, the apparent source of the information. Pickens went so far as to write a letter to his former colleague, Claude A. Barnett, Director of the Associated Negro Press, requesting that the ANP release a statement to African American newspapers to set the record straight. "I am not 'selling bonds' and am not a salesman of any kind, unless we use a figure of speech and call it 'selling ideas'; the great ideas of national defense, national unity, and of financial cooperation through the national treasury," Pickens's personal press release read.[6] Pickens also wrote to the writer of the article, requesting the magazine publish a correction:

> I am not the head of any division. I am a staff member, and the head of our division is Mr. James L. Houghteling. There are many other staff members in the division, whose positions seem to be co-ordinate with mine,—and my skin seems to have more human pigment in it than have the skins of the others. We are on one floor and compose a team.[7]

Although potentially volatile, Pickens's new relationship with the NAACP was for the most part a cooperative one. In the midst of the misunderstanding regarding his title and position with the Treasury, Pickens asked E. Frederick Morrow of the organization for a contact in Butte, Montana, who could serve as local bond committee chair. Morrow's secretary responded with the names of three NAACP members in 1929, the last year in which the organization had members in the area. "It seems that our [current] memberships, etc., in Montana are nil," she wrote to Pickens.[8]

Because the NAACP was the single most influential and powerful African American organization, Pickens relied on the association for more than merely suggesting potential committee chairs in areas of the country with few blacks. Just four days before the bombing of Pearl Harbor, Pickens sent a letter to the NAACP board suggesting they pass a resolution that all organization members purchase defense bonds and stamps. Pickens asked the board,

> What can be better for [NAACP members] than to save [their] money in the world's securest bank,—and to get the unusual rate of interest? And what can be better for our racial minority than for our people to have something to tide them over the terrific period which will follow this emergency as the night follows the day: when there will be, temporarily at least, fewer jobs and many more job-seekers?[9]

Although Pickens was indeed soliciting for bond sales, his underlying agenda here was surely to gain across-the-board NAACP endorsement of the program to parley into future promotion efforts.

Other members of the Treasury's Inter-Racial Section staff sought out help from the NAACP to sell bonds to blacks. In January 1943, Jesse Thomas wrote to Madison S. Jones, youth director of the NAACP, asking Jones for ideas on how to widen "the participation of Negro youth in our all-out war effort through the purchasing of Bonds and Stamps." The request originated with the Inter-Racial Section's launch of its America for Freedom bond campaign, with rallies planned at black colleges across the country. With the campaign to start on February 12 (Lincoln's Birthday) and end on April 6 (Booker T. Washington's birthday), Thomas wanted to give "every Negro student on every college level an opportunity to purchase Bonds and Stamps."[10]

Jones immediately replied to Thomas, saying that he "agree[d] with the idea of holding this project most heartily" and that Thomas could "count on our organization for its endorsement and any support we can give." Jones suggested that the Treasury target other groups of young people in addition to college students, namely high school students and those out of school. For the former, Jones recommended the Treasury promote bonds and stamps at school clubs, at assembly exercises, with poster contests, and in movie theaters. To reach the latter, Jones suggested churches, the YMCA and YWCA, fraternal organizations, and the Civil Defense. Jones was seemingly elated to find a colleague with an equivalent passion for teaching African American youth important lessons: "It [the Treasury's bond program] really can be a wonderful thing and it is just what Negro youth need now to bring them more together not only for what we have at hand, but to impress upon them concerning what their role in the future should be."[11]

John Whitten, promotion specialist for the Inter-Racial Section staff, also contacted the NAACP for help in marketing bonds to African Americans. In September 1943, Whitten asked Walter White for an up-to-date list of all of NAACP branches as the War Finance Committee was "preparing two excellent posters with Negroes on them [an aviator and a baby], and ... desire[d] to have copies of these posters sent to every local N.A.A.C.P. office." White responded by saying that the NAACP had a rule forbidding the release of a list of its branch locations, but that they would be happy to send the poster directly to the organization's six hundred branches, youth councils, and college chapters. Whitten accepted White's offer, adding, "You are doing a swell job for our people through the N.A.A.C.P. and we hope that you may live long to keep up the good fight."[12]

As the war continued, the relationship between Pickens and White seemed to improve through the common ground of bond drives. In July 1944, Pickens sent a form letter to African American organizations, making an appeal for bond purchases to support black soldiers and for investment purposes.[13] White wrote back to Pickens:

> That is an excellent letter you have sent out regarding the purchase of E-Bonds. You will be interested in knowing that the N.A.A.C.P. has invested a very considerable sum for it (in the light of its income) in war bonds, and that we all of us here in the office have personally bought war bonds.[14]

Pickens replied to White, saying that he was "glad to hear that the NAACP is putting a considerable part of its money for safe keeping into United States Treasury Bonds" and that he was "calling this fact to the attention of the Director of my Division and other Treasury officials." Pickens also thanked White for his "generous remark," adding that he "hope[d] and believe[d] that many other sensible people will be equally generous towards the aims of that letter."[15]

In helping to launch the Sixth War Loan four months later, Pickens decided to capitalize on his improved relationship with White. Pickens told White that he was "confident that you are supporting the Sixth War Loan Campaign, and kn[ew] that your endorsement will go a long way with our people." Pickens asked White to cosign (with Lester B. Granger, executive secretary of the National Urban League, and Mary McLeod Bethune, president of the National Council of Negro Women) a joint statement to be distributed to the African American press intended to "stimulat[e] the sale of War Bonds among colored people." White consented to signing the statement, while noting it "was a bit more florid in language than I would written myself."[16]

Many other Treasury officials beside Pickens and his colleagues in the Inter-Racial Section looked to the NAACP to support the bond program. As it did of most larger organizations, the Treasury asked the NAACP to join the payroll savings plan. Because the association represented the national black community, however, the Treasury recognized the greater, symbolic significance of the NAACP's endorsing the plan. In July 1942, White sent a memo to the entire staff in the New York office, asking if they were in favor of the plan. Some of the staff wanted to join, but most preferred buying bonds at their own discretion. In its September board meeting, the organization reached a compromise by formally adopting the payroll savings plan but allowing each employee to join at his or her own discretion.[17]

Communications between the Treasury and the NAACP were truly two-way, with White viewing the administration as a partner in a joint venture. In November 1942, White requested and received from the Treasury one thousand copies of *How to Win the War on the Homefront,* a pamphlet promoting war bonds to and for women. White offered to send the pamphlet to all NAACP branches for use in the field, as part of a dedicated effort to target African American women. A month later, White was invited by Mozelle Swann of the New York War Savings Staff and Nell Hunter of the Inter-Racial Section to a Women's Committee meeting. The committee claimed it had "a most exciting plan . . . for expanding the sale of War Bonds and Stamps [which] if put into operation, will revolutionize the moral and economic life of our Negro community and will prepare the way for our post-war adjustment." With women comprising a large percentage of the NAACP membership, White had a special interest in this campaign, seeing bonds as a singular opportunity to improve these members' and their families' economic position.[18]

In December 1943, White again requested materials from the Treasury, this time a number of the newly issued bond posters featuring an African American aviator. It was somewhat ironic that White was interested in distributing the poster to NAACP members, as the aviator represented the Ninety-ninth Pursuit Squadron trained at Tuskegee airfield. Whereas Pickens supported the segregated training of the pilots, White and the NAACP were opposed to this and any other form of "separate but equal" status for African American military personnel. White intended to distribute the poster to Negro colleges, YMCAs and YWCAs, fraternal organizations, and unions. Willard Allen of the Inter-Racial Section replied he was "thoroughly in accord with your [White's] thought concerning the lack of information on the part of our white citizens relative to the Negro's contribution to the war effort." Allen agreed to send White seven hundred copies of the poster, although the Inter-Racial Section had already sent the poster to many of those on the NAACP's list.[19]

Those involved in publicizing bond drives to African Americans looked to the NAACP for its official stamp of approval. In June 1944, Edgar T. Rouzeau of the Fifth War Loan news desk sent a telegram to the NAACP, asking White or Wilkins for a seventy-five word statement endorsing the drive to African Americans.[20] White gave the bond drive his blessing, while making it clear that African Americans had not yet realized the democracy that the nation was defending:

> Despite the fact that American Negroes so frequently are denied the democracy for which they are asked to fight and pay, it is imperative that all Americans, including thirteen million Negro Americans, make every sacrifice through the purchase of bonds and otherwise to preserve and extend the democratic process. It is for this reason that the Board of Directors of the National Association for the Advancement of Colored People on June 12th invested $40,000 additional dollars of trust funds in war bonds. We urge all Negro organizations and individuals to invest to the limit in democracy while they work to make that democracy real for all irrespective of race, creed, color, or national origin.[21]

White added that his statement should be released to the general press rather than just black newspapers so that "other racial groups may know part Negro is playing in bond drives."

The forty-thousand-dollar purchase of Fifth War Loan bonds White referred to was to honor two African American members of the air force, Captains Charles B. Hall and Lemuel R. Custis. White had recently visited Italy as a war correspondent, getting the opportunity to see the Ninety-ninth Pursuit Squadron and three other black fighter squadrons in action. Through the purchase of the bonds, White declared in a statement to the press,

> It is our hope that America will show these and others of the 700,000 American Negroes now fighting in the war that the democracy they fight to preserve will be more fully given them and other minorities than has been proved in the past. One question asked me anxiously by colored soldiers on all the battlefronts I have visited is, "To what will we return in America? Will it be only to shoe-shining jobs and the Ku Klux Klan?" What will America's answer be?[22]

White's reading of African American soldiers' sentiment is clear evidence that the war and its circulating ideologies did in fact act as a catalyst for the raising of black consciousness. White, in fact, wrote about this very idea in his book, *A Rising Wind*. "World War II," he wrote in 1945, "has immeasurably magnified the Negro's awareness of the disparity between the American profession and practice of democracy ... [and has] given the Negro a sense of kinship with other colored—and also oppressed—peoples." White believed that expectations of equality had been raised among African Americans, and that the United States' failure to grant full equality to blacks could ultimately serve as grounds for the next world war.[23]

Nowhere was this idea better expressed than in Gunnar Myrdal's *An American Dilemma: Modern Democracy and the Negro Problem*. In a manner perhaps incapable by a white American, Myrdal, a Swedish sociologist, directly and frankly confronted the contradiction between the nation's claim to democracy and its actual treatment of blacks. Myrdal recognized that because of the contradiction between the American creed and practiced racism—the American dilemma—the war was a critical juncture for African Americans and the nation's history. With the race supremacy argument significantly weakened because it was now the core of Nazi dogma, Myrdal believed, blacks had a unique opportunity to move forward toward equal rights. The operative caste system in America, particularly in the South, had been exposed due to outside forces, revealing what Myrdal referred to as "the fiction of equality." The United States had been pushed onto the world stage of defending democracy, forcing the administration to promote an ideology of racial tolerance and "inalienable freedoms" for all citizens. He urged African Americans to seize this unprecedented opportunity to combat institutional inequalities by using the Constitution and legal system as weapons. Myrdal also believed the American dilemma would reshape African American identity and accurately predicted that this process would serve as the focal point for an organized civil rights movement. The war would delay the full efforts of this movement, just as the Roosevelt administration planned, but the seeds had been planted for postwar fruition. "The civil rights movement," Bailey and Farber observed, "though still inchoate, was enjoined during the war."[24]

Although the NAACP did on occasion use press releases announcing a purchase of bonds in order to make a point, the organization was ambivalent about public recognition of their investments. After Dr. Channing Tobias, a prominent African American who worked with the New York War Savings Staff throughout the war, asked White to credit a purchase of bonds to Nell Hunter, White reluctantly told Tobias in May 1943, "The [NAACP's] Finance Committee had decided that no publicity would be given to purchase of these bonds."[25] In August 1944, Charles C. Craft, executive manager of the Inter-Racial Section, asked all national African American organizations for information regarding their holdings of war bonds. Craft wrote:

> The War Finance Division of the U.S. Treasury Department is very desirous of giving the proper publicity and credit to all national Negro organizations, with particular regard to their participation in the War Bond program.... May we ask you ... to send us ... a total figure ... showing the consolidated holding of U.S. War Bonds of your organization and its constituent members[?] We will, of course, use the figures only in the process of giving to the American people a complete picture of what various highly patriotic organizations of citizens are actually doing.[26]

White replied to Craft that the NAACP board voted against publicizing the amount of bonds purchased by the organization.[27]

As the headquarters of the organization, the New York office of the NAACP functioned as a clearinghouse for information related to bonds throughout the war. Early in the defense bond program, branches across the country looked to association leaders to determine official policy regarding the selling and buying of bonds. In August 1941, Carl R. Johnson, president of the Kansas City branch, wrote to White asking him what the organization's position was with regard to the sponsoring of bond rallies. Pickens was actively contacting NAACP field offices to campaign for bonds, and Johnson was, expectedly, unsure whether the branch should fully cooperate with Pickens. White took two months to reply to Johnson, bringing the matter to the September board meeting. In typical politically astute fashion, the board determined that Pickens's work was "in accordance with the general resolutions of the Association but ... he is not acting as an office of the Association ... [and] there is no obligation on any branch to arrange such meetings [bond rallies], decision being left entirely to the discretion of the Branch." The board's decision reflected that at this point NAACP leaders were trying to decide whether to show full support for Pickens's work and more broadly, the Roosevelt administration's foreign policy.[28]

Other administrative issues regarding bond selling and buying were brought to NAACP leaders from the field. Immediately after the Pearl Harbor bombing, the Boston branch of the NAACP wished to purchase a $100 bond but was unsure whether a majority or unanimous vote was required by its Executive Committee to go ahead. Wilkins took the matter to the association's Committee on Administration, where again it was decided that such a decision was left to the particular branch. Throughout the war, a variety of individuals and organizations outside the association also looked to the NAACP as the hub of black activity around and support for bonds. In September 1943, John Payne of Newark, New Jersey, wrote to the NAACP, wondering if the association had any authorized agents in the Newark area who could sell him bonds for the Third War Loan. White personally responded to Mr. Payne, telling him that although the national office of the NAACP "has invested a considerable sum of money in war bonds we have no war bond agents in any part of the country."[29]

Although it did not sell bonds, the NAACP did have the ability to persuade African Americans to buy them, a fact well known to many organizations dedicated to promoting bonds. Also in September 1943, Dr. Joseph R. Sizoo, president of the Greater New York Federation of Churches, wrote to area religious leaders, including the NAACP. In a letter cosigned by Nevil Ford, executive manager of the New York State War Finance Committee, Dr. Sizoo asked for

> cooperation in interpreting the moral and significance of the new campaign for the sale of bonds in the Third War Loan, which begins on September 9th. What I am suggesting is not that your church should engage in the selling of bonds, but that there is an opportunity for service which is in full accord with the character of the Church and of the Christian ministry. The greatest need of the nation as it strives to win both the war and the peace is the spirit of sacrifice

and self-denial. At a time when our youth are offering their lives in order that our cherished ideals of freedom and democracy may survive, the least that we at home can offer is our substance. I should greatly appreciate your sounding this note of sacrificial service in connection with the coming effort to persuade the American people to loan their money to their government instead of spending it needlessly or hoarding it. Sunday, September 12, would be an especially effective time for this emphasis.[30]

Although direct selling of bonds from the pulpit was considered bad form, Sizoo linked war finance to Christianity through the common themes of sacrifice and self-denial. With strong connections to the religious community, Sizoo and Ford knew, the NAACP had the power to endorse the promotion of Treasury bonds in black churches.

Similarly, the Social Welfare War Bond Committee approached the NAACP for its cooperation in advancing war savings. In a July 1944 letter to the association (again, cosigned by Ford), Walter W. Pettit, chair of the committee, asked the NAACP to help increase payroll savings plan membership within social service agencies. The committee was sponsored by a variety of local and national agencies including the American Association of Social Workers, the Federation of Jewish Welfare Agencies, New York Catholic Charities, and the Federation of Protestant Welfare Agencies. Like its connections to the church, the NAACP was viewed as an important link to reaching those involved in social services to the foreign born, the aged, families, children, and the handicapped.[31]

The NAACP was frequently asked by outside organizations to support the Treasury program not only because of its influence on the black community but because the association itself was an active, often public investor in bonds. In December 1942, Wilkins suggested to White that the association buy a one-thousand-dollar Series G bond, the first of a number of bond purchases the NAACP would make during the war. After receiving a letter from the Guaranty Trust Company of New York, one of the NAACP's banks, in August 1943 urging its depositors to participate in the Third War Loan, the organization bought a ten-thousand-dollar bond. By the end of 1943, the NAACP had invested a total of fifty-five thousand dollars in war bonds. With each purchase of bonds, the NAACP gave credit for the sale to an African American individual and bond committee. For the organization's forty-thousand-dollar bond purchase in June 1944, White made sure that credit was given to Robert Braddicks, deputy manager of the Harlem Riverside Campaign Committee.[32]

Wilkins was a particularly avid supporter of war bonds, recognizing their value not only as an investment but also for image purposes. In August 1943, the War Finance Committee of New York proposed that the NAACP purchase billboard space in support of the Third War Loan. Wilkins sent a memo to White:

> It occurred to me that the NAACP might want to take some of these billboards. It will be very good advertising for the Association at a low cost. I am taking five in the name of *The Crisis*. The Association ought to be able to afford more than five and I think the returns in goodwill, especially in view of the present feeling would be very much worthwhile.[33]

Upon White's approval (writing on Wilkins's memo, "OK on 5"), the NAACP purchased five billboards at thirty dollars each, requesting that the name of the organization appear on each poster. The NAACP was also interested in where the billboards were to be located. In confirming the purchase, Wilkins made the NAACP's intent clear in a letter to Arthur DeBebian, advertising manager of the War Finance Committee of New York:

> We realize in a porposition [*sic*] of this kind no special location can be requested. We certainly do not want all of these posters confined to the Harlem area or to any "so-called Negro" area. We would like them to be distributed about the City of New York in a way that the advertising committee deems most effective. As I explained to you, we want the general public to know the colored people and their institutions are participating wholeheartedly in this War Bond campaign along with other Americans.[34]

The General Outdoor Advertising Company fulfilled Wilkins's request, locating the NAACP-sponsored posters not only in predominantly black neighborhoods in Harlem and the Bronx but also in mostly white neighborhoods in Brooklyn, New Rochelle, and Stamford, Connecticut.

Wilkins went so far as to have a photographer take pictures of both the *Crisis*'s and NAACP's billboards for use in a press release. Following Wilkins's lead, the NAACP and the *Crisis* each continued their sponsorship of five billboards for the Fourth, Fifth, and Sixth War Loans. For the latter, under Wilkins's urging, the NAACP posters appeared in the white Westchester suburbs of Walden, Nyack, Patterson, Newburgh, and Wallkill.[35]

Although Roy Wilkins was the NAACP's most enthusiastic champion of war bonds, Walter White was the organization's most visible supporter of the program. As the war progressed, White was viewed by the Treasury as instrumental to the success of its Inter-Racial Section. Like labor leaders William Green and Philip Murray, White held sizable power because of his ability to influence great numbers of Americans. Solving "the Negro problem" relied on gaining broad black support, and the Treasury recognized that endorsement of government securities by the leader of the NAACP was potentially a key part of the solution. To White, however, bonds represented not only alignment with national interests but also an opportunity to improve African Americans' economic position and move closer to full equality.

As a notable figure, particularly in the New York City area, White was frequently asked to attend important bond rallies and join influential bond committees. In May 1942, Bayard F. Pope, chair of the executive committee of the New York War Savings Staff, invited White to be a member of the "Citizens Committee of 200,000," its mission to "call on every family in greater New York City" to solicit for bonds. White telegrammed Pope the day after receiving the request, saying he was "pleased to accept membership" on the committee. A week later, the same office asked White to attend an organizing meeting of the Greater New York War Bond Pledge campaign at the Hotel New Yorker. It seemed that the more offers from the Treasury White accepted, the more he received.[36]

White occasionally found himself alongside other noted figures at bond rallies. In June 1942, the War Savings Staff held a Greater New York Inter-Racial Rally at Lewisohn Stadium at the College of the City of New York in Harlem, chaired by Channing Tobias. For maximum publicity value, the program committee of the bond rally sought one hundred sponsors, "equally divided between Negroes and Whites." Nelson Bengston, deputy administrator of the War Savings Staff, asked White to be one of the sponsors, and White accepted. Speaking or performing at the rally, which was free to the public, were Thomas E. Dewey, Marian Anderson, Paul Robeson, Olivia De Havilland, Pearl Buck, Dr. Marshall Shepherd, the Fort Jay Army Band, and the Erskine Hawkins Orchestra.[37]

For the launching of the Second War Loan in April 1943, White was again invited to a high-profile event. The campaign kickoff was held at Carnegie Hall and broadcast nationally, with Secretary Morgenthau, Thomas E. Dewey, Mayor Fiorello LaGuardia, and William Green in attendance. White received his request to attend the event from John W. Davis of the New York War Finance Committee, telling him, "If you have another engagement for that evening, we beg you to cancel it.... For our part this is an invitation, but we should like to have you regard it as a summons to you from your country at war."[38]

For the Fourth War Loan in February 1944, White was asked to help raise the bond quota of $2 million assigned to the Harlem district. More than $1 million was raised in the district during the Third War Loan, and Treasury officials believed they could double that amount with some aggressive promotion. Samuel H. Sweeney, general chairman of the drive, considered White "one of the key people of our community and one to whom many people look for advice and guidance in these crucial days," and asked him to personally solicit for bond sales. "You need no argument from me on the necessity of our section of the City doing its level best," Sweeney told White, "records of this sort constitut[ing] a basis for the demands for justice and fair play in the corporate life of our country, which we are making and shall make in the near future."[39]

Beginning in 1943, "records of this sort" became increasingly important to Treasury officials. Driven by escalating bond quotas with each war loan, the Inter-Racial Section and the National Organizations Division as a whole came under significant pressure to provide firm sales figures. Because White publicly supported the program, members of the Treasury staff repeatedly attempted to quantify how much he individually and the NAACP as an organization had invested in war bonds. In January of that year, Robert Braddicks asked White if he owned war bonds and was continuing to buy them. Braddicks explained that the query was part of a project being pursued by Tobias intended to "obtain a more complete coverage of the field to definitely prove to what extent our people [African Americans] on the home front are evidencing their patriotism." Not wanting to divulge specific numbers, White replied simply, "I wish to say I am continuing to buy them."[40]

Although the NAACP was a firm supporter of Treasury bonds, the organization did not hesitate to protest aspects of the program it felt did not live up to the administration's democratic ideals. In December 1941, a number of people, most black but some white, contacted the NAACP, asking to see more representations of African Americans in bond promotion. No defense bond posters produced and distributed before America entered the war had featured an African American, a fact that did not go unnoticed. One letter to the NAACP came from Virginia Bennett of Bloomfield, New Jersey, a white woman, who told White that "now is the time while artists are making Defense Posters that there should be Negroes represented among the pictures of our men in uniform."[41]

Another, larger source of complaints, however, was a giant mural in Grand Central Terminal in New York that featured a photograph of a group of multiethnic children but no blacks. The mural, covering the entire wall of the east wing of the terminal, could hardly be missed by the one hundred thousand people passing through the train station daily. Designed by Edwin Rosskam, the mural stood nearly one hundred feet tall, the largest of its kind in the world. The mural was sponsored by the Farm Security Administration and featured a collage of photographs of military equipment, farm life, workers and industry, and the group of multiethnic children. The mural also included a dramatic appeal for bonds:

> That government ... by the people shall not perish from the Earth
> That we may defend the land we love
> That these may face a future unafraid
> That we build for a better world
> Buy defense bonds and stamps now![42]

One letter to White (addressed "Dear Walter") about the mural came from G. E. "Kid" Hilton:

> I had the opportunity to view the mural in Grand Central Station depicting the different aspects in our conduct of the war and why we should all buy stamps and Bonds. We as a people are giving our honest effort in everyway [sic] toward keeping democracy safe and I do think a colored childs [sic] face would be quite fitting in the group which the mural depicts. I am writing to you to ask if you will use your good office to bring it before the proper authorities for the correction as I feel it is an oversight.[43]

"Kid" then invited White to the coming baseball season's All-Star game to be played at the Polo Grounds.

On behalf of "Kid" and others, White immediately wrote to Harold Graves, saying that the absence of African Americans in the Grand Central Terminal mural was "not conducive towards Negroes feeling enthusiastic about purchasing or pushing sales." White asked Graves "if some steps couldn't be taken to add to this and other murals dignified Negroes ... who are representative of the type of people who both have the means and vision to invest in Defense Bonds and Stamps." White soon received a letter from S. D. Mahan, associate director of information for the Defense Savings Staff, who explained that the photograph in the mural was of a group of children of California migrant farm workers, intended to "symbolize every American youngster irrespective of creed or color." Mahan assured White that future bond posters would include blacks, and that the Treasury was "very conscious of the contributions that are being made to the Defense Savings Program by the Negroes of this country." Not fully satisfied (and misunderstanding that the images in the mural were photographs rather than illustrations), White wrote back to Mahan, asking him, "I wonder if the painter of the mural was unaware of the fact that there are a good many Negro migrant farm workers in California as in other parts of the country?"[44]

Still, the "mural incident" would not go away. Complaints about the mural continued to arrive at the NAACP's offices, including one from Louise R. McKinney, a member of the Knoxville, Tennessee, branch of the NAACP. This time White wrote directly to Secretary Morgenthau, enclosing McKinney's letter and advising him "of the fact that a good many defense bonds and stamps have been sold to Negroes and, I hope, many, many more will be sold." At Morgenthau's request, Mahan again responded to White's letter, reiterating that Treasury staff members had been instructed "to take every opportunity to afford Negroes proper recognition in all our activities." The mural would rear its ugly head a final time, after the Office of Selective Service featured it on the cover of a bond-themed newsletter titled *Our America*. The John Brown Memorial Association of Philadelphia asked the NAACP to protest distribution of the newsletter, finding it "distinctly discriminatory, inasmuch as it completely ignores the members of the colored or Negro race, as is shown by the pictures exhibited."[45]

Soon after the furor over the mural died down, the NAACP found itself at the center of another cause for protest relating to war bonds. In June 1942, Lora Lewis, a volunteer solicitor for bonds from Queens, New York, was denied pledges by whites because of her color. Lewis, who happened to be the chair of the Education Committee of the Jamaica, Queens, branch of the NAACP, had volunteered only after several whites in the Addesleigh section of St. Albans declined to serve because they were "too busy." The leader of the campaign to refuse to buy bonds from Lewis was Roy Richardson, president of the local property owners association, who stated, "We've got to protect our homes from the Negroes. They want to get into this community and we're doing everything we can to keep them out."[46]

Upon hearing of the incident, Wilkins sent a telegram to John T. Madden, chair of the bond drive in the New York City area:

> We are certain your office deplores this incident and did nothing to encourage such bigotry in the midst of imperative necessity for national unity in support of war effort. But we feel certain, also, you must realize harmful effect upon the Negro minority whose members are rebuffed and insulted when they volunteer services to their country. In order to counteract in some degree the inevitable reaction to this incident, this office is asking its five local chapters in Greater New York to urge our members to ignore prejudice of Queens neighborhood and pledge at least ten percent of income in war bonds. Negro Americans are resentful and bitter over their treatment by many thoughtless persons in all phases of the war effort, but they are determined to support to the limit of their ability our common country in this most critical time so that the Hitlerism which this Queens incident exemplifies shall not become the American pattern of living.[47]

The NAACP put the text of the telegram into a press release and distributed it to newspapers across the country. Although a relatively minor event in a broad sense, the implications are important in terms of better understanding African Americans' national loyalty during the war. Rather than protest the incident by refusing to buy government securities or taking more drastic action through civil unrest, the NAACP reaffirmed their pledge to buy bonds in order to realize the Double V.

Others outraged by the incident literally pledged their support to Lewis. *PM* magazine published an article about the event and asked its readers to designate their bond sales to Lewis and register their protest with Madden. By reproducing a pledge card automatically crediting bond purchases to Lewis, *PM* intended "to prove to this Negro woman who is trying to serve her country that you are with her and her people in the fight for justice."[48] Perhaps the most interesting response, however, was a poem directed to Madden from an NAACP member:

> O Mr. Madden, Mr. Madden, the burden of this song, is to tell you nice and quietly that something sure is WRONG;
> "Excuse it Please—so sorry"—you doubtless have on tap,
> But don't forget 'twas said before (Pearl Harbor) by the Jap!
> Now, WRONG plus WRONG, we do concede, ne'er added up to RIGHT,
> so we wont [sic] scream and rant and rave, and add our WRONG to SPITE;

> But—Mr. Madden, Mr. Madden, please dont [*sic*] try to misconstrue,
> We KNOW that we can do our share—
> The Question is *CAN YOU?*[49]

Madden was far less eloquent in his response to Wilkins's telegram, stating that he was "very grateful for your wholehearted assurances that you will lend this great patriotic campaign every possible assistance" and that "nothing should interfere with our national unity on the war effort."[50]

It was clear from these two incidents that discrimination would not slow the NAACP's support for bonds. Indeed, racism associated with the program seemed to reinforce the belief that defeating enemies at home could be furthered by increasing, not lessening, bond purchases. For its support, the NAACP received a number of citations from the Treasury, the first coming in May 1943. In consideration of its investment in and promotion of bonds, the NAACP was then awarded a citation from the New York War Savings Staff "in recognition of patriotic service through personal and untiring effort." In February 1945, the NAACP received a citation for its sponsorship of outdoor advertising for bonds.[51]

As the war drew to a close, the NAACP remained a devoted backer of the Treasury bond program. In March 1945, Charles Craft asked Wilkins if he could meet with him in New York to discuss the NAACP's continued involvement in the bond program. Wilkins was, coincidentally, visiting black leaders in Tuskegee and Atlanta "regarding the expansion of the War Bond program among our group." In September 1945, the NAACP made its final and largest of government securities when its Finance and Investment Committee voted to invest $60,000 of its general fund account of $125,000 in Victory Bonds. By making such a sizable investment, the NAACP intended to safeguard its liquid assets during what was feared might be a volatile and economically unstable period as the country "adjusted" to peace.[52]

After the war, the Treasury recognized the efforts made by the NAACP and asked the organization for continued support. In March 1946, White was personally awarded the Treasury Silver Medal Award by Secretary Morgenthau, a rare honor.[53] Pickens, still with the Treasury to continue marketing bonds to African Americans, asked White for one more endorsement, this time for the peacetime savings bonds program. In April 1946, Pickens told White that he had "been a constant friend to this U.S. Savings Bonds program, not only because of a patriotic interest in your country and all of its people, but also because of your special interest in the economic welfare and the civic progress of the American Negro."[54]

Pickens asked White and "a few others who are in a position to exert good influence on the colored people of the United States" to recommend savings bonds. In June, White's statement was released to the African American press alongside those from other black leaders from publishing, religion, education, business, and other arenas. Having done its share to help win the war, the NAACP was now dedicated to helping the country "win the peace" and achieve equal rights for African Americans through economic strength.[55]

CHAPTER 8

★ ★ ★ African American Notables and War Bonds

In 1944, Secretary of the Treasury Henry Morgenthau, apparently an observer of African American colloquial speech, made a personal request to Cab Calloway of "Heidi Heide Hi" fame to compose a war bond song in "jive." In response, Calloway composed "Backin 'em Back," which, according to the official 1944 report of the Treasury's Inter-Racial Section, "combin[ed] jive-talk lyrics with a contagious melody." The song urged bondholders to "stash your bonds away," explained by the report as jive for "hide your bonds for safekeeping."[1]

Enlisting the efforts and talents of African American entertainers such as Cab Calloway was part of the Treasury's comprehensive plan to fulfill Morgenthau's vision to "use bonds to sell the war, versus vice-versa." By drawing upon the voluntary support of recognized, notable African Americans, the Treasury's War Finance Division had at its disposal a number of professional pitchmen and pitchwomen who could sell the war through bonds and related causes. The efforts by notable African Americans to sell bonds represents an especially rich part of the development of American identity during World War II, as black celebrities were of immeasurable symbolic value in demonstrating the administration's official brand of pluralistic democracy. A disparate group of notable African Americans would come forward during the war to serve this cause, most prominently the orchestra leader Duke Ellington and the boxer Joe

Louis, two of the most popular and widely known African Americans of the 1930s and 1940s throughout the world.

The first place the Treasury looked to find prominent African Americans to promote bonds to a black audience was, however, within the government itself. The endorsement of the Treasury's program by blacks employed by the government, with William Pickens and his colleagues at the Inter-Racial Section the most visible examples, lent a legitimacy to bond appeals to African Americans. Offering evidence that a variety of African Americans were enjoying successful government careers served as a clear demonstration of the administration's rhetoric of inclusivity and likely contributed to increasing blacks' support of the war effort.

With so much attention paid to the role of black military personnel within the African American community, linking black servicemen and servicewomen to the promotion of bonds was an effective sales technique. Following the heroic performance of Dorie Miller, the African American messman who shot down Japanese planes at Pearl Harbor, the Treasury created a bond poster featuring Miller. The Treasury was also very aware that African Americans in the armed forces held particular symbolic value, as in the case of the Tuskegee Airmen, who were viewed as heroes within the mainstream black community. Musicians from black military units were thus frequently included in bond rallies, as in 1945 when the 404th ASF Band from the First WAC Detachment of Fort Des Moines, Iowa, joined the Squadron F Band from the 3508 AAF Base Unit based in Truax Field of Madison, Wisconsin, in a highly charged downtown Chicago bond drive. Such use of black military personnel helped to bring into focus the direct relationship between the purchase of bonds and the supply of equipment for the protection of African American troops.[2]

Although the United States military was hardly a model example of democracy in action, African American soldiers were featured at bond rallies to encourage higher sales by black attendees. Brigadier General B. O. Davis, the highest ranking African American officer in the army, was a main speaker at the January 1943 Negro Million-Dollar War Bond Dinner at the Parkway Ballroom in Chicago. With Pickens, Graves, Sergeant Joe Louis, Governor Dwight Green, Mayor Edward J. Kelly, and hot dog king Oscar Mayer in attendance, a local black businessman presented a certified check for $100,000 to the Treasury. Entertainers at the dinner included Zasu Pitts, Buddy Ebsen, and Skeets Gallagher (in town on a road show), radio tenor Morton Downey, and the Coast Guard Cutters, a quartet.[3]

The most notable African American promoter of war bonds within the armed forces, with the exception of soldier Joe Louis, was undoubtedly Chief Petty Officer Graham Jackson. Jackson, who taught music and was a nationally recognized musician and entertainer before entering the navy, sold bonds through public performances. Admission to one of Jackson's concerts was typically the purchase of a war bond, with auctions then held for musical numbers, the proceeds of which again were allocated toward bonds. Through such exhibitions, Jackson sold more than $2 million in bonds over the course of the war, including $350,000 in a single evening in Macon, Georgia, and $50,000 at a rally in Athens, Georgia, in October 1943. When not performing at a rally, Jackson, a pianist and accordionist, could frequently be found on a downtown Atlanta street selling bonds for songs. He is best remembered, however, not for his bond efforts but rather from his appearance in a photograph in which he is playing "Going Home" as President Roosevelt's body was being boarded onto a train in Warm Springs, Georgia. Jackson was one of President Roosevelt's favorite musicians, performing often at the White House, Warm Springs, and Hyde Park. He was awarded no less than six War Bond Achievement Citations by the Treasury.[4]

In a highly publicized "photo op" in April 1943, Roosevelt sold bonds to the White House staff to kick off the Second War Loan. The first bond sold by the president was to John H. Pye, an African American messenger who had been Roosevelt's chauffeur when the latter was assistant secretary of the navy during World War I. With newsreel photographers recording the scene and Morgenthau by his side, Roosevelt declared:

> This is just a small cross-section of the White House staff, but this is like a great many other American houses throughout the country—most of us have got one member of the family in the fighting force of the United States and we back home are trying to do our bit, too. We subscribe.[5]

By featuring Pye as a member of the White House "family," the administration was telling African Americans that they were important members of the American family. More broadly, by enlisting African American government employees in the promotion of bonds, the Treasury was symbolically voicing its ideology of national unity and the postponement of what were perceived as domestic squabbles. Allusion to difference or separatism, such as that embodied in the Double V, were not to be found in the administration's promotion of bonds, as recognition of cracks in the

Chief Petty Officer Graham W. Jackson (*left*) receiving a War Bond Achievement Citation from Henry Morgenthau Jr., secretary of the treasury. (National Archives)

American foundation did not fit within the official paradigm of democracy, at least during the wartime emergency.

However, African Americans' special stake in the war could be detected in oblique ways, even within official rhetoric. For the Victory Loan in November 1945, the Treasury called upon Marshall Shepherd, recorder of deeds "and outstanding citizen" to urge Americans to continue to support the bond program. His message reflected mainstream patriotic sentiment, but keeping in mind it was distributed to the black press and designed for a black audience, could be interpreted as holding a set of different meanings for African Americans:

> We must take advantage of every opportunity which presents itself for us to share in shaping the future of America.... We owe to our returning servicemen the fulfillment of our promises of certain security and it is up to us both individually and as a group, to give full support to any program which lends itself to the development of that security. We have won the war but we are yet to win peace.[6]

Read through a lens tempered by the Double V, some of Shepherd's phrases—"shaping the future of America," "certain security," "yet to win peace"—are ambiguous with respect to who exactly is meant by "we." The double meaning of Shepherd's message, intended or otherwise, was an apt reflection of the complexities rooted in the intersection between patriotism and race. The promotion of bonds often resided in that same space, drawing upon the loyalties of African Americans to support the war to serve both causes.

Noted white government officials, as well, occasionally recommended bonds to African Americans. Those involved in America's justice system were in a unique position to endorse bonds for those who had yet to be awarded full civil rights. Hugo Black, former U.S. senator and associate justice of the U.S. Supreme Court during the war, spoke at a bond rally in Chicago in June 1945 and actively promoted bonds late in the war in outside-the-court speeches and writings.[7] In a September 1945 article he wrote for *Negro Digest* titled "The Negro Buys Bonds," Black echoed the administration's aims for bonds to act as a vehicle toward achieving racial harmony: "The bond drive is one example of the way Americans of whatever race or creed may more happily live and work together." As an integrationist, Black viewed bonds as an opportunity for African Americans to demonstrate their patriotism and more firmly establish American as their homeland. Although not going as far to support the Double V, Black emphasized the contributions African Americans were making: "In every war bond drive, as in all the rest of the war effort, the American Negro is doing his job. Thinking only of the common cause he has said to himself: 'This is my war for my country and I will do my part.' And he has done his part."[8]

Another group to promote bonds to African Americans was the intelligentsia of writers and academics. Faculty at black colleges and writers within the black press almost universally supported bond efforts, but it was independent writers and thinkers who offered the most interesting examples of partnership with the Treasury program. The back jacket of a 1945 edition of Richard Wright's *Black Boy*, for example, carried a war bond message. Historical figures of the arts and sciences were also called upon by the administration for promotion purposes, as in the Treasury's printing and circulation of a George Washington Carver Victory Bond poster.[9]

A Victory Bonds promotion involving poets Langston Hughes and Mark Van Doren stands out among bond rallies held by African Americans. With the war over but financial support still being solicited by the Treasury, the National Association of Collegiate Deans and Registrars in Negro Schools sponsored a victory bond contest among seventy-two black colleges in seventeen states and the District of Columbia. The prize for the college whose students purchased the greatest value of victory bonds was a personal visit by Langston Hughes and Mark Van Doren, at which the poets would present original manuscripts to the libraries of the victorious college. Hughes planned to present his manuscript of "Refugee in America" and "Peace Conference in an American Town," in addition to an autographed copy of "Freedom's Plow" (a verse play that had recently been recorded by Frederick March with the Jefferson Chorus). Van Doren planned to present his original draft of *Windless Cabins,* a novel.[10]

Such symbolic gestures by Hughes and Van Doren reflect the remarkable variety of events associated with the sale and purchase of bonds during World War II. These historical snapshots also illustrate how bonds operated as a central point around which a very wide range of individuals and groups found some common ground, profound attempts to defeat an openly racist, antidemocratic regime. Most interesting, voices typically associated with protest were now being used to urge all Americans to lend financial and moral support to the war effort. In May 1941, the Urban League organized a nationwide CBS radio broadcast with "leading Negro entertainers" to protest race discrimination in defense industries. Performers and speakers included Eddie "Rochester" Anderson, Joe Louis, Duke Ellington, and Marian Anderson, each of them a future spokesperson for government bonds.[11]

For wartime entertainers, whose popularity in those more innocent days depended heavily on having a positive and patriotic public image, alignment with the bond program was a wise if not necessary career move. Distancing oneself from war-related activities was considered grounds for suspicion, which in effect left celebrities with little choice but to be involved with bond rallies or other home-front efforts. Men of eligible draft age were at special risk, as questions could be raised as to why they had not enlisted. For African American entertainers, making a public contribution to help win the war was perhaps even more crucial from a career standpoint. Given that a more critical set of standards was likely applied to blacks in measuring national loyalty, it was virtually imperative for African American entertainers to be somehow linked to the war on the home front, and particularly to the Treasury's bond program. Soliciting support from the African American entertainment community, however, presented little difficulty for the Treasury; black musicians, composers, and actors, like most of their white colleagues, were more than eager to help sell bonds by means of their artistic talent and fame.

As with the Defense and, later, War Savings Staff's total bond program, borrowing the services of African American entertainers represented a key component of bond drives directed to a black target audience. For African American audiences, black celebrities held great power in selling bonds, as they stood as visible symbols of having achieved the American Dream. The Treasury's War Finance Division and its Inter-Racial Section capitalized on this symbolic power of black celebrities, calling on a wide variety of the most famous stars of the day to promote bonds. In October 1943, for example, African American members of the City Bond Drive Committee of San Antonio staged a Hollywood cavalcade consisting of "famous movie stars." The price of admission to the show was the purchase of a one-hundred-dollar bond. Following the show, according to one report, "Negroes went out to sell $50,000 in bonds to their people." The proceeds from this particular bond drive exceeded its quota by twenty thousand dollars.[12]

A number of black actors and actresses from the stage made significant contributions to the Treasury's bond program directed toward an African American audience. Black celebrities' personal bond purchases were often used for promotion purposes, as when Muriel Hahn, star of *Carmen Jones,* a popular Broadway show in 1944, bought a one-thousand-dollar bond to "help put over Harlem's quota" for the Fourth War Loan drive. By July 1945, *Carmen Jones* was still running strong, and by playing to capacity audiences at the Curran Theater had generated five hundred thousand dollars in bond purchases over the Seventh War Loan.[13]

Other African American stage notables lent time and effort to promote bonds and contribute to a variety of war-related causes. Hilda Sims, star of the Broadway hit *Anna Lucasta,* teamed up with none other than Tallulah Bankhead in a show performed for wounded sailors at St. Albans Naval Hospital on Long Island. For the Victory Loan campaign in December 1945, a special presentation of *Anna Lucasta* was performed at Chicago's Civic Theater, the price of a ticket a bond worth one hundred or more dollars. A group known as South Center, comprised of African American business leaders, bought out the show, "clinching the city's Victory Loan campaign."[14]

With so much of wartime American music grounded in African American blues and jazz, black musicians had a unique opportunity to contribute to the Treasury's bond program. African American musicians often played bond benefits or made personal appearances in order to help promote bond sales. In September and October of 1943, for example, local bond committee leaders of Memphis persuaded W. C. Handy to come to the city to take part in a series of rallies. At the request of George W. Lee, district manager of the Atlanta Life Insurance Company and chair of the city's African American bond committee, the "Daddy of the Blues" and composer of "Beale St. Blues" helped bond workers reach their $2 million quota for the Third War Loan. In one appearance at Russwood Park on October 3, Handy played "St. Louis Blues" in front of six thousand people during the seventh inning stretch of a Negro League baseball game between the Memphis Red Sox and the Cincinnati Clowns. At another Memphis rally, Eddie Anderson ("Rochester" from Jack Benny's radio program) joined W. C. Handy to help sell war bonds to African Americans.[15]

African American notables were also part of the Treasury's Music Project, which commissioned bond-themed songs to be played at rallies and on the radio and sold as sheet music. In 1944, the Inter-Racial Section formed its own music committee, with its stated mission to "choose the best patriotic song composed by Negroes and to devise adaptation of Negro spirituals." The Inter-Racial Section's music committee consisted of an all-star cast of leading African American notables, including Cab Calloway, Langston Hughes, W. C. Handy, Duke Ellington, and Andy Razaf. Razaf was also part of the "Music for Millions" series, a radio show broadcast nationally during war loan drives. For the Sixth War Loan radio campaign, broadcast over 912 stations in November 1944, Razaf composed two songs, "The War Bond Man" (sung by Frank Sinatra) and "That's Why I Buy Bonds" (sung by Bob Hannon). For his efforts, Razaf received a Treasury citation, signed by Secretary Morgenthau himself. For the "Sing for the Seventh" installment, Razaf teamed up with J. Rosamond Johnson to contribute one of twenty-one bond-related songs, which were broadcast over 700 radio stations across the country. The song, "Idle Dollars—Busy War Bonds" was recorded by Martha Tilton, accompanied by the Mark Wannow orchestra.[16]

As did W. C. Handy, Andy Razaf occasionally made personal appearances at bond rallies when invited. Razaf appeared at the Statue of Liberty movie theater in Times Square for the Sixth War Loan drive, and performed for employees of the Eureka Shipbuilding Corporation in Newburgh, New York, in June 1945 for the Seventh War Loan. Like many defense plants in the Northeast in 1945, Eureka had a large African American work force. For his appearance at Eureka, Razaf was joined by Lucky Roberts, "jiver of the ivories" according to the company's newsletter, the *Eureka Sprinkle*. Managers of both the movie theater in Times Square and the shipbuilding company recognized that bond appeals made to African Americans would be more effective with the presence of a black celebrity such as Razaf.[17]

Although blues artists whose careers had peaked some twenty years earlier still retained some star appeal, it was big band musicians who generated more excitement among both white and black audiences. The Treasury leveraged the broad appeal of big band music during the war years by incorporating bond drives into many concerts. Big band music was heavily segregated during the war, both in band membership and in audience. Big bands led by Harry James, Tommy Dorsey, and Paul Whiteman appealed to a largely white audience, whereas the Duke Ellington, Jimmy Lunceford, and Count Basie bands drew heavy black support. Regional black big bands, such as the Chicago-based Lennie Simmons orchestra, played almost exclusively to African American audiences, entertaining black regiments at armed forces bases and participating in bond drives at clubs such as the Aragon Ballroom. The Golden Gate Quartet, a San Francisco–based group and the first gospel act to reach a secular, national audience, also performed bond benefits before a largely African American audience.[18]

But it was Duke Ellington who emerged as the most important African American entertainer during World War II. Ellington's great popularity stemmed largely from his ability to draw from both black and white audiences. Although Ellington's self-described "Negro music" had roots in "primitive" African rhythms, his compositions were seen as "high-brow" by many critics. "His music," the *Chicago Defender* wrote in November 1942, "is over the heads of the average jitterbugger." It was, however, this paradox that made Duke Ellington such a powerful force in American popular music, leading critics to view him as an African American able to achieve democracy through his actions. As one observer noted in May 1942, "Duke Ellington does almost as good a job for this race of ours as all the combined and concerted efforts of the NAACP." Duke Ellington was considered a role model for many blacks during the war primarily because he was able to negotiate a successful career in entertainment without compromising African Americans' dignity, not an easy task in the 1940s. Ellington achieved this through the nature of his music, his sheer popularity and success as an artist, and by his commitment to breaking color barriers. Ellington emerged as one of the most visible symbols of blacks' involvement in World War II, ultimately enabling him to be a highly successful promoter of bonds for the Treasury.[19]

As did other wartime composers, Ellington contributed war-themed songs with proceeds from sheet music sales allocated for the Treasury. His own compositions, which included "I'll Be Home Soon," "The Swingshifter's Swing," and "What Am I Here For?" never reached hit status. Ellington's band did, however, record "A Slip of the Lip Can Sink a Ship," a popular song written by his son, Mercer Ellington. Ellington also accurately predicted in May 1944 that despite popular opinion, some war-themed songs would indeed stand the test of time: "I have often heard it said that very few good 'war tunes' have come out of the present war, yet I'd like to take a wild guess that twenty years from now people will be singing many of today's hit numbers as 'reminiscent' of World War II."[20]

Although he briefly considered enlisting, Ellington and government officials recognized that he was much more valuable as an artist. Because Ellington was particularly popular among enlisted men and women, he was soon labeled one of the nation's premier "morale boosters." He performed free concerts at army and navy bases throughout the war, including a July 1942 appearance at Chicago's Naval Aviation Training School. He also made an October 1942 appearance at the Hollywood Canteen (a recreation spot for servicemen organized and run by civilian volunteers), and performed at an August 1944 concert for the AAF Training Command at the Sioux Falls Army Air Field. Through direct contact with members of the armed forces, particularly African Americans, Ellington played a major role in enlisting blacks' support for the war. Media coverage of Ellington's frequent army and navy benefits likely had a halo effect on the African American community that translated to greater support for the war and incremental sales of war bonds. Ellington himself purchased three thousand dollars in bonds in the first year of the program alone.[21]

In November 1942, Ellington played for troops at Fort Dix, New Jersey, a concert aired nationally over the American Broadcasting Company's "Blue Network." The show was part of the "Coca-Cola Spotlight Bands" series, a program broadcast from various army camps that included many African American troops. During the first eight weeks of the series, only one African American band—Lionel Hampton's—had been invited to perform, drawing criticism from the black press and African American soldiers. Under pressure, organizers of the series added Ellington to the lineup (as well as the Count Basie and Jimmie Lunceford bands). The explanation for the omission was expressed by one reporter as a classic armed forces SNAFU: "Mentors of the show had considered spotting colored talent in colored camps, but army authorities found out that there are no 'white' or 'colored' camps." The reporter also noted the preferences among black soldiers for big band music led by African Americans: "Some of the camps at which white bands in the 'sweet' category were playing showed a predominance of uniformed Negroes, and producers of the show agree that they might have made happier choices of orks [orchestras]."[22]

Ellington continued his relationship with ABC's Blue Network, playing each Saturday afternoon from 5:00 to 6:00 P.M. during the weeks preceding and during the Seventh War Loan. At the end of each quarter-hour of the hourly concerts, Ellington made personal appeals to listeners to purchase bonds. Ellington's appearances on the Blue Network were made possible at the request of the Treasury and with the approval of Ellington's union, the American Federation of Musicians. Here was another example of representatives from different, and occasionally conflicting, spheres—artist, media, government, and labor—working together to sell bonds to the American people.[23]

Other than gratis performances for the armed forces, Ellington contributed to the war effort by promoting bonds in advertising for his records and by playing benefits for war-related causes. Ellington was the most popular performer of the Swing Shift Dances, a series of concerts held for 140,000 Los Angeles defense workers. He broke attendance records during a run at Chicago's Regal Theater in November 1942, donating a portion of the proceeds to the Treasury and earning a citation for distinguished efforts. His January 1943 Carnegie Hall concert for the Harlem division of the USO is still considered legendary in jazz circles as it marked only the second time that an entire evening of "modern swing" was scheduled at Carnegie Hall. Despite a wartime schedule that included continual composing and one-night stands, Ellington continued to play benefits, even against his doctor's advice.[24]

Ellington also found time to dabble in Hollywood wartime filmmaking, appearing in MGM's *Cabin in the Sky* and Columbia's *Reveille with Beverly*. Like some other wartime films, both *Cabin in the Sky* and *Reveille with Beverly* were patchworks of musical numbers bound by a thin plot. Each of these pictures featured the biggest African American stars of the day, including popular musicians such as Ellington, Louis Armstrong, and Count Basie, who had fallen through Hollywood's cracks primarily because of their race. In April 1943, however, the Office of War Information saw an opportunity to tie in with *Cabin in the Sky*, planning to release a "story for the Negro Press on Negro celebrities, Robson [sic], Rochester, etc., how they save money by buying bonds. Perhaps angled on group of all-Negro cast of 'Cabin in the Sky' (film, starring Ethyl Waters, is in production or will be shortly)."[25]

The greater pluralistic climate of the war years made African American celebrities' omission from the Hollywood scene that much more obvious, as well as exposed greater market opportunities for all-black feature films. Recognition by Hollywood extended Ellington's popularity, with publicity surrounding the making and showing of these films portraying him as an icon of popular music. With Ellington, the Treasury had as best a spokesperson it could hope for to promote bonds and establish African Americans' stake in the war.

The final arena from which African American notables emerged to promote the war through bonds was sports. Boxers in particular played an integral role in bond drives, with a portion of the proceeds from a bout often allocated for bonds or other war-related causes. Because the business of boxing was relatively multicultural, ethnic and racial teamwork (what may be called the "platoon effect" after its popularization in films of and about World War II) was a popular theme in the selling of bonds within the sport. This was summarily captured in August 1944 by Joe Commiskey, a columnist for the *Washington Post*, in his coverage of a benefit fight:

> This is the week when we all should take a deep bow to a couple of Negro kids named Jack and Montgomery. They are the two who drew better than $35,000,000 in War Bonds at the Madison Square Garden gate and drew nothing but blood for their services.... If the Treasury is smart it will try to duplicate last week's show a thousandfold. Somehow, the Stars and Stripes and what we're fighting for runs in a solid pattern right through the whole thing. The Jew (Mike Jacobs) will put it on. The Irish (the managers) will say "Yes." The fighters (mostly Negro) will wait for the bell. And all of them will come out swinging. And together. Isn't that the whole idea?[26]

Although a variety of boxers took part in bond benefits, it was heavyweight champion of the world Joe Louis who most actively and visibly supported the war through bond drives and armed forces relief efforts. Despite practicing in seemingly oppositional fields, Joe Louis and Duke Ellington shared remarkable parallels in their professional and personal lives. Both had risen to phenomenal success during the Depression. To critics and the press, Ellington and Louis were each enigmas, incorporating elements of both "high" and "low" culture and defying traditional African American stereotypes. As well, both Duke Ellington and Joe Louis had exceptional work ethics, each driven by a pursuit for great success and financial gain. This ethic, and the desire to be recognized as the best in their given field, provided the basis for their recognition as American heroes, particularly among blacks. Ellington's and Louis's popularity crossed economic, geographic, and political boundaries within the black community, each of them serving as a symbol of great pride among both the emerging black bourgeoisie and the "people."

Louis was more than eager to position his fights as symbolic attacks against the Nazis. "Boy," he said in September 1941, "how I wish I could get just one punch at that Hitler man.... He'd never get up." In his title defense against Billy Conn in June 1941, Louis invested all his prize money—40 percent of the total purse—in defense bonds. All of the proceeds (eighty-nine thousand dollars) from his January 1942 rematch against Max Baer went to the Navy Relief Society, and a portion of his winnings from his March 1942 fight against Abe Simons were designated for the Army Relief Fund. Following his contribution to the Navy Relief Society, Louis was honored in Congress. "His sportsmanship, his unequaled physical endowments, retained and increased by clean living, are now crowned with supreme generosity," said Senator Brown of Michigan in January 1942. Brown's remarks were even included in the *Congressional Record* as part of the day's proceedings rather than in the appendix, an unusual honor.[27]

Beyond fighting for no or lesser money, Louis was risking his title each time he fought, adding to the personal sacrifice he was making. In September 1945, Supreme Court Justice Hugo Black wrote about how Louis had risked his title without compensation. "You are fighting for nothing tonight, Joe," someone reportedly said to Louis. "No," replied Louis, "I am fighting for my country." Irwin Rosee, a publicist who traveled with Louis when the boxer made appearances at bond drives, recalled a similar anecdote. Rosee remembered "another black man came up to Joe one day and said, 'Why'd you join the Army? This is a white man's country and a white man's war?' And Joe said, 'Lot of things wrong in America, but Hitler ain't gonna fix it.'"[28]

Other than fighting for war bonds and armed forces relief, Louis helped sell the war through other avenues. In March 1942, Louis spoke at a Naval Relief Society rally at Madison Square Garden, declaring that "we're going to do our part ... and we'll win because we're on God's side." The remark was picked up by the media and used in a 1942 government poster, one of very few to feature an African American. Most significant, however, was Louis's much publicized enlistment in the army. Even with his financial contributions, the government recognized that Louis could play a larger role within the military. "He will be of far greater benefit as a morale builder than he can be of benefit to Uncle Sam's treasury as a money maker," said the *Ring* in September 1941. Louis's ability to build morale as a soldier was perceived as having special meaning to African Americans. "Especially will Joe Louis be of great encouragement to members of his own race, who idolize him," wrote the *Ring*. Louis was initially rated 3A, excluded from the draft on grounds of dependency, but outside pressure for him to enlist began to mount by the summer of 1941, and Louis's draft status was changed to 1A, immediate call. Part of Louis's decision to enlist was based on his desire not to make the same mistake Jack Dempsey had made in the previous world war. Dempsey actively avoided the draft to continue to build his aspiring career, a decision he regretted later on.[29]

As a soldier, however, Louis's stature grew to even greater heights. A GI earning twenty-one dollars a month, Louis spent much of his time entertaining troops in wildly popular exhibition bouts. He also successfully defended his professional title on several occasions, becoming the first soldier in American history to box as heavyweight champion. In 1943, soldier Louis appeared (with Ronald Reagan and many other stars of the day) in the movie *This Is the Army,* a propagandistic film designed to sell the war, and specifically war bonds, to the American people. Louis's dedication to his country and his race as both soldier and professional boxer reached nearly mythical proportions. In March 1942, for example, Wendell Willkie publicly praised both Louis and Dorie Miller as outstanding representatives of their race and country.[30] But it was the March 23, 1942, editorial page of the *Daily Mirror* that perhaps painted the most eulogistic picture of Joe Louis:

> The Joe Louis [versus Abe Simon] fight in the [Madison Square] Garden next Friday night transcends the usual appeal of a fight. He's [Louis] is fighting for a hundred other glorious causes; some of the same causes for which Lincoln risked civil war. Joe Louis is fighting for those Negro blood-donors to the Red Cross who were first refused and finally segregated, "so that those receiving transfusions may be given plasma from blood of their own race." Joe Louis is fighting for the morale of the one infantry division and the one armored division and the two pursuit squadrons in the Army that will be manned by patriotic, courageous American Negroes. And Joe Louis is fighting against the prejudice that keeps the people of his race out of certain labor unions, and out of the United States Navy—"our first line of defense." And Friday night, he fights for the Relief Fund of the armed service that permits him and others of his race to wear its uniform—the United States Army. For all these reasons, this fight deserves the support of all the people of New York City.[31]

Although comparing Louis's fight for liberty with Lincoln's might have drawn a little too much on journalistic puffery, the "hundred other glorious causes" Louis was fighting for could not be denied. Joe Louis, Duke

Ellington, and many other notable African Americans were each fighting for the end of Jim Crow and institutionalized discrimination, and ultimately, for William Pickens's "shining star of democracy." To win this war at home, however, the nation had to first win the war abroad, the mandate of the Double V. Driven by both loyalty to their country and their race, these and other recognized African Americans were instrumental in selling a potentially unpopular war to a largely marginalized and disenfranchised group of Americans. Bonds, as the most tangible symbol of the requirements to win the war abroad, lay at the center of this unprecedented campaign of persuasion.

To most African American ears, the rhetoric of democracy was expressed more powerfully and compellingly when delivered by popular and heroic figures of their own race. Although the promotion of bonds and devotion of time and effort to other war-related causes represented the long-term interests of those dependent on popular public image, support from African American notables, like their white counterparts, typically did not have to be coerced or even requested. The broad support of the administration's goals among notable African Americans reflected that demonstrated by the diverse black community. The common ground of war bonds illustrated the flexibility of African Americans to come together to pursue a shared vision, despite different social backgrounds and conflicting political orientations.

Although fulfilling the administration's objectives was not the primary intent of African Americans in backing the war through bonds, the United States would indeed have been a much more fragmented nation had African Americans not supported the bond program. The very strength of the Treasury's bond program, in fact, resided in its ability to meet different objectives for different communities while serving the nation's best interests through its common, symbolic power.

CHAPTER 9

★ ★ ★ African American Investment in War Bonds

In 1942, John Henry Harris, a blind peanut vendor in Greenville, Mississippi, bought his first war bond with saved nickels and dimes, despite having a wife and four children to support. Upon hearing about the upcoming Fourth War Loan drive the following year, Harris told the local committee chairman that he was saving money to be the first bond buyer of the new drive. On September 9, 1943, the first day of the Fourth War Loan, the committee chairman called on Harris, who turned over 995 pennies, $8.75 in nickels and dimes, and a nickel from his coat pocket in exchange for a $25.00 bond.[1]

Harris's story of personal sacrifice was one of many that offered vivid proof that African Americans across the country were supporting the war effort through the purchase of bonds.

Spurred by national loyalty and the administration's effort to present the bond program as uniquely opportunistic for blacks, millions of African Americans bought bonds in order to achieve a double victory. Because war bond sales were recorded only by geography, however, there were and are no reliable statistics regarding African Americans' or any other particular group's contribution to the bond program. Early in the war, some banks in the South would stamp bonds sold to blacks *Negro* or *Colored,* but this practice was soon ordered stopped because it violated the democratic intent of the program. Nevertheless, to Treasury officials, there was little doubt African Americans were backing the war effort on all fronts, including the bond program. As Ted R. Gamble, national director of the War Finance Division, stated in 1944, "When the record of this war effort shall have been written, it will show that Negroes not only fought the enemy in the front lines of the battle overseas, but met him on the home front on the assembly lines and the bond-purchasing lines." A year later, in response to some hefty praise awarded by the Treasury to African Americans for their contribution to the bond program, William Pickens said simply, "Negroes are merely doing their share. They too are stockholders in the greatest corporation the world has ever known—America."[2]

The government's refusal to record purchases by demographics such as gender, age, religion, and race was an intentional measure taken to ensure the program remain voluntary and nondiscriminatory. Pickens himself regularly commented on this aspect of the bond program in both reports to his superiors and as part of speeches to various audiences. "No full report of the part which colored citizens have so far borne or will yet bear in the war finance program is possible," he wrote in his report of the Inter-Racial Section for 1943. "In our democracy," he continued, "any citizen of any race or color has the privilege of buying his bonds through all the issuing agencies. No records are made by race."[3]

Delivering on Morgenthau's mission to sell the war via bonds rather than vice versa, Pickens emphasized the qualitative aspects of the bond program as directed to African Americans. "For evaluating the contribution by Negro Americans," he wrote in the 1943 report, "attention is called to the Negro's general economic position and to the priceless spiritual factors involved in these contacts with colored groups—in lifting and sustaining morale, in building and protecting their good will, and in helping to perpetuate their devotion and loyalty to the Government and to the Nation." Pickens's emphasis on the qualitative aspects of the program was sincere, but was also a necessary tactic to deflect the impossibility to produce hard numbers. Given his penchant of producing facts regarding contributions made by blacks throughout American history in order to correct popular misperceptions, Pickens would likely have made full use of accurate statistics had they been available.[4]

Although reliable figures regarding African Americans' bond sales were not available, Pickens's emphasis on the qualitative aspects of the program did not always satisfy his superiors. A September 1943 memo, for example, sent by Pickens's boss, James Houghteling, to the entire Inter-Racial Section staff reflects the pressure Houghteling and other high-level executives of the Treasury were under as the war debt grew to mammoth levels:

> The program of the Inter-Racial Unit has heretofore been aimed at educating a large section of the population on the subject of the war needs and war finance and has resulted in the sale of War Bonds beyond what we had dared to hope for when the program was initiated. However, with the momentum already attained it is essential that our work from now on be measured by actual production in the form of recorded sales of War bonds. The visits of members of the Unit to communities which do not result in an actual increase in the purchase of War Bonds in those communities must be regarded as failures. From now on we must measure the success of our work by results actually recorded.[5]

Houghteling's note indicates that despite the founding mission of the program to build morale and the Treasury's own decision to not record purchases by race, Pickens was expected to produce some estimates on bond sales by African Americans. Quantifying the Inter-Racial Section's impact on the black community, however, was difficult at best; estimating blacks' total contribution was virtually impossible. The only hard sales numbers the Treasury kept were based around quotas, justified as a geographical measure. Quotas for bond drives were set in cities, counties, or states with a sizable black population, giving the Inter-Racial Section and Treasury some idea of sales during these high-volume periods. Other contribution figures, however, covering nondrive periods or from the payroll savings deduction plan, simply did not exist.[6]

Because there were so many variables to consider, estimates of African Americans' investment in bonds varied wildly. Actual sales generated at rallies attended by the Inter-Racial Section were estimated as $9,213,241 and $10,719,052 for 1943 and 1944, respectively, but this obviously represented only a small portion of blacks' total investment. In order to estimate total contributions by African Americans, Pickens had to make extrapolations from these figures using assumptions that would probably have made a Treasury statistician very nervous. For example, based on estimated attendance figures from Inter-Racial Section rallies in 1943, Pickens determined that the section had met with 2.3 percent of the nation's fifteen million blacks (the number assumed by Pickens) in 1943. From these numbers, and some unknown variables, Pickens somehow arrived to the conclusion that "we might state that the Negro people of the United States, during 1943, must have bought more than $300,000,000 in Government Bonds." Consistently, a document dated June 2, 1944, estimated African American bond purchases as "more than $250 million" prior to the Fourth War Loan (January 18 to February 15, 1944), excluding revenue from the payroll deduction plan.[7]

In his 1944 report, however, Pickens used a set of different assumptions to arrive at a much higher estimate of bond investment among African Americans. Based on 10 percent of the Treasury's estimate of 27 million payroll plan enrollees, Pickens estimated there were 2.7 million African Americans participating in the payroll savings plan. If each of these 2.7 million individuals were purchasing one $25 bond per month, African Americans were investing $67.5 million per month or $810 million a year in the payroll plan alone. Given other sources of revenue, Pickens stated in his report, this "would undoubtedly raise Negro participation well above ONE BILLION DOLLARS per year." At such levels of support, African Americans were investing in bonds at a per capita rate exceeding that of the program as a whole.[8]

Although their bond sales could not be accurately estimated, there is no doubt that African Americans were eager supporters of the Treasury's bond program. Bonds were considered a particularly attractive financial investment by blacks because they represented a safe and reliable alternative to local white banks, which often cheated blacks. In fact, after Treasury sales data indicated that African Americans were redeeming bonds at a significantly greater than average rate early in the war, the Inter-Racial Section had to take steps to prevent blacks from purchasing bonds they could not afford. African Americans' substantial and sustained contribution to the program is clear given the many individual reports of black individuals, groups, businesses, and communities purchasing bonds that were published in local media and often subsequently replayed in Treasury public relations material. The history of World War II bonds is, in fact, better told not through statistics but through the many and diverse stories in which bonds played an important role in the lives of home-front Americans.[9]

For some individuals, for example, war bonds served as the bridge connecting the experiences of two world wars. This was the case for one African American veteran of World War I, Florida Anderson, who was putting 80 percent of his income into bonds. Another World War I veteran, James Ragan of Perry, Georgia, carried a dirt-caked flour sack filled with old, oversized five-dollar bills into an authorized bond office in July 1943 to purchase war bonds. Ragan had been saving the money—buried on his land—since the First World War. Other African Americans were making equally extraordinary sacrifices to support the war effort through bonds. In October 1942, for example, Eliga Gordon purchased bonds with the one-thousand-dollar prize money he was awarded for becoming national champion of cotton pickers. Sometimes stories of personal sacrifice reached extreme, almost mythic proportions, as when Jim Kearse purchased nine

Jim Kearse (*left*), serving a life sentence for murder, being presented with nine war bonds by B. Frank Wilkes, captain of the guard at the South Carolina State Penitentiary. Kearse, according to prison authorities, was "actuated by a fine spirit of patriotism and a homespun philosophy of thrift." (National Archives)

war bonds while serving a life sentence for murder in a Columbia, South Carolina, prison. "I'll tell you why I'm buying war bonds," said Kearse. "I like the interest and I'm building a stake for the future. Another thing, I want to help whip the Japs. I don't like the way they treat our boys."[10]

As in the case of John Henry Harris and many others, the conversion of change into war bonds made particularly good copy for the African American press and the Treasury Department. Purchasing bonds with saved change conveyed both thrift and sacrifice, themes central to the selling of bonds and the war itself, and values the administration were trying to instill among blacks. For the Third War Loan in October 1943, for example, a Jackson, Tennessee, railroad worker with a salary of $135 a month purchased a $1,000 war bond using eight one-quart fruit jars filled with precisely $750 in quarters and half dollars. Cases of children converting change for stamps or bonds were even more compelling, as when five-year-old Wilbur Othello Merriweather of Cleveland turned in his life savings—3,750 pennies—for a $50 war bond for the Seventh War Loan in July 1945. Reporting such stories of thrift and sacrifice let other African Americans know the extent to which some blacks were going to support the war, a device very likely to have a positive impact upon attitudes toward the administration and its policies.[11]

Individuals, skilled or otherwise, also often offered their services in exchange for the purchase of bonds. Women wanting to serve the cause occasionally offered to do housework or prepare food for people who would make a sizable bond purchase. Such was the case in October 1943, when Minnie Edwards, a San Antonio air warden, offered to do a half day of housework for someone willing to buy a one-hundred-dollar bond. She found four takers and sold a twenty-five-dollar bond on top of the four hundred-dollar bonds she helped sell. Cooking for bonds was an equally interesting promotional device, as suggested by the following ad that appeared in a New York newspaper in 1944: "Colored girl, War bond worker, will cook and serve dinner any Sunday for anyone who will buy or pledge $1,000 up in War Bonds, Box 2424, Times-Union." The cooking-for-bonds theme could also be embellished to generate higher interest and sales. This was the case when Susan Tokes, a well-known caterer in Winchester, Virginia, cooked "an old Virginia dinner of fried chicken and ham" for a June 24, 1944, bond rally in Winchester, Massachusetts, with the price of admission a bond purchase. On that very same day in Winchester, Virginia, two cooks from Winchester, Massachusetts, were preparing "a traditional New England dinner of beans and codfish," also for the price of a bond. The two cities were engaging in a friendly competition, another recurring theme in bond promotion. Tokes, it might be noted, was the daughter of a slave, and had prepared food for Senator Harry Byrd's annual picnics for the past seventeen years.[12]

Because of their symbolic value, bonds were often purchased or awarded to commemorate a special occasion. Both the black press and the Treasury expressed great interest in commemorative bond purchases, particularly those associated with black federal government employees, as such visible demonstrations of African American support for the war were ideal to further promote bond sales. In December 1944, for example, the Treasury announced that James W. Johnson, a collector in Internal Revenue, had purchased extra bonds (beyond those through the payroll deduction plan) to celebrate his first anniversary in his position. A local newspaper forwarded to the Treasury Department the story of Maceo Rutherford, a Denver mail carrier, who bought a bond valued at one thousand dollars as a twenty-fifth anniversary gift for his wife. Sometimes the government itself used bonds as a promotional technique, as in June 1945, when the navy awarded a seventy-five-dollar bond to William Smith for an idea he had submitted. Using bonds to showcase supportive government employees was a way the administration attempted to influence African Americans' view of the war and their role within it. Linking bond purchases to successful African Americans also indirectly communicated that bonds were a wise investment likely to pay off in the future.[13]

War bond drives held special meaning in the rural South, connecting typically isolated communities to the national scene. Although predominantly poor, African American farmers demonstrated remarkably strong support for bonds through both the purchase and sale of bonds. Children of farmers—young farmers themselves associated with various groups—were particularly active in bond activities. The New Farmers of America, for example, a group of nineteen thousand African American farm students from eleven southern states, had already purchased more than $150,000 of bonds and stamps through July 1943. On a more local level, thirteen African American boys and girls from the Marion, South Carolina, 4-H Club invested $243.74 in bonds and stamps by selling hogs they had raised. The Future Farmers of America, which included more than two hundred thousand African American boys and girls, canvassed rural areas throughout the nation, and were credited with more than $8 million in sales of bonds by 1945.[14]

Throughout the country, African American farmers showed support for the war by exchanging whatever resources they had for bonds. Robert Bissic, for example, a farmer in Grambling, Louisiana, sold several head of cattle for money to participate in the 1943 Victory Club. His wife sold poultry and eggs for the same drive, as did the Bissic's eleven-year-old son, who sold peas to purchase a twenty-five-dollar bond. In another reported pea episode in October 1942, a farmer unable to afford the price of a war bond sought to donate his peas to feed American soldiers. One year later, G. L. Archie, a watermelon farmer, split his farm income in two, half going toward a new house and half toward war bonds. Such case histories illustrate the desire of many African American farmers to preserve their version of the American Way of Life through the purchase of war bonds.[15]

Other occupations or industries with large numbers of African Americans were obvious targets for bond promotions by the Inter-Racial Section, and most blacks in these groups responded enthusiastically through bond purchases. One million African Americans were estimated to be employed in "industry" by 1945, the vast majority of which were working in defense plants. The federal government, which essentially mandated

E. M. Graham (*left*), president of the Pullman Porters Benefit Association, handing a fifty-thousand-dollar check to Major C. Udell Turpin, deputy administrator of the Illinois War Savings Staff, during the Second War Loan. (National Archives)

purchases through payroll deduction, employed 270,000 blacks. The 100,000 African American railroad workers (about 8 percent of the total industry's work force in 1945) were strong supporters of the bond program despite consistently protesting job discrimination, led by A. Philip Randolph, president of the Brotherhood of Sleeping Car Porters. Blacks accounted for a significant share of the $127 million invested in bonds by railroad workers through the Seventh War Loan.[16]

Whereas the purchase of bonds by individuals demonstrated personal commitment to winning the war, purchases by organizations stood as signs of institutional power within the African American community. Because bonds were financial investments, local, regional, and national businesses had a vested interest in bond-related activities. Investment in bonds by businesses served a number of beneficial functions attractive to shareholders, present and potential customers, and employees. First, it demonstrated a commitment to national defense and thus stood as a sign of faith in America; second, with a ten-year maturity, bonds represented a long-term

Ashley L. Totten (*right*), international secretary-treasurer of the Brotherhood of Sleeping Car Porters, AFL, presenting a check for one hundred thousand dollars to Arthur T. MacManus, deputy manager for the State Labor Division, New York War Finance Committee, during the Seventh War Loan. (National Archives)

orientation, a sign of conservatism in a still thrift-oriented society; and third, as they were for individuals, bonds were one of the few places businesses could store liquid assets and earn interest while the consumption side of the economy was essentially stalled.

The African American business community played an important role in the purchase and promotion of bonds throughout the war. African American–owned and –managed businesses represented the economic power bloc of urban black life and thus served as a critical liaison between the Treasury and the broader black community. More so than in the economic arena at large, institutional power was concentrated in the black community, with bonds often serving as the principal wartime link among African American businesses and media. For the black business community, war bonds represented a rare, unprecedented opportunity to participate in the national economy. As a fusing of patriotism and capitalism, war bonds were an irresistible financial instrument for organizations with resources to invest, an opportunity for black businesses to carve out a bigger piece of the American pie.

As in the general bond program, the biggest African American investors in bonds thus came from the business community. Despite the Treasury's effort to tailor the bond program to the average individual's investment needs, war bonds were an attractive investment option for companies with large amounts of cash on hand, particularly insurance companies and banks. In fact, investment in conservative government financial securities was business as usual for corporations with sizable assets. With additional regulations placed on bank holdings of bonds, insurance companies emerged as the industry to dominate the bond program. As case in point, the total holding of the thirty-nine largest African American insurance companies through August 1944 was nearly $18 million, the single largest amount of any African American investor group. The Treasury awarded its highest citation to the National Negro Insurance Association, a group of fifty-two insurance companies and thirteen underwriters, for its outstanding support of the bond program.[17]

Instances of insurance companies investing heavily in bonds, such as the Mammoth Life and Accident Insurance Company of Louisville purchasing $53,000 in defense bonds in October 1941, became relatively common. In October 1943, E. M. Martin, secretary of the Atlanta Life Insurance Company, announced the company's total investment in bonds as $1,528,500. His company, Martin said, was "investing the people's money in the best securities in the world." During the same month, the Afro-American Life Insurance Company of Jacksonville purchased $100,000 in war bonds in order "to equip and support the 37 A.L.I.C. employees now in the armed services of the United States government." Although grounded in the best interests of their customers, employees, or the nation itself, bonds were also the smartest way for large businesses to safeguard excess cash.[18]

Investment in bonds within the African American business community was, of course, not limited to large organizations. Mom-and-pop businesses in local communities were just as likely to invest in bonds for the same reasons as large companies—patriotism, financial common sense, and customer goodwill. Businesses central to black community life backed the attack through bond drives, such as in May 1943, when the T. H. Hayes Funeral Home of Memphis sponsored a bond drive for the Third War Loan. Fifteen thousand dollars' worth of bonds were sold, as the *Southern Frontier* put it, "to the average Negro earning a living over the wash tub, in kitchens, factory, and the small grocery business." Owners of independent businesses were often the single largest investors in local bond drives, as it was typically these individuals who had the most money in town. This was perhaps the case in October 1943, when H. M. Morgan, owner of the Tyler Barber College in Smith County, Texas, led the way in the local Third War Loan drive with a five-thousand-dollar bond purchase.[19]

African American employees of small businesses were also active in the payroll deduction plan. A lumber company in Tchula, Mississippi (population 861), for example, had 100 percent participation in the plan among its African American employees, totaling one thousand dollars a month. During the Third War Loan drive, however, 50 of the company's employees bought an extra fifty-dollar bond, bringing the plan total to more than three hundred dollars. Rumors that many employees were cashing in their bonds soon after purchase, always a concern by the Treasury, proved to be false after a company audit.[20]

Beauticians, a strong coalition in many local black communities and on a national scale, were very active contributors to bond drives. On a local level, for example, two hundred Memphis beauticians exceeded their quota of $50,000 in bonds in May 1943. The previous month, beauticians in New Jersey held a bond rally at their annual meeting and conference, raising $27,900 in cash sales and another $2,250 in pledges. In attendance at the Paterson YMCA rally were Pickens, NAACP officials, pastors, an American Legion color guard, and heroes of World War I. After a poet read "The Colored Soldier's Prayer," Pickens told the beauticians that "Fascism makes no place for the Negro in humanity.... This is distinctly our war." On a national level, the Beauticians Volunteer Corps, a subgroup of the National Beauty Culturists' League, pledged $1,123,000 for the Seventh War Loan. Because beauty culturists held a prominent place in the life of most major cities for African American women in the first half of the twentieth century, beauticians' endorsement of bond rallies undoubtedly had a rippling effect throughout many black communities.[21]

The organization of Negro Savings Clubs represented another means of appealing to African Americans on a local level. As did general war bond savings clubs, Negro clubs reported to state War Finance Committees, which in turn reported to the Treasury's War Finance Division. A club's one hundred members would generally purchase one twenty-five-dollar bond a month for deposit in a local bank. Numbering forty-seven in September 1944, Negro Savings Clubs were particularly popular in the South; Mississippi, strangely, accounted for almost half (twenty-two) of all clubs during the Sixth War Loan. Ironically, the government's segregation of war bond savings clubs by race demonstrated its policy toward blacks as "separate but equal," reflecting the rhetorical nature of America's pluralistic democracy and revealing the biases embedded within the ideological consensus it was espousing.[22]

Although not a government agency, Negro Savings Clubs had strong ties to the Inter-Racial Section and were led by a National Organizing Committee whose members represented the core support block for the African American bond program. Vice chairmen of the committee included a cross-section of the leaders of the most influential organizations of the black bourgeoisie: Mary McLeod Bethune, president of the National Council of Negro Women; Bishop James A. Bray, president of the Fraternal Council of Negro Churches in America; Lester B. Granger, executive secretary of the National Urban League; Shellie Northcutt, supervising Jeanes teacher; Fannie B. Peck, president of the National Negro Housewives League; Dr. Frederick D. Patterson, president of the National Negro Land Grant College Presidents' Association; P. L. Prattis, executive editor of the *Pittsburgh Courier;* and J. Finley Wilson, grand exalted ruler of the IBPOE (Elks).[23]

The bylaws of the general plan of Negro Savings Clubs outlined that it was the responsibility of the national chairman to file a copy of progress reports from state War Finance Committees with the Inter-Racial Section. With these reports, Pickens gained direct knowledge of activities related to war bond purchases in every state in which there was a club. Negro Savings Clubs thus operated in some ways as a field sales force for the Inter-Racial Section, branch offices that sold the government's product at a local level. The Inter-Racial Section in turn made its services available to local clubs, such as helping to organize rallies and parades, providing subjects for discussion groups, and recognizing attainment of bond goals.[24]

It was P. L. Prattis of the *Pittsburgh Courier* who originally proposed the idea for Negro Savings Clubs (another indication of the broad support the mainstream black press showed for the administration's bond program), but the National Negro Business League was the clubs' driving force. Dr. J. E. Walker, president of the league, served as the club's national chairman; its secretary was Albon L. Holsey, executive secretary of the league; and its treasurer was J. B. Blayton, treasurer of the league and vice president of the Citizens Trust Company in Atlanta. Although Negro Savings Clubs operated much like other savings clubs, a Treasury promotional brochure indicated secondary motives behind the National Negro Business League's strong interest in the clubs, that is, to document African

American's contribution to the bond program when the Treasury refused to keep records by race:

> The National Negro Business League regards it as highly desirable that a more complete record be assembled to demonstrate how loyally and generously the Negro population has Backed the Attack by buying War Bonds. It has been difficult to get together figures to prove how many millions of dollars have been invested in War Bonds by Negroes. The organization of a large number of War Bond Savings Clubs will help to prove this point. If the League can supply the Treasury Department with such records it will be most helpful in improving the recognized economic standing of the Negro throughout the country. Lively competition between War Bond Savings Clubs and extra good records on the part of individual clubs or their members will help the record and the cause of national unity.[25]

With Negro Savings Clubs designed to serve the business interests of black communities, some clubs offered members the opportunity to pool their war bond purchases for designation toward commonly shared business ventures or for reinvestments at bonds' maturation. In these programs, the value of war bonds was allocated not to a single purchaser but to a group, with profits (or losses) distributed among contributors to the venture. Here then was an interesting case of what can be considered "black capitalism" at work, the combining of African American resources in pursuit of common financial gain. Spurred by Pickens, leaders in the African American business community recognized that war bonds not only served a national cause but also represented a means for blacks to make socioeconomic progress. As greater economic power offered a direct path toward the ultimate goal of equality, a link can be established between the purchase of war bonds and the pursuit of African American civil rights.[26]

As in the general bond program, African American students, religious groups, and fraternal organizations were strong supporters of bonds. As the Treasury's Schools at War program preached, the thrift value of bonds carried extra weight, with scarcities lingering from the Depression and as a result of the war an everyday reality. Quite often in school bond drives, dollar amounts were translated into material, tangible terms, making the program easier for students to conceptualize and establishing clear goals. Students, as well as many religious groups and fraternal organizations, preferred purchasing noncombative, "friendlier" military equipment, such as Jeeps, ambulances, or other support vehicles. African American children at Booker T. Washington School in San Antonio, for example, bought three thousand dollars in stamps and bonds to go toward the army's "pur-

African American Investment in War Bonds 199

Dedication of the two Jeeps students at Eliza Randall Junior High School in Washington, D.C., "purchased" by selling and buying war bonds and stamps. The twelve hundred pupils of the school raised more than fourteen thousand dollars in bonds and stamps between March 1, 1942, and March 1, 1943. For half an hour each morning, the students sold bonds and stamps to parents and residents of the neighborhood. During a one-week rally that began April 1, 1943, they raised two thousand dollars' worth of bonds and stamps, enough to buy the two Jeeps. (National Archives)

chase" of a Jeep, and black students in Memphis raised enough revenue in stamps and bonds to buy a trainer plane for the air force during the Seventh War Loan.[27]

Bond drives at black schools represented much more than fund raising activities, serving as a real-life lesson in history, civics, and economics. Such was the case at Bond Day at Palmer Memorial Institute in Sedalia, North Carolina, on February 4, 1942. All of the school's 175 students and teachers purchased stamps or bonds, following the singing of patriotic songs, cheers, and a ten-minute address by the institute's president, Charlotte Hawkins Brown. Seemingly inspired by William Pickens, Brown told the students of African American patriotism in previous wars, even citing the faithfulness of slaves who guarded the homes of their white masters during the Civil War. Regardless of America's flaws, Brown said, this nation offered blacks the greatest opportunities in the world.[28]

The Taylors Musical Strings, a St. Paul, Minnesota–based ensemble of African American girls aged seven to fourteen. The group devoted its entire earnings from radio and religious concerts to buying bonds and stamps. (National Archives)

As part of bond drives, African American students also frequently served as bond salespeople. For the Third War Loan in May 1943, students at Manassas High School in North Memphis organized themselves as Minute Men and Minute Women and went door to door throughout the community soliciting for bonds. Even college students, infamously poor supporters of the bond program, occasionally raised money for bonds. This was the case in October 1943, when the Kappa Alpha Pi fraternity held a Negro bond rally dance, with the price of admission a purchase of a bond, as well as at a bond rally at A&I State College.[29]

In its bond drives, African American religious groups created a heady mix of spirituality, patriotism, and, often, race consciousness. With the church such a major presence in most black communities, maintaining the right to pursue the religion of one's choice emerged as a primary reason to support the war through bonds. As Nazi atheism was cast alongside its racism, church-going African Americans had a double mission to financially back an Allied victory. Such reasoning was perhaps the case when students at an African American school run by the Sisters of the Blessed

Sacrament in Beaumont, Texas, bought $18,145 in bonds and stamps in just the first two months of 1943. Despite an enrollment of only 260 pupils, this represented the "second largest amount of all schools, white or Negro, in the city."[30]

Sometimes the sale of bonds became entwined with centuries-old religious rituals, with racial identity yet another dimension associated with the event. A classic case of this occurred in New Orleans in September 1943, when thousands of African American Catholics incorporated the Third War Loan into their annual celebration honoring a seventeenth-century monk, St. Peter Claves, the "Apostle of the Negroes." The drive, held at St. Monica Church, was coordinated to coincide with the birthday of the patron saint. A month later in South Boston, Virginia, the Independent Order of St. Luke held a Negro war bond auction, with all proceeds from the sale going toward the purchases of bonds. Such case histories illustrate the extreme fluidity inherent in war bonds, the sale of which was seemingly capable of fitting into virtually any existing American ritual.[31]

Fraternal organizations, many of which already had a foundation in patriotism, were a natural fit for the selling and buying of bonds. As one of the cornerstones of many African American communities for both men and women, a wide variety of black fraternal organizations spearheaded bond drives throughout the war. The New York City chapter of the Sons of Georgia, for example, were early investors in the program, purchasing ten thousand dollars in defense bonds in September 1941. Soon after Pearl Harbor in February 1942, the Stringer Grand Lodge of Free and Accepted Masons of Mississippi pooled funds with a women's organization, the Grand High Court of Heroines of Jerico, to purchase bonds. In order to make the investment, the two groups used ten thousand dollars that had been set aside in their respective building funds. More typical of African American fraternal investment in bonds was the May 1943 purchase of an ambulance by the Ohio black chapter of the IBPOE. As it was for religious groups, the freedom to join a society of one's choice became the principal reason for members of fraternal organizations to support the war through bonds.[32]

Perhaps the most compelling bond drives, however, were those involving entire communities. African American communities as a whole occasionally appeared to be making the kinds of sacrifices that individuals were making. For example, in October 1943, Mound Bayou, Mississippi, an "all-Negro town of 1,000," neared its quota, "even though the cotton crop upon which this Delta town depends had not been marketed." When Macon, Georgia, exceeded its Third War Loan quota, the chair of the local African American committee spoke for his community's display of patriotism: "If colored people are given a fair chance to do their part, they will do it and then do some more." In August 1943, Indiana African Americans gathered at Victory Field in Indianapolis and purchased $55,900 of war bonds. Present at the rally were Pickens, the governor, the mayor, a state senator, the actress Hattie McDaniels, and "noted Negro soprano" Dorothy Maynor. "Speakers generally referred to recent attempts to alienate Negro citizens of the United States," a Treasury press release reported, "and termed the success of the Sunday rally the Hoosier Negro's answer to Nazi and Fascist charges."[33]

As they did for social groups, bonds became incorporated into the daily life of many communities, fused together with public and popular activities. Bond rallies located within the civic or public sphere brought people literally and ideologically together, just as Secretary Morgenthau believed they would. For African Americans, whose lives often revolved heavily around the public sphere, bond rallies represented a source of civic and racial pride. While acting as a vehicle for national unity, bonds could also act as an instrument of difference, a way to proclaim racial separateness within a patriotic cause. African American bond rallies within large communities were thus the largest scale evidence of the Double V in action.

Activities grounded in both consumer and popular culture were thus often used as sites for African American community bond drives. For the Seventh War Loan, for example, $450,000 in war bonds were sold at the Fashion Rhapsody in Chicago. More than two thousand African Americans attended the fashion show, which was "filled with high grade entertainment and modeling" by acts such as the Club de Lisa Dancing Chorus and Sammy Dyer's Kiddies. In Washington, D.C., almost $750,000 was raised at the twenty-four Lichtman theaters through the first six war loans. Stamps and bonds were sold in the lobbies of the movie theaters since October 1941. The general manager of the chain, Graham Barbee, believed that it was the individual theater managers, all of them African American, who were most responsible for Lichtman surpassing its quota. He viewed these twenty-four men as soldiers, fighting the war at home by selling war bonds through clever promotional schemes: "The boys on the theater front—the managers—[get] the credit for seeing the plans mature. They do the job."[34]

Bond drives became linked with community celebrations, a merging of national, local, and racial pride. A June 1945 bond rally held in conjunction with American Negro Day in Buffalo, New York, was such a multi-identity celebration. Bond drives frequently became part of or employed parades, the most visible public demonstrations of support for the war. On

July 5, 1943, in Atlanta, the city's Council of Negro Women and Service Group War Bond Committee held a huge parade and bond rally, described by one observer as a "far-reaching demonstration by Negroes in high and low stations of life." "While other communities are torn by strife and dissension," the reporter continued, "Atlanta Negroes are sponsoring successful rallies to show their faith in the American way of life and its people."[35]

In large urban bond drives that included parades, the participation of African American military units was often a cause for great celebration. Along Chicago's Michigan Avenue, also in July 1943, a U.S. Treasury Salute to Victory Parade "drew a crowd of an estimated 300,000 persons, both races." Units of African American military police, WACs, and sailors marching in the parade, one reporter wrote, "added the necessary color to the military process at a huge War Bond Rally held in [Chicago's] Washington Park, netting the U.S. Treasury $350,000." African American bond drives appeared to reach a higher level of enthusiasm when black military troops were represented in parades, as their presence served as the clearest proof of blacks' contribution to the war effort.[36]

Relatedly, the incentive to name a piece of military equipment after a prominent African American provided a great boost to bond drives involving black communities. Making a direct connection between the "war" on the home front and the one overseas was an effective strategy to motivate Americans to purchase bonds. A $2 million bond drive in May 1943, for example, was presented to blacks as an opportunity to name a cargo ship "Frederick Douglas." The *Frederick Douglas* would in fact be the third such ship to be named after a prominent African American (all of them with a black ship master), the first being the *Booker T. Washington* and the second the *George Washington Carver*. Harlem also had a quota of $2 million for the Third War Loan in October 1943, the goal being to purchase a Flying Fortress bomber to be named the *Harlem Express*. Simultaneously, prisoners at the District Reformatory in Lorton, Virginia, were also raising money to go toward the purchase of a Flying Fortress. Coincidentally, they too were considering the name "Harlem Express," although the convicts were also open to the names "Haile Selassie" and "Life-timer."[37]

Meanwhile, citizens of Birmingham, Alabama, were taking a more sober approach to the purchase and naming of an airplane. Bond purchases totaling $300,000 made by the black community were being allocated for a B-24 Liberator bomber to be christened *The Spirit of Ellsberry*, in honor of Julius Ellsberry, an African American citizen of Birmingham killed at Pearl Harbor. During the same drive, African American citizens of Kansas City were raising $250,000 in bonds to purchase, as the slogan went, "a

Brown Bomber for our Brown Flyers." Many African Americans were employed at defense plants in Kansas City, building the very planes they were raising money to purchase. The slogan referred to the color of the airplanes and the black flying squadrons training at various air force bases around the country. Again, a connection between home-front efforts and military operations was being made through the purchase of war bonds.[38]

Finally, in Memphis in December 1943, another three hundred thousand dollars in bonds was dedicated for a Consolidated Liberator bomber, to be named *The Spirit of Beale Street*. During the Second War Loan, African American citizens of Memphis had raised an equivalent sum for a Flying Fortress named *Memphis Blues,* but it had been shot down and destroyed. This effort for the Third War Loan demonstrated the resolve Memphis blacks had toward participating in the war effort and stood as an exceptional example of civic and racial pride. Popularly attributed as the birthplace of the blues, an African American art form, Memphis's Beale Street was a perfect symbol to commemorate the contribution African Americans were making to win a Double V.[39]

As this and many other stories suggest, there was a clear racial component to African Americans' investment in bonds. The sale and purchase of a war bond to and by whites was, in simple terms, an act of patriotism revolving around a "Single V"—defeating the enemy abroad to restore the American Way of Life at home. The sale to and purchase of war bonds by African Americans, however, reveals a more complex version of patriotism reflective of both sides of the Double V. Blacks' enthusiastic "consumption" of war bonds was thus not only a mainstream display of patriotism but also an independent attempt to achieve equality in America by gaining greater social and economic power. With virtually all other avenues of socioeconomic progress closed off to blacks in the early 1940s, bonds represented a rare opportunity by which to improve their individual and group lot in American society. There was, then, an additional, political agenda attached to bonds, an agenda embracing both national unity and racial difference in the pursuit of greater black social and economic power. This pursuit of greater socioeconomic power was neither exclusively separatist or assimilationist in nature, but rather a complex negotiation between African Americans' racial and national identities.

Although the net result was the same—a purchase of a bond—the administration's aim and that of the African American people often differed within the context of the consumer culture of bonds during World War II. The federal government used bonds as an ideological and financial tool, targeting African Americans to ease racial unrest, galvanize all

Americans around the war effort, and broaden the consensus. America's pluralism could be espoused, without giving up perceived power through the enforcement of antidiscrimination laws. Just as African Americans were offered war-related jobs in significant numbers only when it served the administration's needs, extending an offer to blacks to join the consensus was done to demonstrate outward strength during the war.

Irrespective of the administration's objectives, however, African Americans enthusiastically purchased bonds to demonstrate their national loyalty and gain greater equality by improving their socioeconomic status. As white ethnic immigrants purchased war bonds on a level exceeding their numbers in order to demonstrate loyalty to their adopted country, African Americans showed higher than per capita support to take action against an exponentially more racist regime. War bonds were sold to and purchased by African Americans because they were in fact the best opportunity to achieve the Double V and carve out a piece of the American Dream. In the middle stood William Pickens, advocate for both the Roosevelt administration and the African American community. An ideological power struggle was at work, although all parties saw the purchase of war bonds as the means to winning the struggle.

Viewing African Americans' significant investment in war bonds as a display of ideological alignment with the consensus or basic act of patriotism would be an incomplete and inaccurate conclusion. African Americans purchased war bonds as an act of empowerment and means to strengthen their individual and group racial identities in addition to their national one. Whereas the government was selling war bonds to African Americans in an attempt to defuse a separatist ideology (i.e., to have them literally and figuratively "buy into" the war), African Americans were purchasing bonds for reasons that both supported and redefined the administration's aims. Uncovering such evidence leads to a conclusion that the formation of the consensus society during World War II was more multidimensional than we have been taught, predicated on the unique American experiment of pluralistic democracy.

★ ★ ★ **Conclusion**

Immediately following V-J day, the Truman administration officially charged the Treasury with the mission to sell United States savings bonds to the American people. The public image of bonds was virtually instantly transformed from a means of winning the war to a vehicle of privatized financial well-being. Only months after the war's end, riders of New York City buses and subways sat beneath advertising placards reading "U.S. Savings Bonds Will Help You Get There: Now Back Your Future." Posters for Savings Bonds in banks and post offices depicted a young couple with a son waving a flag, looking toward a house lit up by a rainbow. The single word "Security" hung as a protective halo over the house.[1]

How did the Treasury segue so quickly and smoothly from agent of war to agent of domestic bliss? The seeds of postwar prosperity had of course been sown throughout the war via the bond program, with a privatized narrative of Americanism "presold" to the nation. With war and Victory bonds especially grounded in a fusion of patriotism and individual interests, the lines between consumerism and nationalism had already been effectively blurred during the war. War bonds were presented and perceived not just as expressions of national loyalty but as the means to greater materialism and acquisition of goods. In July 1944, for example, the Office of War Information, in collaboration with the Treasury and a number of other agencies, prepared a pamphlet titled *Planned Spending and Saving*. The pamphlet showed Americans how wartime taxes, higher living costs, and bonds were the means to "assure yourself of the benefits of peacetime tomorrow." Spending and saving during the war were directly linked to ability to buy automobiles, take vacations, and invest in children's education after the war. Tocqueville's nineteenth-century observation that consumerism is an integral part of the American idea and experience, that our national identity is inseparable from our common desire for things, was affirmed through the dynamics of the wartime economy and, specifically, through World War II bonds.[2]

The development of a consumption-based version of national identity was largely due to the full-scale entry of the state into arenas normally recognized as private. As the most literal conversion of private money into public funding, bonds have always served this end. More than any other time in American history, however, the public and private spheres became almost indistinguishable as banks, businesses, and other nonpublic institutions integrated war bond promotions into their daily activities. The successful efforts by the Treasury to have commercial banks sell government securities and have private businesses sell bonds through the payroll savings plan were major steps taken by the administration to inject civic affairs into realms historically outside the state's domain. While the nation thus fought for democracy, freedom, and individual liberties, American society became on an operative level more centralized and bureaucratic, an irony in a war full of contradictions and paradoxes. The infusion of the state into private life via bonds would carry over into postwar America, contributing to the formation of the ideologically aligned triumvirate of government, business, and the academy.

Through the Treasury's democratic economic policies, the full force of the state was deployed, promising future prosperity for all. The state's power was extended as New Deal ideology moved to the center, embracing the interests of business capital. The presence of the state in traditionally private arenas was perhaps most visible in the commercial arts as the state coopted popular culture, imprinting movies, music, and other creative media with promotions for war bonds. Filmmakers, authors, composers, and other artists/producers were themselves eager to integrate bond and other war-related themes into their works, an example of the bottom-up dynamics of World War II nationalism that crossed paths with top-down ones. Again the irony of the state's shaping the ultimate expression of individualism—the creative act—in a war being waged against totalitarianism and fascism cannot be ignored. The greater acceptance for the government to determine social roles of popular culture carried over into the postwar years, most visibly through HUAC's infiltration of the film industry.

The blending of the state and private interests via war bonds had further implications for the postwar economy. Just as the government borrowed from the private sector in creating the bond program, postwar corporate America took advantage of innovations in marketing developed by the government. As seen, the Treasury drew heavily upon market segmentation strategies and techniques, and postwar businesses embraced the government's approach toward dividing the marketplace into segments or niches when the economy reverted back to private interests. The Schools at War program, for example, was one of the earliest and most dedicated marketing efforts to target children as a distinct, legitimate consumer group. The program helped lay the groundwork for marketers to recognize children and teenagers as population segments with particular wants and needs, key to consumer culture of the 1950s and 1960s.

Via the nexus of World War II bonds, we gain a greater understanding of how the war created the foundation for what has been commonly referred to as the consensus society of the postwar years. During the war emergency, all Americans were asked to give up or at least postpone any opposition to institutional forms of power for the sake of national unity. Signs of divisiveness, such as class conflict or forms of prejudice, became less acceptable as the administration defined outward strength as internal harmony. War finance emerged as a central focal point around which the vast majority of Americans rallied, acting as a catalyst or spark toward the creation of a broader and more deeply felt sense of national loyalty. At the same time, attention was diverted from certain internal tensions, as support for the Treasury's bond program helped to defuse opposition to many of the Roosevelt administration's international and domestic policies. As the buying and selling of bonds penetrated deeply into everyday life, appealing to virtually all segments of society, traditional divisions in American society were bridged, including those of personal identity (gender, age, geography, religion, ethnicity, and race), economic status (class and labor-capital), and political affiliation (party loyalty). As a touchstone of common cause, the core of a united home front, war bonds helped lay a path toward a postwar cultural climate encouraging conformity to prescribed social norms. The postwar consensus clearly traded on bonds' role as a central wartime activity by extending the trajectory of consumerism as nationalism, that is, the American Way of Life.[3]

Without contradicting their role as a unifying force, a legitimate argument can be made that the enduring legacy of World War II bonds was that as agent for a new, pluralistic narrative of American identity. Comparing the dynamics of the World War I Liberty Bond program with those of the World War II program clearly marks the progression of American pluralism, which had germinated in the Depression and flourished during the war. Although outright opposition to national policy was taboo in each war, different interpretations of nationalism were allowed to coexist only during the second world war. In response to populist and official pluralism, white ethnic and African American culture became more validated elements of Americanism. Similarly, the simple fact that the administration recognized African Americans as a vital constituency of society during World War II but not during the first world war is evidence of the great shift in the terms of American identity. In view of this, Treasury bond promotion proves to be a valuable time capsule of wartime sentiment, especially those messages directed to ethnic groups and African Americans. William Pickens's speeches stand out as important narratives of myth and symbol ideology specific to blacks, narratives largely missing from early American studies intellectual history. War bond promotion thus adds a significantly more pluralistic dimension to our interpretations of the utopian American mythologies originally proposed by nineteenth-century Enlightenment figures such as Emerson, Whitman, and Thoreau.[4]

Aided by a half century plus of hindsight, the many examples of sacrifice made by Americans via the selling and buying of bonds, particularly those made by white ethnic and African Americans, stand as important evidence that the consensus created during the war was a genuinely pluralistic one. The design and execution of the Treasury's bond program was in the true spirit of tolerance, providing a climate in which Americans could create their own interpretation of patriotism. Upon reflection, then, World War II may indeed have been "the Good War," but only because of a set of different reasons than those popularly believed. The war's "goodness," if there was any, resided in its ability to foster and accommodate diversity in both ideology and practice. Although World War I bond drives shared the common values of patriotism and fighting for freedom, the terms of American identity and expression were much different in World War II, a function of both Nazi racism and the legacy of the New Deal. In World War I, race and ethnicity outside the Anglo-Saxon ideal were considered threats to national defense, whereas in World War II the administration allowed, even encouraged, white ethnic groups and African Americans to celebrate their "difference" as part of bond drives. Markers of ethnicity and race commingled with those of classic patriotism, creating a form of cultural synergy. Sites of bond consumerism thus frequently reconciled the dynamics of a dominant, official culture with those of subcultures, illustrating the tolerance and flexibility of national identity.

The corollary legacy of the Treasury's bond program of World War II—the emergence of African Americans into the liberal consensus—suggests that issues of race represented both the greatest advancements and limitations of the war. The patriotic support displayed by African American leaders such as Walter White, Roy Wilkins, Joe Louis, and Duke Ellington was tempered by an awareness of a "two-ness" or "double self," symbolizing the complexities associated with racial and national identity during World War II. The participation of blacks in bond drives vividly illustrated their wartime experience, functioning as the clearest expression of the pursuit of a Double V. Unlike in the previous war, blacks refused to postpone their "special grievances," seizing the opportunity to force the administration to take action. The case of war bonds provides direct access to blacks' dual purpose in World War II, to achieve two victories as a means to realize the equal rights they were promised and deserved. Perhaps most indicative of blacks' ambivalence toward the war, many African Americans who were protesting racial discrimination were also likely investing in war bonds, as each activity was viewed as a step toward achieving equal rights. Such evidence is a reminder that acts of patriotism can at the same time be acts of protest, again demonstrating the elasticity of American nationalism.

Although the loosening of the United States' immigration restrictions offers some evidence of the country's greater pluralistic climate during World War II, it was the offering of a fuller citizenship to African Americans that most clearly demonstrated a paradigmatic shift in American nationalism. During this critical juncture in American history, a pluralistic narrative of American identity was forged, an identity much different from that in place during the First World War. In contrast to World War I, when assimilation to dominant Anglo-Saxon values was prescribed for ethnic and African Americans, World War II, and specifically war bonds, had the effect of advancing a version of American identity that had begun to form in earnest during the Depression. This cultural shift is clear evidence that nationalism is not a constant, homogeneous experience but a fluid, heterogeneous one that mutates over time and relies heavily upon personally defined dimensions of identity. On a closer level, bonds represented a common ground in which Americans negotiated their unique mix of identity within the powerful and pervasive rubric of pluralistic democracy, creating a unique exchange of top-down and bottom-up dynamics.

A significant portion of this book examined the relationship between African Americans and bonds because it was within this sphere that the country's democratic principles were most tested during the war. The tensions between accepting and rejecting the pluralistic consensus that emerged during the war and jelled in the postwar period were played out most clearly and compellingly in African Americans' experience. As C. L. R. James wrote in 1950, "The Negro question in the united [*sic*] States is the No. 1 minority problem in the modern world ... because if this cannot be solved, then there is no possibility of the solution of any minority problem anywhere." Alongside their protests against the institutional racism of the war years, blacks showed great support for the administration's bond program, a clear example of many African Americans' ambivalence toward the war. This dual conflict took on especially interesting and revealing forms with regard to notable African American entertainers and sports figures, as it was they who stood as the most visible symbols of the possibilities of American democracy. Bonds acted as a vehicle by which African Americans could help reconcile this ambivalence, an opportunity to simultaneously help defeat the racist Nazi regime, demonstrate national loyalty, and express racial pride.[5]

Like other aspects of the war that worked to blacks' advantage—more jobs, greater mobility, and the devaluation of racial superiority theories—war bonds improved the socioeconomic status of African Americans during and after the war. Widespread holdings of government securities among blacks generated economic clout and financial stability, a primary means of achieving greater civil liberties. Thus although bonds played a significant role in the lives of most Americans during and after the war, they were particularly important to blacks who, quite simply, had more to gain. Soon after the war, F. D. Patterson, president of Tuskegee Institute, confirmed the gains African Americans had made through war bonds:

> From the number of homes being built by Negroes, I am sure many of them experienced substantial earnings during the war ... and were wise enough to invest these earnings in such a way as to have them available for expenditure at this time. I know that among the good investments which were made, U.S. Savings Bonds were at the head of the list.[6]

Despite the gains made by African Americans via bonds, however, the Treasury's Inter-Racial Section remained first and foremost an organization designed to control racial tensions during the war emergency. Like other forms of governmental hegemony, the section's primary function was to elicit blacks' support for the war in order to serve national interests. And although true, the Treasury's claim that the purchase of war bonds served the individual and group interests of African Americans was, fundamentally, strategic fodder intended to sell them the idea of the war. Bonds contributed to helping blacks move up the socioeconomic ladder as promised, but in fact did little to promote interracial harmony or equality on a national scale. Democratic in intent but largely segregationist in practice, the Inter-Racial Section was itself a metaphor for the country's pervasive racist attitudes and behavior, which thrived during and after the war. War bonds were then one of many forms of propaganda intended to solve or at least ease Gunnar Myrdal's "American dilemma," a means to keep the lid on racial unrest by promoting the utopian themes of democracy, brotherhood, and interracial cooperation. Separate and unequal status for African Americans would remain the norm during and following the war, as "official racism" continued to pervade both the public and private arenas. Although the idea of pluralism was validated—a critical event that should by no means be dismissed—the war and bonds specifically did not create a real exchange of power along the lines of race. The American people as a whole would not endorse the noble pursuit of governmental rhetoric, as whites resented blacks competing for equitable employment, housing, and recreation opportunities.

The looming failure on the part of the administration was thus its inability or refusal to extend the bond program's mission of "democracy in action" by eliciting the full participation of African Americans in the consensus. Although cultural forms of inclusion were realized for white ethnic groups and the working class, the limits of practiced American democracy were made equally evident for people of color. Opening the door to blacks for legitimate citizenship—a necessary step given the ideological dynamics of the war—would in many ways serve to backfire against the administration's aims. Despite the government's attempts to create racial and class unity as an ideological weapon against the Nazis, the consensus would prove to flounder throughout and after the war because of the persistence of "the Negro problem." The war therefore both created and reflected the contradictions of fighting a war overseas to preserve individual freedoms while institutional racism and segregation flourished in both the public and private spheres at home.

Precisely because of these contradictions, however, blacks' racial consciousness was raised during the war as the government's full promise of democracy fell short of its potential. The persistent gap between official idealism and wartime reality would prove to serve as the basis for the postwar civil rights movement, as the administration's failure to guarantee the rhetorical rights of inclusion awarded to African Americans compelled blacks to mobilize. As agent for the Double V, bonds played a critical role in this mobilization process, and helped build the economic resources of the black bourgeoisie, who would serve as the power bloc within the mainstream African American civil rights movement. Healthy roots of the postwar struggle for civil rights can thus be clearly detected in the war years and in war bonds, as blacks fought for their place in an imagined democracy predicated on class harmony and enjoying the fruits of an abundant society.

The ultimate question is, of course, whether the World War II bond program succeeded or failed to meet its various objectives. The overwhelming popularity of the bond program among essentially all sectors of the population lends support to the argument that the administration did indeed succeed in its objective to give Americans a personal stake in the war. Most "failures" of the program were relatively insignificant, matters of questionable judgment or the overstepping of boundaries. The low level opposition to the Schools at War program, suspect retailer practices, and potential inappropriateness of the Stars over America tour or defense chain letters would fall into this category of failures. Similarly, the judge who sentenced a defendant to buy stamps or serve time and the politician who suggested Americans abstain from alcohol in order to buy bonds were probably just overzealous patriots, and the paternalistic approach the Treasury employed toward women and blacks was essentially emblematic of the times. Other failures of the program, however, had more of a social impact. The Treasury's implied claims that winning the war was contingent on bond and stamp sales was simply not true, equivalent to much of the puffery associated with wartime propaganda. In its marketing of bonds, the Treasury entirely overestimated Americans' concern of wartime and postwar inflation and drastically underestimated the importance of having a personal connection to someone serving in the armed forces. It is reasonable to say that the bond program was successful beyond anyone's expectations, but for a different set of reasons than originally believed.[7]

Judging the program's relative success from an economic standpoint is as difficult as evaluating it as a tool of propaganda. Bonds did indeed help to stem inflation and serve as a safe way for Americans to store excess cash resulting from the wartime boom. Defense, war, and victory bonds advanced the fledgling savings bond program of the 1930s, and solidified Americans' trust in the national economy, government securities, and the government itself. The administration's objective to encourage thrift was achieved, as the U.S. savings bond program emerged as a popular, respected form of investment. Unlike in World War I, the administration

Conclusion

was able to mobilize the nation's centralized banking system, and bring private banks, the federal government, and the American people together in common pursuit of financial stability and prosperity. World War II bonds thus played a large part in reversing Americans' experience of both the World War I Liberty Bond program and the Depression and helped to drive the optimistic, imperialistic course of the postwar economy. If the industrial buildup for the war got the country out of the Depression, as popularly believed, widespread investment in war bonds helped lead the country toward a fiscally stable future.[8]

The effect of World War II bonds on the postwar American economy is equally difficult to quantitatively measure. When the first defense bonds sold in 1941 matured in the spring of 1951, the American economy was "artificially" inflated due to the Korean War. A "mixed" economy characterized late 1951 and 1952, and the country went through a relatively mild contraction through 1953 and 1954. In 1955, when bonds from the Seventh and Victory War Loans matured, the national economy rapidly expanded, fueled by an active real estate market and high automobile sales.[9]

Although too many variables obscure the net effect of war bonds on the early 1950s economy, there is no doubt that maturing bonds did have a significant impact on the national and worldwide security market. In February 1954, ten years after the Fourth War Loan, the Treasury refunded $21 billion in government loans, the largest amount in history. Ten months later, the ten-year anniversary of the Sixth War Loan, the Treasury refunded $17.3 billion, the second largest amount in history. To fund these exchanges, the Treasury offered short- and medium-term securities at 2.5 percent interest, an appealing proposition to banks which held a disproportionate share of war bonds. Ninety-eight percent of the matured bonds were, in fact, rolled over into the new offerings, with only $345 million in bonds cashed. Efforts such as these by the Treasury were successful in lengthening out the national debt stemming from the war.[10]

Although bonds were highly successful from a propaganda standpoint, the Treasury's foremost objective to sell a large percentage of Series E "people's" bonds generally failed. The Series E may have been considered "boring" to the professional investor, as the Treasury intended, but Series F and G bonds were highly attractive to banks and other large investors. The proportion of government securities held by nonbank investors rose during the war, but banks, insurance companies, and other large financial institutions still dominated the program (see Table 1). Bank profits more than doubled from 1940 to 1946, much more a result of interest gains from government securities than in loaning money to private investors. These

TABLE 1. BOND HOLDINGS BY INVESTOR, 1946

Investor	Bond Holdings ($ billion)	Share (%)
Commercial banks	68.3	34
Individuals	53.8	27
Other corporations and associations	22.8	11
Federal Reserve banks	21.3	11
Insurance companies	18.8	9
Mutual savings banks	8.4	4
State/local banks	6.1	3
Total	199.5	100

Source: T. R. Martin, "Inflation: The Second World War," *Current History* (April 1953): 298, from *Federal Reserve Bulletin* and *Annual Report of the Secretary of the Treasury,* 1946.

profits were largely achieved through a process called "free [or quota] riding," in which commercial banks exchanged currently held bonds for new offerings, resulting in quick interest gains. The Federal Reserve repeatedly recommended that the Treasury restrict such resales to banks, but pressure from bond sales organizations trying to meet assigned quotas was the determining factor to allow the practice to continue. As Woodlief Thomas suggested in his 1955 essay "Lessons of War Finance," the pursuit of sales volume prevailed over the program's "purity."[11]

The postwar audit of the country's wartime economy revealed that 46 percent of the government's operating budget was sourced through taxes, and 54 percent was realized through borrowing, that is, bonds. The government's attempt to slow inflation by taking "excess dollars" out of the economy through higher taxes and borrowing was only partially successful. From 1940 to 1946, the consumer price index rose 30 percent, an unusually high amount (but still significantly less than the 50 percent rise during World War I). Money in circulation from 1940 to 1945 rose nearly four times, going from $6.7 to $25.1 billion, whereas personal income over this same period more than doubled, rising from $78.3 to $171.9 billion.[12]

Perhaps the most interesting postwar audit of the Treasury's bond program came from *American Mercury,* a magazine with a distinct lean toward the Right. *American Mercury* supported the bond program during the war, even running ads for the Treasury at no cost. Writing in April 1951, however, while the Treasury pitched bonds to help fund the Korean War, Christopher Bliss of the magazine astutely observed that the Treasury never mentioned in its sales promotion the inevitable impact of postwar inflation on war bonds as an investment:

> Exactly ten years ago this government began selling war bonds. And the clever soap salesmen of the New Deal decided that something new should be added to the sales pitch. The bonds for the First War were sold on patriotism.... But so much cynicism had been injected by 1941 that the salesmen decided to lure us with "the selfish point of view." Well, ten years have passed; the first bonds have matured; and what can the small investor get for his investment?... The disillusioning fact is that the *smart* investor who loaned his Government $75 in 1941 can now get back, in purchasing power, only $57. He didn't *make* one-third; he lost almost one-third.... Moreover, since the bonds are not tax exempt, those who invested in 1941 will pay an income tax—at the higher 1951 rates—on the ephemeral $25 "profit."[13]

Although Bliss was pursuing a political agenda, his numbers regarding the effect of postwar inflation were correct. Consumer prices of food rose significantly from May 1941—the month the defense bond program debuted—to January 1951:[14]

Item	**May 1941**	**January 1951**
Round steak/pound	$.37	$.97
Coffee/pound	$.22	$.86
Sugar/5 pounds	$.28	$.50
Butter/pound	$.41	$.79

Bliss furthered his argument against bonds by citing the case of Edwin Pauley, a California financier. Pauley publicly denounced bonds as a poor investment in 1942, putting his money instead into commodities that were almost sure to continue to rise in value through and after the war. Pauley got rich in the commodity market due to short supplies and increased demand, far richer than if he had purchased war bonds with his original 1942 investment. "Instead of buying bonds in 1942 to insure a diet of beefsteak in your old age, wouldn't it have been 'smarter' to have bought a deep freeze and a ton of steak?" Bliss asked his readers.[15]

Even if Bliss was right that they were a losing venture, bonds remained an important factor in the dominant consumer capitalism paradigm of the postwar era. Defense and war bonds maturing between 1951 and 1955 provided many Americans with the necessary funds to purchase or make a down payment on houses, automobiles, and large consumer durables.

Besides the connection between war bonds and the privatization and "leisurization" of American life that characterized postwar society, the Treasury's bond program contributed to instilling the postwar savings ethos, a compelling financial orientation for those who had lived through the Depression. Those not redeeming bonds at their ten-year maturity rolled them over into other investments, including U.S. savings bonds, helping to fuel the broad prosperity of the late 1950s and early 1960s. Ultimately, war bond nest eggs often went toward raising and educating the children of wartime and postwar Americans, thereby creating a trickle-down of benefits that continues to this day. Baby boomers' high rates of college education and professional occupations can be seen as part of the legacy of the Roosevelt administration's World War II bond program, a legacy being passed on to this generation's own children that will continue to shape American life into the twenty-first century.

 Notes

Introduction

1. "They're Giving," *New Orleans Times Picayune,* 18 May 1941; U.S. Treasury, "Bond Bursts: Sidelights on 3d War Loan," Release No. 93, RG 56, National Archives (hereafter cited as NA); "1944 Report of Inter-Racial Section," William Pickens Papers, Box 19, Schomberg Center, New York Public Library, New York City (hereafter cited as "1944 Report of Inter-Racial Section," WPP).

2. "Often described in the press as 'the greatest sales operation in history'..." War Finance Division Special Release No. 13, 15 February 1946, NA.

3. Alan Brinkley, *The End of Reform: New Deal Liberalism in Recession and War* (New York: Alfred A. Knopf, 1995), 26–33. Gary Gerstle, "The Working Class Goes to War" (paper presented at American Historical Association Conference, Chicago, March 1992); Studs Terkel, *"The Good War": An Oral History of World War II* (New York: Pantheon, 1984); Richard Polenberg, "The Good War? A Reappraisal of How World War II Affected American Society," *Virginia Magazine of History and Biography* 100, no. 3 (July 1992): 295–23.

4. John Morton Blum, *V Was for Victory: Politics and American Culture During World War II* (New York: Harcourt Brace Jovanovich, 1976), 147; Lizbeth Cohen, *Making a New Deal: Industrial Workers in Chicago, 1919–1939* (Cambridge: Cambridge University Press, 1990); John Higham, "The Transformation of the Statue of Liberty," in *Send These to Me: Jews and Other Immigrants in Urban America* (New York: Atheneum, 1975), 78–87.

5. Philip Gleason, "American Identity and Americanization," in *Harvard Encyclopedia of American Ethnic Groups,* ed. Stephan Thernstrom (Cambridge: Harvard University Press, 1980), 43–49.

6. Richard Oestricher, "Urban Working-Class Political Behavior and Theories of American Politics, 1870–1940," *Journal of American History* 74, no. 4 (March 1988): 1263–64, 1283.

7. Philip Gleason, "Pluralism, Democracy, and Catholicism in the Era of World War II," *Review of Politics* 49, no. 2 (Spring 1987): 220; Richard Polenberg, *One Nation Divisible: Class, Race, and Ethnicity in the U.S. Since 1938* (New York: Viking Press, 1980), 40; Gary Gerstle, *Working-Class Americanism: The Politics of Labor in a Textile City, 1914–1960* (Cambridge: Cambridge University Press, 1989), 301; Philip Gleason, "Americans All: World War II and the Shaping of American Identity," *Review of Politics* 43, no. 4 (1981): 518. For more on the formation of a pluralistic narrative of American identity as the war approached, see Richard W. Steele, "The War on Intolerance: The Reformulation of American Nationalism, 1939–1941," *Journal of American Ethnic History* (Fall 1989): 11–33.

8. Jarvis M. Morse, "Paying for a World War: The United States Financing of World War II," manuscript, p. 11, U.S. Treasury Library.

9. Beth Bailey and David Farber, *The First Strange Place: The Alchemy of Race and Sex in World War II Hawaii* (New York: Free Press, 1992); Blum, *V Was for Victory;* Neil A. Wynn, "The Impact of the Second World War on the American Negro," *Journal of Contemporary History* 6 (May 1971): 42–54.

10. Harvard Sitkoff, "Racial Militancy and Interracial Violence in the Second World War," *Journal of American History* 58 (December 1971): 661–81. For important findings related to Du Bois's motives in asking African Americans to put aside their grievances during the war, see Mark Ellis, "'Closing Ranks' and 'Seeking Honors': W. E. B. Du Bois in World War I," *Journal of American History* 79, no. 1 (June 1992): 96. According to Ellis, Du Bois was more interested in becoming a captain in the Military Intelligence Branch than furthering blacks' rights during the war, a priority which slowed the civil rights movement and ultimately damaged Du Bois's reputation.

11. Blum, *V Was for Victory,* 208. For an interesting examination of the dynamics of the Double V campaign in Hawaii, see Beth Bailey and David Farber, "The 'Double V' Campaign in World War II Hawaii: African Americans, Racial Ideology, and Federal Power," *Journal of Social History* (Summer 1993): 817–44.

12. Frank W. Fox, *Madison Avenue Goes to War: The Strange Military Career of American Advertising, 1941–45* (Provo, Utah: Brigham Young University Press, 1975).

Chapter 1. The Voluntary Way

1. U.S. Treasury, *A History of U.S. Savings Bonds* (Washington, D.C.: U.S. Treasury, 1963); U.S. Treasury, *A History of U.S. Savings Bonds* (Washington, D.C.: U.S. Treasury, 1987). For more on the history of public debt, see Donald R. Stabile and Jeffrey A. Cantor, *The Public Debt of the United States: An Historical Perspective, 1775–1990* (New York: Praeger, 1991); William G. Anderson, *The Price of Liberty: The Public Debt of the American Revolution* (Charlottesville: University Press of Virginia, 1983); and Committee on Public Debt Policy, *Our National Debt: Its History and Its Meaning Today* (New York: Harcourt, Brace, 1949).

2. U.S. Treasury, *History of U.S. Savings Bonds* (1963); U.S. Treasury, *History of U.S. Savings Bonds* (1987); Kittleson Collection, Minneapolis Public Library, Minneapolis, Minnesota (hereafter cited as Kittleson Collection); World War I and II Poster Collection, Immigration Research History Center, University of Minnesota, St. Paul, Minnesota (hereafter cited as World War I and II Poster Collection); Warshaw Poster Collection, Smithsonian Institution, Washington, D.C. (hereafter cited as Warshaw Poster Collection); *Miscellaneous Man Catalog 48: Vintage Patriotic Posters 1914–1946* (New Freedom, Pa.: Miscellaneous Man, n.d.).

3. Walter Lafeber and Richard Polenberg, *The American Century: A History of the United States Since the 1890s* (New York: John Wiley and Sons, 1975), 97, 101. For a full discussion of Wilson's political agenda, see Lloyd E. Ambrosius, *Wilsonian Statecraft: Theory and Practice of Liberal Internationalism During World War I* (Wilmington, Del.: SR Books, 1991).

4. Leslie J. Vaughan, "Cosmopolitanism, Ethnicity, and American Identity: Randolph Bourne's 'Trans-national America,'" *Journal of American Studies* 25, no. 3 (December 1991): 443, 447; Nelson Lichtenstein, "The Making of the Postwar Working Class: Cultural Pluralism and Social Structure in World War II," *Historian* 51, no. 1 (November 1988): 53. For surprising revelations regarding the extent to which the Wilson administration went to suppress both ethnic and leftist publications, see Mick Mulcrone, "'Those Miserable Irish Hounds': World War I Postal Censorship of the Irish World," *Journalism History* 20, no. 1 (Spring 1994): 15–25. For more on the intersection of Americanization propaganda and the public sphere during the World War I, see Wayne A. Wiegand, *"An Active Instrument for Propaganda": The American Public Library During World War I* (New York: Greenwood Press, 1989) and Larry Wayne Ward, *The Motion Picture Goes to War: The U.S. Government Film Effort During World War I* (Ann Arbor, Mich.: UMI Research Press, 1985).

5. Amos B. Hulen, "War Bonds and Mob Spirit," *Christian Century*, 4 June 1941; "Voluntary Henry," *Time*, 25 May 1942. For a full examination of the role of Mennonites during the war, see Arlyn John Parish, *Kansas Mennonites During World War I* (Hays: Fort Hays Kansas State College, 1968).

6. Lafeber and Polenberg, *American Century*, 102; "Better Buy Some Bonds," *Colliers*, 3 May 1941, 74.

7. Kittleson Collection.

8. World War I and II Poster Collection.

9. *Miscellaneous Man Catalog 48;* Charles Flint Kellogg, *NAACP: A History of the National Association of Colored People, Volume I, 1909–1920* (Baltimore: Johns Hopkins University Press, 1967), 265–66.

10. Morse, "Paying for a World War," 22.

11. Ibid., 31.

12. Ibid., 34.

13. Ibid., 35.

14. *Annual Report of the Secretary for 1941*, in Henry C. Murphy, *Public Debt in War and Transition* (New York: McGraw-Hill, 1950), 36.

15. Morse, "Paying for a World War," 37.

16. Ibid., 6, 9, 42. For an in-depth discussion of the Four Freedoms, see Frank Robert Donovan, *Mr. Roosevelt's Four Freedoms: The Story Behind the United Nations Charter* (New York: Dodd, Mead, 1966).

17. "These potentially dangerous dollars can be put to work fighting and winning the war through the purchase of War Bonds." Office of War Information (hereafter cited as OWI), *Office of War Information Program on Third War Loan Drive*, 8, Boxes 8–9, File "Photographs, Information Kits, and Posters, NA; Morse, "Paying for a World War," 14–15.

18. Morse, "Paying for a World War," 16–21; Murphy, *Public Debt*, 63–65. For Keynes's original thesis, see John Maynard Keynes, *How to Pay for the War: A Radical Plan for the Chancellor of the Exchequer* (New York: Harcourt, Brace, 1940). For a comparative analysis of British views of World War II finance, see E. F. M. Durbin, *How to Pay for the War: An Essay on the Financing of War* (London: G. Routledge and Sons, 1939).

19. Murphy, *Public Debt*, 79; Brinkley, *End of Reform*, 26.

20. Ira Katznelson and Bruce Pietrykowski, "Rebuilding the American State: Evidence from the 1940s," *Studies in American Political Development* 5 (Fall 1991): 322; Woodlief Thomas, "Lessons of War Finance," *American Economic Review* 41 (September 1951): 620.

21. Brinkley, *End of Reform*, 26–33.

22. Robert Lekachman, in Gerstle, *Working-Class Americanism*, 267.

23. Murphy, *Public Debt*, 72, 84–87.

24. For more on Morgenthau, see Henry Morgenthau III, *Mostly Morgenthau: A Family History* (New York: Ticknor and Fields, 1991); John Morton Blum, *Roosevelt and Morgenthau* (Boston: Houghton Mifflin, 1970); John Morton Blum, *From the Morgenthau Diaries* (Boston: Houghton Mifflin, 1959–67).

25. Robert K. Merton, *Mass Persuasion: The Social Psychology of a War Bond Drive* (New York: Harper and Brothers, 1946).

26. U.S. Treasury, *History of U.S. Savings Bonds* (1987), 8; Morse, "Paying for a World War," 2–3, 40, 11.

27. Morse, "Paying for a World War," 93, 42–43; Murphy, *Public Debt*, 33.

28. U.S. Treasury, *History of U.S. Savings Bonds* (1987), 8; Morse, "Paying for a World War," 106; Blum, *V Was for Victory*, 17.

29. Peter H. Odegard and Alan Barth, "Millions for Defense," *Public Opinion Quarterly* (Fall 1941): 399–401.

30. "Lesson in Merchandising for Banks," *American Banker*, 17 April 1941. For a discussion on how the administration controlled investment and finance during the war, see Gregory Hooks, "The Weakness of Strong Theories: The U.S. State's Dominance of the World War II Investment Process," *American Sociological Review* 58, no. 1 (February 1993): 37–54.

31. Morse, "Paying for a World War," 39. For the most thorough examination of psychological appeals in advertising during the war, see Fox, *Madison Avenue Goes to War*.

32. U.S. Treasury, *History of U.S. Savings Bonds* (1987).

33. "Our National Bargain," *Woman's Home Companion*, January 1942, 2; "Better Buy Some Bonds," *Colliers*, 3 May 1941, 74; Morse, "Paying for a World War," 30.

34. U.S. Treasury, *History of U.S. Savings Bonds* (1987); for a detailed look at the role of elementary schools and specifically social studies during the war, see Sherry Lynn Field, "Doing Their Bit for Victory: Elementary School Social Studies During World War II" (Ph.D. diss., University of Texas, Austin, 1991).

35. Morse, "Paying for a World War," 25.

36. Ibid., 28.

37. U.S. Treasury, *History of U.S. Savings Bonds* (1987), 8; John Morton Blum, *The Morgenthau Diaries: Years of Urgency, 1938–1941* (Boston: Houghton Mifflin, 1965), 301–2.

38. Morse, "Paying for a World War," 1; Blum, *Morgenthau Diaries*, 304.

Chapter 2. Democracy in Action

1. "Defense Bond Sales Better than Hoped, Morgenthau Says," *Washington Star*, 22 May 1941.

2. Morse, "Paying for a World War," 48–49, 54, 65.

3. Ibid., 62–64, 144.

4. Ibid., 43–50; Sheldon Avery, *Up from Washington: William Pickens and the Negro Struggle for Equality, 1900–1954* (Newark: University of Delaware Press, 1989), 184.

5. Morse, "Paying for a World War," 54.
6. Ibid., 54–56.
7. Ibid., 62–63.
8. Brinkley, *End of Reform,* 145–46, 171–74; Morse, "Paying for a World War," 63.
9. D'Ann Campbell, *Women at War with America: Private Lives in a Patriotic Era* (Cambridge: Harvard University Press, 1984), 66–69; Brinkley, *End of Reform,* 147.
10. Campbell, *Women at War with America,* 69–71, 220–25.
11. Morse, "Paying for a World War," 66–71.
12. Ibid., 75–76; Blum, *Morgenthau Diaries,* 302.
13. Morse, "Paying for a World War," 1.
14. Odegard and Barth, "Millions for Defense," 399–400; U.S. Treasury, *History of U.S. Savings Bonds* (1987).
15. "Contracts in Bond Sales," *Philadelphia Bulletin,* 28 May 1941.
16. H. I. Phillips, "The Once Over," *Washington Post,* 27 May 1941.
17. "Defense Checkoff," *Business Week,* 7 June 1941.
18. George Rothwell Brown, "The Political Parade," *New York Journal-American,* 14 May 1941.
19. "Gratitude," *Philadelphia Bulletin,* 24 January 1942; Stanley High, "The U.S. Pocketbook Enlists," *Reader's Digest,* March 1942, 12–13; Morse, "Paying for a World War," 75. The 1942 propaganda film *December 7,* directed by John Huston, is a particularly interesting narrative of the impact of Pearl Harbor on American society. Also see Archie Satterfield, *The Day the War Began* (Westport, Conn.: Praeger, 1992) and Stanley Weintraub, *Long Day's Journey into War: December 7, 1941* (New York: Dutton, 1991).
20. "Bonds for Bombs," *Washington Star,* 17 December 1941; "Give Defense Bonds," *Saginaw News,* 19 December 1941.
21. "From Installments on Autos to Installments on Defense," *American Banker,* 18 December 1941.
22. "Don't Kill the 'Goose,'" *Chattanooga News Free Press,* 11 January 1942; "Alcohol and National Defense," *Hartford Times,* 9 January 1942; Harry Scherman, "Invisible Greenbacks," *Reader's Digest,* August 1942, 108.
23. Scherman, "Invisible Greenbacks," 108; "Bonds in Every Family," *Great Falls Tribune,* 22 January 1942.
24. "Buy U.S. Bonds! U.S. Spurs Drive to Draw in a Billion a Month, *Newsweek,* 6 July 1942, 44.
25. "Voluntary Henry," 78; "Uncle Sam's Bonds," *Business Week,* 11 April 1942, 72.
26. Murphy, *Public Debt,* 130.
27. Morse, "Paying for a World War," 76, 36, 163–66. For a history of company savings plans, see the *National Industrial Conference Board's Employee Savings Plans in the United States* (New York: National Industrial Conference Board, 1962).
28. Morse, "Paying for a World War," 166, 75, 91; "Voluntary Henry," 79.
29. Morse, "Paying for a World War," 101, 130.
30. Ulric Bell and William B. Lewis to Archibald MacLeish, 3 February 1942 (Henry Pringle MSS), in Polenberg, *One Nation Divisible,* 47; Morse, "Paying for a World War," 106. For more on Roosevelt ideology during the war, see Wayne S. Cole, *Determinism and American Foreign Relations During the Franklin D. Roosevelt Era* (Lanham, Md.: University Press of America, 1995); William E. Leuchtenburg, *The FDR Years: On Roosevelt and His Legacy* (New York: Columbia University Press, 1995); Frederick B. Pike, *FDR's Good Neighbor Policy: Sixty Years*

of Generally Gentle Chaos (Austin: University of Texas Press, 1995); Robert Dallek, *Franklin D. Roosevelt and American Foreign Policy, 1932–1945* (New York: Oxford University Press, 1995); Franklin D. Roosevelt, *FDR's Fireside Chats*, ed. Russell D. Buhite and David W. Levy (Norman: University of Oklahoma Press, 1992); Warren F. Kimball, *The Juggler: Franklin Roosevelt as Wartime Statesman* (Princeton, N.J.: Princeton University Press, 1991); Sean J. Savage, *Roosevelt: The Party Leader, 1932–1945* (Lexington: University Press of Kentucky, 1991); Philip Abbott, *The Exemplary Presidency: Franklin D. Roosevelt and the American Political Tradition* (Amherst: University of Massachusetts Press, 1990); Sean Dennis Cashman, *America, Roosevelt, and World War II* (New York: New York University Press, 1989); and Waldo Heinrichs, *Threshold of War: Franklin D. Roosevelt and American Entry into World War II* (New York: Oxford University Press, 1988).

31. Defense Savings Staff, "The Call to Colors Calls for Dollars," *Our America* (Washington, D.C.: GPO, 1941).

32. Odegard and Barth, "Millions for Defense," 409.

33. Ibid., 410; U.S. Treasury, *Fifth War Loan Campaign Book*, June 1944, Wilson Library Government Center, University of Minnesota, Minneapolis, 37.

34. Morse, "Paying for a World War," 171–72.

35. Ibid., 174–75. For more on Eleanor Roosevelt's many activities during the war, see Doris Kearns Goodwin, *No Ordinary Time: Franklin and Eleanor Roosevelt: The Home Front in World War II* (New York: Simon and Schuster, 1994).

36. "Helping Your Uncle Sam," *Patriotic Plays and Programs* (Darien, Conn.: Educational Publishing, 1942), 74.

37. Morse, "Paying for a World War," 175.

38. William M. Tuttle Jr., *Daddy's Gone to War: The Second World War in the Lives of America's Children* (New York: Oxford University Press, 1993), 123–26.

39. Morse, "Paying for a World War," 176–77, 173. For a full study of the academy during the war, see V. R. Cardozier, *Colleges and Universities in World War II* (Westport, Conn.: Praeger, 1993).

40. Morse, "Paying for a World War," 176–78.

41. Ibid., 180–82.

42. U.S. Treasury, War Finance Division and *Ladies' Home Journal*, *Home Front Journal* 2, no. 11 (November 1943), Civil Reference Branch, Boxes 8–9, NA; Morse, "Paying for a World War," 181.

43. Morse, "Paying for a World War," 183; OWI, "The OWI News Bureau's Activity in Support of the Second War Loan Drive," April 1943, Civil Reference Branch, Boxes 8–9, NA.

44. OWI, "OWI News Bureau's Activity." For a discussion of other propaganda directed at women during the war, see Susan Mathis, "Propaganda to Mobilize Women for World War II," *Social Education* 58, no. 2 (February 1994): 94–98.

45. Susan M. Hartmann, *The Home Front and Beyond: American Women in the 1940s* (Boston: Twayne, 1982). Also see Nancy Baker Wise and Christy Wise, *A Mouthful of Rivets: Women at Work in World War II* (San Francisco: Jossey-Bass, 1994); Elizabeth Fox-Genovese, "Mixed Messages: Women and the Impact of World War II," *Southern Humanities Review* 27, no. 3 (Summer 1993): 235–46; Doris Weatherford, *American Women and World War II* (New York: Facts on File, 1990); and Robert B. Westbrook, "I Want a Girl, Just Like the Girl that Married Harry James: American Women and the Problem of Political Obligation in World War II," *American Quarterly* 42, no. 4 (December 1990): 587–615. Ruth Milkman, *Gender at Work: The Dynamics of Job Segregation by Sex During World War II* (Urbana: University of Illinois

Press, 1987); Sherna Berger Gluck, *Rosie the Riveter Revisited: Women, the War, and Social Change* (Boston: Twayne, 1987); Maureen Honey, *Creating Rosie the Riveter: Class, Gender, and Propaganda During World War II* (Amherst: University of Massachusetts Press, 1984); and Karen Anderson, *Wartime Women: Sex Roles, Family Relations, and the Status of Women During World War II* (Westport, Conn.: Greenwood Press, 1981).

46. Morse, "Paying for a World War," 184.
47. Ibid., 183.
48. U.S. Treasury, "War Bond Promotions," 1944, Civil Reference Branch, Boxes 8–9, NA.
49. Morse, "Paying for a World War," 185.
50. Ibid., 189–92.
51. Lichtenstein, "Making of the Postwar Working Class," 42.
52. Morse, "Paying for a World War," 200–202. For more on labor relations during the war, see Nelson Lichtenstein, *Labor's War at Home: The CIO in World War II* (Cambridge: Cambridge University Press, 1982) and Howard Kimeldorf, "World War II and the Deradicalization of American Labor: The ILWU as a Deviant Case," *Labor History* 33, no. 2 (Spring 1992): 248–77.
53. Morse, "Paying for a World War," 205, 207.
54. Mark H. Leff, "The Politics of Sacrifice on the American Home Front in World War II," *Journal of American History* 77 (March 1991): 1296–1313.

Chapter 3. The Biggest Selling Campaign in History

1. Morse, "Paying for a World War," 1. Note that Henry C. Murphy in his 1950 *Public Debt in War and Transition* cites total sales as $156.9 billion.
2. Morse, "Paying for a World War," 124.
3. Ibid.
4. U.S. Treasury, *History of U.S. Savings Bonds* (1987); Blum, *Morgenthau Diaries*, 303. For more on the construction of the consensus through the consumer sphere, see Robert Griffith, "The Selling of America: The Advertising Council and American Politics, 1942–1960," *Business History Review* 57, no.3 (Autumn 1983): 388–412, and Leff, "Politics of Sacrifice on the American Home Front," 1296–1318.
5. Morse, "Paying for a World War," 266, 271–74; *CIO News* 5, no. 5 (2 February 1942): 1.
6. "All-Out for Defense Savings," *New York Herald Tribune,* 10 January 1942; U.S. Treasury, "Let's All Back the Attack," *4th War Loan Campaign Bulletin for Field Force*, No. 13, 24 January 1944, NA; U.S. Treasury, "Bond Bursts," Release No. 93, NA; "Pastors and War Bonds," *Christian Century,* 24 March 1943.
7. Morse, "Paying for a World War," 235.
8. Ibid., 222; Blum, *Morgenthau Diaries,* 303. For more on radio during the war, see K. R. M. Short, ed., *Film and Radio Propaganda in World War II* (Knoxville: University of Tennessee Press, 1983) and Mary Ann Watson, "Seems Radio is Here to Stay," *Media Studies Journal* 7, no. 3 (Summer 1993): 184–98.
9. Morse, "Paying for a World War," 232; "Bond Marathon," *Newsweek,* 20 July 1942, 84; "No. 1 Selling Job," *Business Week,* 30 May 1942.
10. Morse, "Paying for a World War," 232; my reading of posters corresponds roughly to the themes elicited by the singer Kate Smith during the Third War Bond Day radio campaign on CBS on 21 September 1943 as described by Robert K. Merton. In *Mass Persuasion,* Merton

describes six major themes used by Smith in ranked order of reason for a bond purchase: sacrifice (51 percent), participation (16 percent), competition (12 percent), facilitation (7 percent), familial (6 percent), personal (6 percent), and miscellaneous (2 percent).

11. U.S. Treasury, "Attachment to Special Memorandum," 7 December 1945, Civil Reference Branch, Boxes 8–9, NA; Warshaw Poster Collection; Princeton University Poster Collection, Smithsonian Institution; Kittleson Collection; World War I and II Poster Collection. See also Derek Nelson, *The Posters that Won the War* (Osceola, Wisc.: Motorbooks International, 1991); Denis Judd, *Posters of World War II* (New York: St. Martin's Press, 1973); G. H. Gregory, *Posters of World War II* (New York: Gramercy Books, 1993); George C. Marshall Research Foundation, *Posters of World War I and World War II in the George C. Marshall Research Foundation*, ed. Anthony R. Crawford (Charlottesville: University Press of Virginia, 1979); *Posters for Victory: The American Home Front and World War II: Posters from the West Point Museum* (West Point, N.Y.: U.S. Military Academy, 1978); *The Bowman Gray Collection of World Wars I and II* (Chapel Hill: University of North Carolina Library, 1986); *Miscellaneous Man Catalog 48;* Anthony R. Crawford, "Your Country Needs You! Posters from Two World Wars," *Gateway Heritage* 1, no. 4 (1981): 32–41; and Mary M. Rider, "Images of Propaganda: World War I and World War II Posters," *Queen City Heritage* 41, no. 3 (1983): 31–36.

12. Rider, "Images of Propaganda."
13. Ibid.
14. Ibid.
15. Ibid.
16. Ibid.
17. Ibid.
18. "Sale of Defense Issues 'Better than Expected,'" *New York Herald Tribune,* 13 May 1941; Morse, "Paying for a World War," 262, 275. For the definitive work on advancements in advertising, marketing, and marketing research between the wars, see Roland Marchand, *Advertising the American Dream: Making Way for Modernity, 1920–1940* (Berkeley and Los Angeles: University of California Press, 1985). Also see T. J. Jackson Lears, *Fables of Abundance: A Cultural History of Advertising in America* (New York: Basic Books, 1994); T. J. Jackson Lears, "Some Versions of Fantasy: Toward a Cultural History of American Advertising, 1880–1930," *Prospects* 9 (1984): 349–405; T. J. Jackson Lears, "From Salvation to Self-Realization: Advertising and the Therapeutic Roots of the Consumer Culture, 1880–1930," in *The Culture of Consumption,* ed. Richard Wightman Fox and T. J. Jackson Lears (New York: Pantheon, 1983), 3–38; and Stuart Ewen, *Captains of Consciousness: Advertising and the Social Roots of Consumer Culture* (New York: McGraw-Hill, 1976).

19. Blum, *Morgenthau Diaries,* 20.
20. U.S. Treasury, "Fight by His Side," 37, June 1944, Boxes 8–9, File "Photographs, Information Kits, and Posters."
21. "Defense Bonds," *Raleigh News and Observer,* 20 May 1941; "Where the Bond $ Go," *CIO News* 8, no. 28 (9 July 1945): 9.
22. U.S. Treasury, Release No. 95, 19 September 1943, Defense Savings Staff Press Releases, Box 1, NA.
23. George Fort Milton, "How Many Bonds Should You Buy?" *New Republic,* 13 April 1942.
24. U.S. Treasury and OWI, "The Sixth War Loan Drive and Psychological Warfare in the Far East," Civil Reference Branch, Boxes 8–9, NA.
25. Ibid.
26. Ibid.

27. Morse, "Paying for a World War," 90, 169, 210–14; "Buy Bonds! U.S. Spurs Drive to Draw in a Billion a Month," *Newsweek*, 6 July 1942, 46; U.S. Treasury, Release No. 107, Defense Press Releases, Box 1, NA; U.S. Treasury, News Material Release No. 134, 3 February 1942, Box 1, File "Defense Savings Staff (DSS) Press Releases," NA. For more on how Hollywood contributed to the war effort, see Robert Fyne, *The Hollywood Propaganda of World War II* (Metuchen, N.J.: Scarecrow Press, 1994); Roy Hoopes, *When the Stars Went to War: Hollywood and World War II* (New York: Random House, 1994); Thomas Doherty, *Projections of War: Hollywood, American Culture, and World War II* (New York: Columbia University Press, 1993); Clayton R. Koppes and Gregory D. Black, *Hollywood Goes to War: How Politics, Profits, and Propaganda Shaped World War II Movies* (New York: Free Press, 1987).

28. Gypsy Rose Lee, "About Those War Bonds," *Mailway: News and Ideas on Direct-Mail* 7, no. 2 (July–August 1943): 1.

29. Morse, "Paying for a World War," 214.

30. Letter from Ted R. Gamble, National Director, War Finance Division, to NAACP, May 1944, NAACP Records, Group II-A, Box 666, File "War Savings Bonds, 1943–1944," Library of Congress (hereafter cited as File "War Savings Bonds, 1943–1944," LC).

31. "War Film News Letter," No. 27, April 1945, NAACP Records, Group II-A, Box 666, File "War Savings Bonds, 1945–1946," Library of Congress (hereafter cited as File "War Savings Bonds, 1945–1946," LC).

32. "Bond Marathon," *Newsweek*, 20 July 1942.

33. U.S. Treasury, Release No. 94, 17 September 1943, Box 1, File "Defense Savings Staff (DSS) Press Releases," NA; *Daily Worker* 19, no. 30 (4 February 1942): 8; U.S. Treasury, "Bond Bursts: Sidelights on 3d War Loan," Release No. 93, NA.

34. Morse, "Paying for a World War," 216; U.S. Treasury, "Music Educators Bulletin," Field Memorandum No. 386, 10 September 1942, Civil Reference Branch, Boxes 8–9, NA. For an interesting comparative study of the impact of patriotic songs during World War II, see B. Lee Cooper, "Popular Songs, Military Conflicts, and Public Perceptions of the United States at War," *Social Education* 56, no. 3 (March 1992): 160–69.

35. Morse, "Paying for a World War," 217–19.

36. Ibid., 219–20; "Defense Bonds Prizes for Short Plays," *Daily Worker* 19, no. 53 (3 March 1942): 7; *Minute Man* 2, no. 24 (15 May 1943): 27.

37. U.S. Treasury, "Let's All Back the Attack," *4th War Loan Campaign Bulletin for Field Force*, No. 14, 25 January 1944, Boxes 8–9, File "Photographs, Information Kits, and Posters," NA; U.S. Treasury, "Bond Bursts: Sidelights on 3d War Loan," Release No. 57, Box 1, File "Defense Savings Staff (DSS) Press Releases," NA; U.S. Treasury, "Let's All Back the Attack," *4th War Loan Campaign Bulletin for Field Force*, No. 31, 14 February 1944, Box 1, File "Defense Savings Staff (DSS) Press Releases," NA. For a full backdrop on economic conditions during the war, see Harold G. Vatter, *The U.S. Economy in World War II* (New York: Columbia University Press, 1985).

38. Morse, "Paying for a World War," 194; "Defense Bond Plan," *Waterbury Republican*, 30 January 1942.

39. Morse, "Paying for a World War," 194, 196.

40. Ibid., 196.

41. Ibid., 193, 197–98.

42. Ibid., 197; OWI, "Payroll Savings Plan—Freedom's Promise," Domestic Radio Bureau Fact Sheet M-5791, 14 May 1943, Boxes 8–9, File "Photographs, Information Kits, and Posters," NA; U.S. Treasury and the Hecht Company, "The War Bond Show," April/May 1943,

Civil Reference Branch, Boxes 8–9, NA. For a full analysis of the role of the *Saturday Evening Post* in American culture, see Jan Cohn, *Creating America: George Horace Lorimer and the Saturday Evening Post* (Pittsburgh: University of Pittsburgh Press, 1989). For more on the role of the OWI during the war, see Allan M. Winkler, *The Politics of Propaganda: The OWI, 1942–1945* (New Haven, Conn.: Yale University Press, 1978).

43. "They Also Serve," *Columbus Citizen*, 3 February 1942; U.S. Treasury, "Bond Bursts: Sidelights on 3d War Loan," Release No. 76, NA; U.S. Treasury, Release No. 92, 17 September 1943, Box 1, File "Defense Savings Staff (DSS) Press Releases," NA.

44. U.S. Treasury, "Bond Bursts," Release No. 76, NA; "Keep 'Em Respectable," *New Haven Register*, 31 January 1942; Bailey and Farber, *First Strange Place*, 127.

45. "Bonds for Conchies," *Newsweek*, 20 July 1942, 65; Hulen, "War Bonds and Mob Spirit." For the relationship between Catholicism and nationalism during the war, see Philip Gleason, "Pluralism, Democracy, and Catholicism," 208–31.

46. "They're Giving," *New Orleans Times-Picayune*, 18 May 1941; "Bond-Buying Spirit," *Indianapolis News*, 25 December 1941; "Award for the First Bomb," *Portland Oregonian*, 25 January 1942; U.S. Treasury, "Let's All Back the Attack," No. 31.

47. U.S. Treasury, "Bond Bursts," Release No. 76, NA; High, "U.S. Pocketbook Enlists," 14; "100 Percent Towns," *Fairmont Times*, 18 January 1942; Morse, "Paying for a World War," 256; "Accent on Bonds," *Business Week*, 17 October 1942.

48. Lloyd E. Partain, Agriculture Section, War Finance Division, quoted in U.S. Treasury Press Release, number and date unknown, Box 1, File "Defense Savings Staff (DSS) and War Savings Staff (WSS) Unnumbered Releases," NA; *Minute Man* 2, no. 19 (1 March 1943): 40.

49. "Alcohol and National Defense," *Hartford Times*, 9 January 1942; "Defer Bond Pay for Overtime," *Daily Worker* 19, no. 68 (20 March 1942); U.S. Treasury, Release No. 28, 4 September 1943, Box 1, File "Defense Savings Staff (DSS) Press Releases," NA.

50. "Buy Bonds! U.S. Spurs Drive to Draw in a Billion a Month," *Newsweek*, 6 July 1942, 46; Stanley High, "The U.S. Pocketbook Enlists," *Reader's Digest*, March 1942, 14.

51. Morse, "Paying for a World War," 280, 321.

52. Ibid., 281–82, 323, 329.

Chapter 4. On This We Are United

1. Lichtenstein, *Labor's War at Home*, 18, 27, 37, 42.

2. Gerstle, *Working-Class Americanism*, 292, 298.

3. Charles S. Maier, "The Politics of Productivity: Foundations of American International Economic Policy After World War II," *International Organization* 31, no. 4 (1977): 607–32.

4. Gerstle, *Working-Class Americanism*, 302, 311, 301.

5. Elizabeth A. Fones-Wolf, *Selling Free Enterprise: The Business Assault on Labor and Liberalism, 1945–1960* (Urbana: University of Illinois Press, 1994), 4, 19; Lichtenstein, *Labor's War at Home*, 207, 232.

6. Lichtenstein, *Labor's War at Home*, 73, 196.

7. *CIO News* 5, no. 6 (9 February 1942).

8. *CIO News* 5, no. 52 (21 December 1942).

9. *CIO News*, 27 November 1944, 17.

10. *CIO News* 8, no. 25 (18 June 1945): 5.

11. Fones-Wolf, *Selling Free Enterprise*, 139–40.

12. Roy Gould, "St. Louis CIO Hits at 'Defense Savings Committee,'" *Labor Action* 6, no. 5 (2 February 1942): 3; "US Labor Unites on Billion-a-Month War Bond Drive," *CIO News* 5, no. 17 (27 April 1942): 2; Maier, "Politics of Productivity," 612.

13. Marc Stone, "Publishers Seek $$$ for U.S. Bond Ads," *CIO News* 5, no. 12, 2.

14. Conrad Komorowski, "Chicago Tribune Prints Attack on Sale of U.S. Defense Bonds," *Daily Worker* 19, no. 70 (23 March 1942): 3.

15. Henry Judd, "War Bonds: Forced Savings in the Offing," *Labor Action* 6, no. 36 (7 September 1942): 4.

16. *CIO News* 5, no. 4 (26 January 1942): 6; "Shipyard Snubs Bonds," *CIO News* 5, no. 12 (23 March 1942): 1.

17. "News Guild Leader to Aid Bond Sales; Locals Cooperate," *CIO News* 5, no. 18 (4 May 1942): 18, 3; "Urge U.S. Buy Bond a Month for Soldiers," *CIO News* 5, no. 20 (18 May 1942): 3.

18. "Buy Defense Bonds!" *CIO News* 4, no. 50 (15 December 1941): 3; *CIO News* 4, no. 52 (29 December 1941): 2; *CIO News* 4, no. 52 (29 December 1941): 2; "CIO Union to Raise $6,000,000 for Submarine," *Daily Worker* 19, no. 26 (30 January 1942): 4. "Five Unions Pledge Huge Bond Sales to Replace Ships," *CIO News* 5, no. 13 (30 March 1942): 2.

19. *CIO News* 4, no. 52 (29 December 1941): 2; "Use Back Wages for War Bonds," *CIO News* 5, no. 43 (26 October 1942): 3; "CIO Woman Puts All in War Bonds," *CIO News* 7, no. 14 (27 March 1944): 11.

20. *CIO News* 5, no. 5 (2 February 1942): 1; "UAW Baby Given $500 Bond," *CIO News (Serviceman's Edition)*, 5 March 1945, 7; "Shipbuilders Buy Bonds to Launch Liberty Ship, the SS Philip Murray," *Daily Worker* 19, no. 94 (20 April 1942): 3.

21. "CIO Barbers Aid War; Bond Sales Talk Comes with Shaves, Haircuts," *CIO News* 5, no. 24 (15 June 1942): 1; "Clothe the Army, Slogan of CIO Union Bond Drive," *CIO News* 6, no. 36 (6 September 1943): 2; "CIO Backs the Attack with War Bonds—Millions More of 'Em," *CIO News* 6, no. 41 (11 October 1943): 1.

22. "CIO, AFL, RR Union Women Hold Joint Bond Sale Rally," *Daily Worker* 19, no. 78 (1 April 1942): 3.

23. Clara Bodian, "Women Have Big Role in Bond Drive," *Daily Worker* 19, no. 58 (9 March 1942): 5.

24. "Candidate Sells $3,050 Worth of Defense Bonds," *Daily Worker* 19, no. 52 (2 March 1942): 5.

25. "City CIO-AFL Join Efforts in Bond Drive," *Daily Worker* 19, no. 49 (25 February 1942): 5; "Labor Unites to Urge More Bond Buying," *CIO News* 7, no. 3 (27 January 1944): 2.

26. "Hosiery Union, Employers in Joint Bond Campaign," *CIO News* 5 (3 August 1942): 7.

27. "Rubber Union, Companies in Joint Bond Drive," *CIO News* 5, no. 34 (24 August 1942): 6; "CIO, Rubber Drive for More Bond Sales Ends, Huge Success," *CIO News* 5, no. 41 (5 October 1942): 8; "L-M Companies Top Nation's Bond Sales," *CIO News* 6, no. 36 (6 September 1943): 1.

28. "Workers Buy Bonds, and They Don't Go 'By By' Either!" *CIO News* 6, no. 9 (1 March 1943): 2.

29. "2nd War Loan Drive Opens Soon," *CIO News* 6, no. 14 (5 April 1943): 6; "Four Fifths of Workers Buying War Bonds," *CIO News* 6, no. 16 (19 April 1943): 2; "Unionists Tops as War Bond Buyers," *CIO News* 6, no. 30 (26 July 1943): 1.

30. "Auto Union Buys $50 Million Bonds," *Daily Worker* 19, no. 92 (17 April 1942): 3; "Big CIO Union Puts 75% in War Bonds," *CIO News* 7, no. 19 (8 May 1944): 8.

31. "Steel Bond Drive Nears 100% Goal," *CIO News* 5, no. 50 (14 December 1942): 1; "War Bond Films," *CIO News* 7, no. 46 (13 November 1944): 11; "Films for Union Showings," *CIO News* 8, no. 15 (9 April 1945): 10.

32. *CIO News* 5, no. 5 (2 February 1942): 1; "Treasury Ups Union Bond Limit to $100,000," *CIO News* 5, no. 26 (29 June 1942): 1.

33. Henry C. Fleisher, "'Workers Know Score on War' Morgenthau Tells Labor Press," *CIO News* 5, no. 47 (23 November 1942): 2; "Workers Buy Bonds, and They Don't Go 'By By' Either!"

34. "Union Bond Buying Record Tops, Says Treasury Official," *CIO News* 7, no. 4 (24 January 1944): 1; "Union Labor Urged to Back 6th War Loan," *CIO News* 7, no. 46 (13 November 1944): 3.

35. Philip Murray, "Buy Bonds," *CIO News*, 21 May 1945; *CIO News* 8, no. 21, 1.

36. "Say It with Bonds," *CIO News* 5, no. 52 (21 December 1942): 1.

Chapter 5. Consent of the Governed

1. U.S. Treasury, "Let's All Back the Attack," No. 31; "Buy Bonds! U.S. Spurs Drive to Draw in a Billion a Month," *Newsweek*, 6 July 1942, 46. For more on the political activity of Einstein and other refugee physicists during the war, see William Lanouette, "Bumbling Toward the Bomb," *Bulletin of the Atomic Scientists* 45, no. 7 (September 1989): 7–12.

2. Morse, "Paying for a World War," 208: "The Foreign Origin Section ... sold the idea that the United States derived its strength from the 'consent of the governed,' and that its strength was greatest when the largest possible numbers of its people were able to do their share on a free-will basis in the planning and financing of great national projects."

3. Horace Kallen, *Culture and Democracy in the United States* (New York: Boni and Liveright, 1924); Gary Gerstle, "The Protean Character of American Liberalism," *American Historical Review* (October 1994): 1063; Gerstle, *Working-Class Americanism*, 290–93.

4. "Foreign Nationality Groups in the United States: A Handbook," 2d ed. (Washington, D.C., 1945), vii–x, in Lorraine M. Lees, "National Security and Ethnicity: Contrasting Views during World War II," *Diplomatic History* 11, no. 2 (1987): 114–17, 120–21.

5. "Fight by His Side," *Fifth War Loan Campaign Book* (U.S. Treasury), June 1944, 37–38, NA.

6. Ibid.; *Minute Man* 2, no. 24 (15 May 1943): 3.

7. World War I and II Poster Collection; "Buy Bonds!" 46; Morse, "Paying for a World War," 207; *Minute Man* 2, no. 24 (15 May 1943): 3.

8. "Treasury Opens Laugh Drive to Boost Defense Bonds Sale," *Washington Star*, 24 May 1941; Odegard and Barth, "Millions for Defense," 406. More recent investigation has revealed that Thomas Mann's daughter, Erika Mann, acted as an informer to the FBI during the war (only to face deportation orders soon after). See *New York Times*, 18 July 1993, pp. 11N, 25L.

9. Memo from Lew Frank Jr., President of Office for Emergency Management, to Herman Hettinger, 18 December 1943, Boxes 8–9, File "Photographs, Information Kits, and Posters," NA.

10. Defense Savings Staff Press Releases (U.S. Treasury), No. 123, 14 January 1942, Box 1, NA.

11. *Minute Man* 2, no. 24 (15 May 1943): 3.

12. "It is Not Too Late" (U.S. Treasury), transcription of CBS radio broadcast made by Eve Curie on behalf of Defense Savings Program, 11 June 1941, Boxes 8–9, File "Photographs, Information Kits, and Posters," NA.

13. *Minute Man* 2, no. 12 (1 November 1942): 31.

14. Memo from R. W. Coyne, Field Director, War Savings Staff, to State Administrators, Field Memorandum No. 371, 11 August 1942, Boxes 8–9, File "Photographs, Information Kits, and Posters," NA.

15. Dowsley Clark, Chief, News Bureau, DB, and Herbert C. Plummer, Assistant Chief, News Bureau, DB, "Sixth War Loan Drive," 19 December 1944, Boxes 8–9, File "Photographs, Information Kits, and Posters," NA; M. S. Szymczak, "Faith and Freedom," *Minute Man* 2, no. 12 (1 November 1942): 28.

16. U.S. Treasury, War Savings Staff Radio Announcement, 1 February 1943, Boxes 8–9, File "Photographs, Information Kits, and Posters," NA.

17. Morse, "Paying for a World War," 208; *Minute Man* 2, no. 24 (15 May 1943): 39.

18. "2 Groups Purchase Big Defense Bonds," *New York Times,* 13 May 1941; U.S. Treasury, "Reports from National Organizations," 1944, Boxes 8–9, File "Photographs, Information Kits, and Posters," NA; U.S. Treasury, Release No. 113, 20 September 1943, Box 1, File "Defense Savings Staff (DSS) Press Releases," NA. For the larger role of American Jews during the war, see I. Kaufman, *American Jews in World War II: The Story of 550,000 Fighters for Freedom* (New York: Dial Press, 1947).

19. "Benny's Fiddle Puts Purchaser in the Limelight," *New York Herald Tribune,* 25 February 1943.

20. *Minute Man* 2, no. 23 (1 March 1943): 42.

21. Tuttle, *Daddy's Gone to War,* 180; "Patriotic Partnership," *Tampa Tribune,* 26 December 1941; U.S. Treasury, Release No. 77, 14 September 1943, Box 1, File "Defense Savings Staff (DSS) Press Releases," NA; *Minute Man* 2, no. 12 (1 November 1942): 31. For an interesting examination of discrimination against Italian Americans during the war, see Stephen R. Fox, *The Unknown Internment: An Oral History of the Relocation of Italian Americans During World War II* (Boston: Twayne, 1990).

22. Release No. 77; U.S. Treasury, "Bond Bursts," Release No. 93, NA; *Minute Man* 2, no. 24 (15 May 1943): 3.

23. Photograph Reference Files, Box 10, Civil Reference Branch, U.S. Treasury, NA (hereafter cited as Photographic Reference Files, NA).

24. "Chinese Women Win Bond Honor," newspaper clipping, Photograph Reference Files, NA.

25. "Filipinos to Sponsor Bond Sale from Victory Wagon," newspaper clipping, Photograph Reference Files, NA.

26. *Minute Man* 2, no. 24 (15 May 1943): 26.

27. "Slogan Contest Winners Revealed," *Nippu Jiji,* 7 March 1942, newspaper clipping, Photograph Reference Files, NA. For more on Hawaiian Japanese Americans during the war, see Bailey and Farber, *First Strange Place;* Tomi Kaizawa Knaefler, *Our House Divided: Seven Japanese American Families in World War II* (Honolulu: University of Hawaii Press, 1991); and John Rademaker, *These Are Americans: The Japanese Americans in Hawaii in World War II* (Palo Alto, Calif.: Pacific Books, 1951).

28. John Okada, *No-No Boy* (Seattle: University of Washington Press, 1992); Photograph Reference Files, NA. For nonfictional accounts of the lives of Japanese Americans during the war, particularly related to their internment, see Page Smith, *Democracy on Trial: The Japanese-American Evacuation and Relocation in World War II* (New York: Simon and Schuster, 1995); Roger Daniels, *Prisoners Without Trial: Japanese Americans in World War II* (New York: Hill and Wang, 1993); Lillian Baker, *American and Japanese Relocation in World War II: Fact, Fiction and Fallacy* (Medford, Oreg.: Webb Research Group, 1990); Donald E. Collins, *Native*

American Aliens: Disloyalty and the Renunciation of Citizenship by Japanese Americans During World War II (Westport, Conn.: Greenwood Press, 1985); and Leonard Broom and John I. Kitsuse, *The Managed Casualty: The Japanese-American Family in World War II* (Berkeley and Los Angeles: University of California Press, 1973).

29. Photograph Reference Files, NA.

30. Photograph Reference Files, NA; "Indian Bond Buyers," *Toledo Blade*, 17 December 1941.

31. Photograph Reference Files, NA; Leslie Marmon Silko, *Ceremony* (New York: Viking Penguin, 1977); Tuttle, *Daddy's Gone to War*, 178–79; Eric Hobsbawm and Terence Ranger, ed., *The Invention of Tradition* (Cambridge: Cambridge University Press, 1983); George Lipsitz, *Time Passages: Collective Memory and American Popular Culture* (Minneapolis: University of Minnesota Press, 1990), 136. Also see Margaret T. Bixler, *Winds of Freedom: The Story of the Navajo Code Talkers of World War II* (Darien, Conn.: Two Bytes, 1992); Alison R. Bernstein, *American Indians and World War II: Toward a New Era in Indian Affairs* (Norman: University of Oklahoma Press, 1991); Lynn Escue, "Coded Contradictions: Navajo Talkers and the Pacific War," *History Today* 41 (July 1991); Albert Hemingway, *Ira Hayes: Pima Marine* (Lanham, Md.: University Press of America, 1988); Laurence M. Hauptman, *The Iroquois Struggle for Survival: World War II to Red Power* (Syracuse, N.Y.: Syracuse University Press, 1985); and Broderick H. Johnson, ed., *Navajos and World War II* (Tsaile, Ariz.: Navajo Community College Press, 1977).

32. Photograph Reference Files, NA; *Minute Man* 2, no. 23 (1 May 1943): 37.

33. *Minute Man* 2, no. 19 (1 March 1943): 42; Photograph Reference Files, NA; *Minute Man* 2, no. 24 (15 May 1943): 23.

34. Photograph Reference Files, NA; "Scottish Pipers to Drone for 6th Loan Tomorrow," *Seattle Times*, 15 December 1944, newspaper clipping, Photograph Reference Files, NA.

35. *Minute Man* 2, no. 23 (1 May 1943): 37.

36. Photograph Reference Files, NA; *Minute Man* 2, no. 19 (1 March 1943): 42.

37. *Minute Man* 2, no. 24 (15 May 1943): 3; *Minute Man* 2, no. 12 (1 November 1942): 31; *Minute Man* 2, no. 23 (1 May 1943): 39.

38. *Minute Man* 2, no. 19 (1 March 1943): 42; *Minute Man* 2, no. 24 (15 May 1943): 23; *Minute Man* 2, no. 23 (1 May 1943): 38–39; *Minute Man* 2, no. 24 (15 May 1943): 23.

39. *Minute Man* 2, no. 12 (1 November 1942): 29–30.

40. Ibid., 30.

41. Ibid.

42. *Minute Man* 2, no. 19 (1 March 1943): 41–42.

Chapter 6. William Pickens and the Inter-Racial Section

1. "1944 Report of the Inter-Racial Section," WPP; U.S. Treasury, "William Pickens in the U.S. Treasury," press release, 9 September 1941, WPP.

2. William L. Andrews in William Pickens, *Bursting Bonds: The Autobiography of a "New Negro"* (Bloomington: Indiana University Press, 1991), xi–xviii; Benjamin Hooks in Pickens, *Bursting Bonds*, ix.

3. Avery, *Up from Washington*, 10, 135–41, 158–60.

4. Ibid., 168–69.

5. U.S. Treasury, "William Pickens in the U.S. Treasury."

6. Ibid.
7. Ibid.
8. Blum, *V Was for Victory,* 183–89; Polenberg, *One Nation Divisible,* 69.
9. Robin D. G. Kelley, "The Riddle of the Zoot: Malcolm Little and Black Cultural Politics During World War II," *Malcolm X: In Our Own Image,* ed. Joe Wood (New York: St. Martin's Press, 1992), 155–82. Also see Bruce Tyler, "Zoot Suit Culture and the Black Press," *Journal of American Culture* 17, no. 2 (Summer 1994): 21–34.
10. Clayton R. Koppes and Gregory D. Black, "Blacks, Loyalty, and Motion-Picture Propaganda in World War II," *Journal of American History* 73, no. 2 (September 1986): 389; Blum, *V Was for Victory,* 8.
11. "1944 Report of the Inter-Racial Section," WPP; "Why Crucify Pickens?" *Richmond Times-Dispatch,* 6 February 1943; "Women in the War Finance Program," in "1943 Report of the Inter-Racial Section," WPP; U.S. Treasury, Special News Release NN-2, 25 October 1945, Victory Loan Special Releases (Rural and Negro), Box 5, Civil Reference Branch, NA (hereafter cited as Victory Loan Special Releases, NA).
12. "Labor & Fraternal Activities" in "1943 Report of the Inter-Racial Section," WPP.
13. U.S. Treasury, Release N-788, WPP; Morse, "Paying for a World War," 209–10.
14. "Negroes Ask About Democracy," *Propaganda Analysis,* 26 August 1941, 8.
15. "1944 Report of the Inter-Racial Section," WPP; OWI, "Summary of OWI Cooperation in the Fourth War Loan Drive," 1944, NA. For a study of the black press during the war, see Patrick S. Washburn, *A Question of Sedition: The Federal Government's Investigation of the Black Press During World War II* (New York: Oxford University Press, 1986) and Lee Finkle, *Forum for Protest: The Black Press During World War II* (Rutherford, N.J.: Fairleigh Dickenson University Press, 1975). For a comparative analysis of the black press during the previous world war, see Mark Ellis, "America's Black Press, 1914–18," *History Today* 14 (September 1991): 20–28. Despite Du Bois's call for African Americans to temporarily ease their protests against discrimination, the black press during World War I actively pointed out the hypocrisy of the government's goal to "make the world safe for democracy."
16. "1944 Report of the Inter-Racial Section," WPP; U.S. Treasury, Release N-1506, Minute Man Section, Box 2 ("Interracial Material") and Box 10 ("Colored"), NA.
17. Memo from Ted Poston, Office of Emergency Management, to Louis J. Gale, 2 June 1944, Minute Man Section, Box 2, File "Interracial Material," RG 56, NA (hereafter cited as File "Interracial Material," NA).
18. *Southern Frontier,* October 1943.
19. *Southern Frontier,* January 1944.
20. *Negro Quarterly* 1, no. 2 (Fall 1942); *Brown American* (Fall–Winter 1942).
21. Letter from William C. Page, Promotion Manager, *Pittsburgh Courier,* to Ted Poston, OWI, 9 February 1942, Minute Man Section, Boxes 2 and 10, NA.
22. Robert L. Vann, Editor, *Pittsburgh Courier,* 13 December 1941; Koppes and Black, "Blacks, Loyalty," 387; Blum, *V Was for Victory,* 208.
23. Washburn, *Question of Sedition,* 7–8, 100–101; Herbert Garfinkel, *When Negroes March: The March on Washington Movement in the Organization Politics for FEPC* (Glencoe, Ill: Free Press, 1959), 32–33. For more on the government's investigation of African Americans' political activities during the war, see Kenneth O'Reilley, "The Roosevelt Administration and Black America: Federal Surveillance Policy and Civil Rights During the New Deal and World War II Years," *PHYLON* 48, no. 1 (March 1987): 12–26.

24. U.S. Treasury, Defense Savings Staff Press Release, 20 August 1941, WPP. Excerpt of Pickens speech to the National Medical Association of Negro Doctors, Chicago, 20 August 1941.

25. "1944 Report of the Inter-Racial Section," WPP; Morse, "Paying for a World War," 173: "The lack of enthusiastic response from colleges was in some cases due to the fact that many college students had no funds to invest. Meager college response to the Treasury's program was also due to academic preoccupation with the intellectual rather than the practical aspects of citizenship."

26. U.S. Treasury, Defense Savings Staff Press Release, 22 December 1941, WPP.

27. U.S. Treasury, Defense Savings Staff Press Release, 3 December 1941, WPP.

28. U.S. Treasury, Release N-1587, WPP; William Pickens, "Democracy of War Savings," *Crisis,* July 1942, 232.

29. U.S. Treasury, Defense Savings Staff Press Release, 29 August 1941, WPP. Excerpt of Pickens speech to National Negro Business League, Memphis, 29 August 1941.

30. "1944 Report of the Inter-Racial Section," WPP.

31. U.S. Treasury, Release N-1486, Minute Man Section, Boxes 2 and 10, NA.

32. Pickens, "Democracy of War Savings," 221.

33. "1944 Report of the Inter-Racial Section," WPP; Pickens, "Democracy of War Savings," 232.

34. U.S. Treasury, Defense Savings Staff Press Release, 15 July 1941, WPP. Excerpt of Pickens speech to the Summer School Teachers and the Public, Atlanta University, 15 July 1941.

35. Pickens, "Democracy of War Savings," 221.

36. OWI/Treasury Department press release N-214, 29 October 1942, Box 1, File "Defense Savings Staff (DSS) Press Releases," NA.

37. "1944 Report of the Inter-Racial Section," WPP; Atlanta University speech, 15 July 1941.

38. Cohen, *Making a New Deal,* 148; Letter from Pickens to *Richmond Times Dispatch,* 27 April 1942, WPP. For another version of "black capitalism" at work in an urban economy, see Joe William Trotter Jr., *Black Milwaukee: The Making of an Industrial Proletariat, 1915–45* (Urbana: University of Illinois Press, 1985).

39. U.S. Treasury, Defense Savings Staff Press Release, 12 September 1941, WPP. Excerpt of Pickens speech to the National Baptist Convention, Shreveport, 11 September 1941, and the National Baptist Convention, Cleveland, 12 September 1941; Atlanta University speech, 15 July 1941.

40. OWI, "OWI News Bureau's Activity."

41. Letter from Pickens to Mr. and Mrs. Howard W. Coles of Rochester, New York, 20 September 1943, WPP.

42. Letter to Pickens to Pauli Murray of Howard University, Washington, D.C., 21 July 1944, WPP.

43. John Scharr, "The Case for Patriotism," *American Review,* No. 7 (May 1973): 62; Atlanta University speech, 15 July 1941.

44. Memo from William Pickens to Peter Odegard, "The American Negro and His Country in War," 20 May 1944, WPP.

45. U.S. Treasury, Defense Savings Staff Press Release, 18 August 1941, WPP. Excerpt of Pickens speech to the National Convention of the Agents of the Mme. C. J. Walker Manufacturing and Beauty Culture Company, Indianapolis, 18 August 1941; Atlanta University speech, 15 July 1941; for a conceptual analysis of "containment" and its role within gender

roles in postwar society, see Elaine Tyler May, *Homeward Bound: American Families in the Cold War Era* (New York: Basic Books, 1988).

46. Memphis speech, 29 August 1941; for more on "myth and symbol," see especially Bruce Kuklick, "Myth and Symbol in American Studies," *American Quarterly* 24(4) (1972): 435–50, and Philip Gleason, "World War II and the Development of American Studies," *American Quarterly* 36 (1984): 343–58.

47. Garry Wills, *Lincoln at Gettysburg: The Words that Remade America* (New York: Simon and Schuster, 1992); Indianapolis speech, 18 August 1941.

48. Atlanta University speech, 15 July 1941.

49. Benedict Anderson, *Imagined Communities* (New York: Verso, 1983), 16.

50. Avery, *Up from Washington*, 171–78; The Tuskegee Airmen continue to be a highly charged site of historical examination. See Lawrence P. Scott and William M. Womack Sr., *Double V: The Civil Rights Struggle of the Tuskegee Airmen* (East Lansing: Michigan State University Press, 1994); Stanley Sandler, *Segregated Skies: The All-Black Combat Squadrons of World War II* (Washington, D.C.: Smithsonian Institution Press, 1992); and Robert J. Jakeman, *The Divided Skies: Establishing Segregated Flight Training at Tuskegee, Alabama, 1934–1942* (Tuscaloosa: University of Alabama Press, 1992).

51. Avery, *Up from Washington*, 181–84; Brinkley, *End of Reform*, 141; *Crisis*, March 1943, 72.

52. "Why Crucify Pickens?" *Richmond Times-Dispatch*, 6 February 1943.

53. Letter from James Houghteling to Sidney Osborn, 22 December 1943, WPP.

54. Memo from William Pickens to James Houghteling, 13 August 1945, WPP.

55. Letter from James Houghteling to William Pickens, 29 October 1945, WPP.

56. Memo from William Pickens to James Houghteling, 1 March 1945, WPP.

Chapter 7. The NAACP and War Bonds

1. Robert Korstad and Nelson Lichtenstein, "Opportunities Found and Lost: Labor, Radicals, and the Early Civil Rights Movement," *Journal of American History* (1988): 786–87, 797.

2. Michael K. Honey, *Southern Labor and Black Civil Rights: Organizing Memphis Workers* (Urbana: University of Illinois Press, 1993), 218; Korstad and Lichtenstein, "Opportunities Found and Lost," 787; for the most recent biography of A. Philip Randolph, see Paula F. Pfeffer, *A. Philip Randolph, Pioneer of the Civil Rights Movement* (Baton Rouge: Louisiana State University Press, 1990); for a full-length study of the march, see Garfinkel, *When Negroes March*.

3. Avery, *Up from Washington*, 153, 170; Edward Franklin Frazier, *Black Bourgeoisie* (Glencoe, Ill.: Free Press, 1957).

4. William Pickens, "The American Negro Participates in War Finance," *Opportunity* 23 (Winter 1945): 25.

5. Letter from Lorimer D. Milton, Staff Advisor, Defense Savings Staff, to Roy Wilkins, Assistant Secretary, NAACP, 24 May 1941, NAACP Records, Group II-A, Box 225, File "Defense Bonds, 1941," Library of Congress (hereafter cited as File "Defense Bonds, 1941," LC); letter from Wilkins to Milton, 6 June, File "Defense Bonds, 1941," LC; letter from White to L. D. Milton, Citizens Trust Company, 21 April 1941, File "Defense Bonds, 1941," LC.

6. Letter from Claude A. Barnett, Director, Associated Negro Press, to Roy Wilkins, 6 August 1941, File "Defense Bonds, 1941," LC.

7. Letter from William Pickens, Staff Assistant, Defense Savings Staff, to Kathryn Close, *Survey Graphic,* 14 September 1941, File "Defense Bonds, 1941," LC.

8. Letter from William Pickens to E. Frederick Morrow, NAACP, 30 August 1941, File "Defense Bonds, 1941," LC; letter from Secretary to Morrow, 4 September 1941, File "Defense Bonds, 1941," LC.

9. Letter from Pickens to Arthur B. Spingarn, President, NAACP, Walter White, Secretary, NAACP, Louis T. Wright, Chair, NAACP, and Mary White Ovington, Treasurer, NAACP, 3 December 1941, File "Defense Bonds, 1941," LC.

10. Letter from Jesse O. Thomas, National Organizations Division, to Madison S. Jones Jr., Youth Director, NAACP, 4 January 1943, File "War Savings Bonds, 1943–1944," LC.

11. Letter from Jones to Thomas, 6 January 1943, File "War Savings Bonds, 1943–1944," LC.

12. Letter from John W. Whitten, Promotion Specialist, Inter-Racial Section, to White, 4 September 1943, File "War Savings Bonds, 1943–1944," LC; letter from White to Whitten, 6 October 1943, File "War Savings Bonds, 1943–1944," LC; letter from Whitten to White, 12 October 1943, File "War Savings Bonds, 1943–1944," LC.

13. Letter from Pickens to NAACP, 10 July 1944, File "War Savings Bonds, 1943–1944," LC.

14. Letter from White to Pickens, 20 July 1944, File "War Savings Bonds, 1943–1944," LC.

15. Letter from Pickens to White, 22 July 1944, File "War Savings Bonds, 1943–1944," LC.

16. Letter from Pickens to White, 20 November 1944, File "War Savings Bonds, 1943–1944," LC; letter from Pickens to White, 24 November 1944, File "War Savings Bonds, 1943–1944," LC; letter from White to Pickens, 27 November 1944, File "War Savings Bonds, 1943–1944," LC.

17. Letter from White to Treasury Department, 28 July 1942, NAACP Records, Group II-A, Box 666, File "War Savings Bonds, 1941–1942," Library of Congress (hereafter cited as File "War Savings Bonds, 1941–1942," LC); memorandum from White to executive and clerical staffs, NAACP, 28 July 1942, File "War Savings Bonds, 1941–1942," LC; memorandum from White to executive and clerical staffs, NAACP, 23 September 1942, File "War Savings Bonds, 1941–1942," LC.

18. Letter from Helen Dallas, Chief, Materials Unit, Women's Section, Treasury Department, to White, 3 November 1942, File "War Savings Bonds, 1941–1942," LC; letter from White to Dallas, 1 December 1942, File "War Savings Bonds, 1941–1942," LC; letter from Mozella Swann, Chairman, Women's Committee, New York War Savings Staff and Nell Hunter, Inter-Racial Section, 4 December 1942, File "War Savings Bonds, 1941–1942," LC.

19. Letter from Willard W. Allen, Chief Executive Officer, Interracial Section, to White, 23 December 1943, Box 498, File "Publicity—War Bond Posters: NAACP and *Crisis,* 1943–1946," Library of Congress (hereafter cited as File "Publicity," LC).

20. Telegram from Edgar T. Rouzeau, Fifth War Loan Desk, to NAACP, 14 June 1944, File "War Savings Bonds, 1943–1944," LC.

21. Telegram from White to Rouzeau, 15 June 1944, File "War Savings Bonds, 1943–1944," LC.

22. Statement by White, undated, File "War Savings Bonds, 1943–1944," LC.

23. Walter White, *A Rising Wind* (Garden City, N.Y.: Doubleday Doran, 1945); Blum, *V Was for Victory,* 219. See also White's autobiography, written shortly after the war, *A Man Called White: The Autobiography of Walter White* (New York: Viking Press, 1948).

24. Gunnar Myrdal, *An American Dilemma: The Negro Problem and Modern Democracy* (New York: Harper and Brothers, 1944); Bailey and Farber, *First Strange Place,* 138.

25. Letter from White to Dr. Channing Tobias, 13 May 1943, File "War Savings Bonds, 1943–1944," LC.

26. Letter from Charles C. Craft, Executive Manager, Inter-Racial Section, to White, 23 August 1944, File "War Savings Bonds, 1943–1944," LC.

27. Letter from White to Craft, 15 September 1944, File "War Savings Bonds, 1943–1944," LC.

28. Letter from Carl R. Johnson, President, Kansas City Branch, NAACP, to White, 13 August 1941, File "Defense Bonds, 1941," LC; letter from White to Johnson, 17 October 1941, File "Defense Bonds, 1941," LC.

29. Letter from Raymond Guild, President, Boston Branch, NAACP, to Wilkins, 16 December 1941, File "War Savings Bonds, 1941–1942," LC; letter from White to Guild, 31 January 1942, File "War Savings Bonds, 1941–1942," LC; letter from John T. Payne to White, 4 September 1943, File "War Savings Bonds, 1943–1944," LC; letter from White to Payne, 6 October 1943, File "War Savings Bonds, 1943–1944," LC.

30. Letter from Dr. Joseph R. Sizoo, President, Greater New York Federation of Churches, to NAACP, 1 September 1943, File "War Savings Bonds, 1943–1944," LC.

31. Letter from Walter W. Pettit, Chairman, Social Welfare War Bond Committee, to NAACP, 6 July 1944, File "War Savings Bonds, 1943–1944," LC.

32. Memorandum from Wilkins to White, 30 December 1942, File "War Savings Bonds, 1941–1942," LC; letter from E. W. Stetson, President, Guaranty Trust Company of New York, to NAACP, 19 August 1943, File "War Savings Bonds, 1943–1944," LC; memorandum from White to Wilkins, 7 December 1943, File "War Savings Bonds, 1943–1944," LC; NAACP document titled "Monies Invested 1943," 13 December 1943, File "War Savings Bonds, 1943–1944," LC; telegram from Bob Braddicks, Deputy Manager, Harlem Riverside Campaign Committee, to White, 11 July 1944, File "War Savings Bonds, 1943–1944," LC; telegram from White to Braddicks, 12 July 1944, File "War Savings Bonds, 1943–1944," LC.

33. Memorandum from Wilkins to White, 26 August 1943, File "Publicity," LC; for more on Wilkins, see his autobiography, *Standing Fast: The Autobiography of Roy Wilkins* (New York: Viking Press, 1982).

34. Letter from Wilkins to Arthur DeBebian, Advertising Manager, War Finance Committee of New York, 27 August 1943, File "Publicity," LC.

35. Memorandum from Wilkins to "Miss Harper," 5 October 1943, File "Publicity," LC; letter from Wilkins to Debebian, 28 December 1943, File "Publicity," LC; Outdoor Advertising Association contract for Fifth War Loan, 19 April 1944, File "Publicity," LC; letter from Wilkins to General Outdoor Advertising Company, 8 September 1944, File "Publicity," LC.

36. Telegram from Bayard F. Pope, Chairman, Executive Committee, New York War Savings Staff, to White, 21 May 1942, File "War Savings Bonds, 1941–1942," LC; telegram from White to Pope, 22 May 1942, File "War Savings Bonds, 1941–1942," LC; letter from John T. Madden, chairman, to White, 1 June 1942, File "War Savings Bonds, 1941–1942," LC.

37. Letter to NAACP from Nelson Bengston, Deputy Administrator, Defense Savings Staff, 21 May 1942, File "War Savings Bonds, 1941–1942," LC; New York War Savings Staff press release, 17 August 1942, File "War Savings Bonds, 1941–1942," LC.

38. Letter from John W. Davis, New York War Finance Committee, to White, 1 April 1943, File "War Savings Bonds, 1943–1944," LC.

39. Letter from Samuel H. Sweeney, General Chairman, Defense Savings Staff, to NAACP, 5 February 1944, File "War Savings Bonds, 1943–1944," LC.

40. Letter from Braddicks to White, 5 January 1943, File "War Savings Bonds, 1943–1944," LC.

41. Letter from Virginia Bennett to White, 17 December 1941, File "War Savings Bonds, 1941–1942," LC.
42. *Our America,* Office of Selective Service, U.S. Printing Office, undated, File "War Savings Bonds, 1941–1942," LC.
43. Letter from G. E. "Kid" Hilton to White, 20 December 1941, File "War Savings Bonds, 1941–1942," LC.
44. Letter from White to Harold Graves, Assistant to the Secretary of the Treasury, 30 December 1941, File "War Savings Bonds, 1941–1942," LC; letter from S. D. Mahan, Associate Director of Information, Defense Savings Staff, to White, 6 January 1942, File "War Savings Bonds, 1941–1942," LC; letter from White to Mahan, 13 January 1942, File "War Savings Bonds, 1941–1942," LC.
45. Letter from Louise R. McKinney to White, 12 January 1942, File "War Savings Bonds, 1941–1942," LC; letter from White to Henry Morgenthau, Secretary of the Treasury, 16 January 1942, File "War Savings Bonds, 1941–1942," LC; letter from Mahan to White, 26 January 1942, File "War Savings Bonds, 1941–1942," LC; letter from Dr. John W. Shirley, President, and John C. G. Temple, Secretary, John Brown Memorial Association, to White, 25 January 1942, File "War Savings Bonds, 1941–1942," LC.
46. Willard Wiener, "Race Hate Fights the Minute Men," *PM Daily,* 24 June 1942, 2.
47. Telegram from Wilkins to Madden, 24 June 1942, File "War Savings Bonds, 1941–1942," LC.
48. Memorandum from NAACP to NAACP members, 25 June 1942, File "War Savings Bonds, 1941–1942," LC; "Race Hate Fights the Minute Men."
49. Letter from "John D. & the Misses" to White, 30 June 1942, File "War Savings Bonds, 1941–1942," LC.
50. Telegram from Madden to Wilkins, 26 June 1942, File "War Savings Bonds, 1941–1942," LC.
51. Citation from New York War Savings Staff to NAACP, 24 May 1943, File "War Savings Bonds, 1943–1944," LC; Citation from Treasury Department to NAACP, 16 February 1945, File "War Savings Bonds, 1945–1946," LC.
52. Letter from Craft to Wilkins, 27 March 1945, File "War Savings Bonds, 1945–1946," LC; memorandum from White to NAACP Finance Committee, 25 September 1945, File "War Savings Bonds, 1945–1946," LC.
53. Letter from Vernon L. Clark, National Director, U.S. Savings Bonds Division, to White, 25 March 1946, File "War Savings Bonds, 1945–1946," LC.
54. Letter from Pickens to White, 27 April 1946, File "War Savings Bonds, 1945–1946," LC.
55. Pickens to White, 27 April 1946; letter to White from Pickens, 11 June 1946, File "War Savings Bonds, 1945–1946," LC.

Chapter 8. African American Notables and War Bonds

1. "1944 Report of Inter-Racial Section," WPP. For more on Cab Calloway, see his autobiography, *Of Minnie the Moocher and Me* (New York: Crowell, 1976).
2. U.S. Treasury, Release N-1501, NA.
3. OWI press release N-281, 15 January 1943, File "War Savings Bonds, 1943–1944," LC.
4. U.S. Treasury, Release N-1528, File "Interracial Material," NA; *Southern Frontier,* October 1943.

5. "Roosevelt Sells Bonds to Staff at White House," *New York Herald Tribune,* 7 April 1943, p. 8.

6. U.S. Treasury, Release NN-13, 23 November 1945, Victory Loan Special Releases, NA.

7. Memo titled "Program Material" from Theodore R. Poston, OWI, to Herbert Plummer, News Bureau, 23 June 1945, File "Interracial Material," NA.

8. Hugo Black, "The Negro Buys Bonds," *Negro Digest,* September 1945. Of the many biographies of Hugo Black, see Roger K. Newman, *Hugo Black: A Biography* (New York: Pantheon Books, 1994) and Tony Freyer, ed., *Justice Hugo Black and Modern America* (Tuscaloosa: University of Alabama Press, 1990).

9. Memo titled "Program Material." See Richard Wright, *Black Boy: A Record of Childhood and Youth* (New York: Harper and Brothers, 1945).

10. U.S. Treasury, Release NN-23, 30 November 1945, Victory Loan Special Releases, NA; Mark Van Doren, *Windless Cabins* (New York: H. Holt, 1940).

11. *Brown American,* May 1941, 17.

12. *Southern Frontier,* October 1943.

13. *Chicago Defender,* 26 February 1944; U.S. Treasury, Release N-1589, 4 July 1945, File "Interracial Material," NA.

14. U.S. Treasury, Release N-1498, File "Interracial Material," NA; U.S. Treasury, Release NN-14, 23 November 1945, Victory Loan Special Releases, NA.

15. *Southern Frontier,* October 1943; "1943 Report of Inter-Racial Section," WPP. For more on Handy, see Elizabeth Rider Montgomery, *William C. Handy: Father of the Blues* (Champaign, Ill.: Garrard, 1968).

16. "1944 Report of Inter-Racial Section," WPP; U.S. Treasury, Release N-1498, NA; "Race Artists Prominent in 6th War Loan Drive," *Los Angeles Tribune,* 20 November 1944; Letter from Maurice H. Kafka, Coordinator, Music Promotion Unit, War Finance Division, to Andy Razaf, 9 November 1944, Andy Razaf Papers, Schomberg Center, New York Public Library, New York City (hereafter cited as Razaf Papers); letter from David Levy, Special Radio Consultant, War Finance Division, to Andy Razaf, 4 May 1945, Razaf Papers.

17. Letter from Fred N. Tracy to Andy Razaf, 4 January 1945, Andy Razaf Papers; *Eureka Sprinkle,* 26 June 1945, in Razaf Papers.

18. "1944 Report of Inter-Racial Section," WPP; Memo titled "Program Material" from Theodore R. Poston, OWI, to Herbert Plummer, News Bureau, 16 June 1945, NA.

19. "Hint Broadway is Blacked Out to Duke Ellington," *Chicago Defender,* 21 November 1942, in Duke Ellington Archives, Archives Center, National Museum of American History, Smithsonian Institution, Washington, D.C. (hereafter cited as DEA); Peter Susskind, "Duke Ellington, Ambassador of Good Will," *San Francisco Chronicle,* May 1942, DEA.

20. "The Duke to Face Hollywood Cameras After Appearance Here," news clipping, DEA; "'Lip Slip Sinks Ship' New Ellington Tune," *People's Voice,* 28 November 1942, DEA; Duke Ellington, "Judging the Radio Programs," news clipping, DEA.

21. "Duke Ellington to Play for Air Cadets," *Chicago Herald-American,* July 1942, news clipping, DEA; "Thousands Hear Famed Orchestra in Post Theater," *Polar Tech,* 25 August 1944, DEA; Pickens, "Democracy of War Savings," 221.

22. "Duke on 'Spotlight' This Week; Lunceford, Dec. 8th," *Pittsburgh Courier,* 14 November 1942, DEA; "Spotlight on Duke Spotlights Thrills," *Metronome,* December 1942, 16, DEA; "Ellington and Lunceford Bands Set for Coca-Cola [sic] Spotlight," *People's Voice,* 21 November 1942, DEA; "Coca-Cola Signs More Sepia Orks," *Billboard,* 31 October 1942, DEA.

23. U.S. Treasury, Release N-1498, NA.

24. "Loads of Dough for Orks, Halls in 'Swing Shift Hops,' and War Workers on West Coast Love 'Em," *Billboard*, 4 July 1942, DEA; "Duke Ellington Comes to Regal with Hopes," *Chicago Defender*, 31 October 1942, p. 15, DEA; "Duke Plays Carnegie Concert on January 23; Sets Precedent," *People's Voice*, 14 November 1942, DEA; Daniel Richman, "Ellington Set for Carnegie," *New York Post*, 7 November 1942, DEA; Earl Wilson, "Broadway Proves Itself Not Very Race-Minded," *Record*, 5 April 1944, DEA. Also see Richard Schickel and Michael Walsh, *Carnegie Hall: The First One Hundred Years* (New York: Abrams, 1987).

25. "Top Colored Bands Hit Film Spotlight in Hollywood, Calif.," *Pittsburgh Courier*, news clipping, DEA; "Pair King Together," news clipping, *Chicago Defender*, DEA; OWI, "OWI News Bureau's Activity in Support of the Second War Loan Drive," April 1943, Civil Reference Branch, Boxes 8–9, NA. For histories of African Americans in film, see Donald Bogle, *Toms, Coons, Mulattos, Mammies, and Bucks: An Interpretive History of Blacks in American Films* (New York: Continuum, 1994); Thomas Crippes, *Making Movies Black: The Hollywood Message Movie from World War II to the Civil Rights Era* (New York: Oxford University Press, 1993); and Edward Mapp, *Blacks in American Films: Today and Yesterday* (Metuchen, N.J.: Scarecrow Press, 1972).

26. Joe Commiskey, *Washington Post*, 5 August 1944, in "1944 Report of Inter-Racial Section," WPP.

27. Sid Mercer, "Louis Will Not Surrender Title," *New York Journal-American*, 30 September 1941, Julian Black Scrapbooks of Joe Louis, 1935–1944, Archives Center, National Museum of American History, Smithsonian Institution, Washington, D.C. (hereafter cited as JBS); Harold Conrad, "Louis Picked to Kayo Conn within 4 Rounds," *Brooklyn Eagle*, 18 June 1941, JBS; "Extra—Joe Louis to Risk Title for Navy," *Louisville Defender*, 22 November 1941, JBS; "Joe Louis Fighting for Great Causes," *Daily Mirror*, 23 March 1942, Joe Louis Scrapbook, Archives Center, National Museum of American History, Smithsonian Institution, Washington, D.C. (hereafter cited as JLS); "Joe Louis Eulogized in Congress," *Southern Frontier*, February 1942.

28. Black, "Negro Buys Bonds," 3; Ira Berkow, "Sports of the Times; Tyson is a Boxing Exception," *New York Times*, 4 February 1992, sec. B (Sports Desk), p. 7.

29. *Brown American* (Winter/Spring 1944); Daniel M. Daniel, "Louis in Army, Will Raise Morale," *Ring*, September 1941, JBS.

30. Joseph C. Nichols, "Louis Thrilled by Willkie Visit to Dressing Room After Victory," *New York Times*, 10 January 1942, JLS.

31. "Joe Louis Fighting for Great Causes," *Daily Mirror*, 23 March 1942, JLS.

Chapter 9. African American Investment in War Bonds

1. "Blind Peanut Vendor Buys First Bond," *Southern Frontier*, October 1943.
2. Morse, "Paying for a World War," 210; "1944 Report of Inter-Racial Section," WPP; U.S. Treasury, Release N-1593, WPP.
3. "1943 Report of Inter-Racial Section," WPP.
4. Ibid.
5. Memo from James Houghteling to Inter-Racial Section staff, 4 September 1943, WPP.
6. "1943 Report of Inter-Racial Section," WPP.
7. Ibid.; "1944 Report of Inter-Racial Section," WPP; Memo from Ted Poston, Office of Emergency Management, to Louis J. Gale, 2 June 1944, NA.
8. "1944 Report of Inter-Racial Section," WPP.

9. Elizabeth Cohen, *Making a New Deal;* Morse, "Paying for a World War," 209.

10. Dowsley Clark, Chief, News Bureau, and Herbert Plummer, Assistant Chief, News Bureau, "Sixth War Loan Drive," 11 December 1944, NA; "1943 Report of Inter-Racial Section," WPP; *Southern Frontier,* October 1942; "1944 Report of Inter-Racial Section," WPP; OWI/Negro Press release (undated), by W. J. Cormack, War Finance Committee, Columbia, South Carolina.

11. U.S. Treasury, "Bond Bursts," Release No. 93, NA; U.S. Treasury, Release N, Defense Savings Staff and War Savings Staff Unnumbered Releases, File "Interracial Material," NA.

12. *Southern Frontier,* October 1943; "1944 Report of Inter-Racial Section," WPP; Photograph Reference Files, NA.

13. Clark and Plummer, "Sixth War Loan Drive"; Photograph Reference Files, NA; memo titled "Program Material" from Theodore R. Poston, OWI, to Herbert Plummer, News Bureau, 30 June 1945, NA.

14. U.S. Treasury, "Negroes in the War Bond Program," Sixth War Loan campaign brochure, November 1944, 43, File "Interracial Material," NA; "1943 Report of Inter-Racial Section," WPP; U.S. Treasury, Release N-1500, NA; U.S. Treasury, Release N-1589, NA.

15. "1943 Report of Inter-Racial Section," WPP; "Has Right Spirit to Whip Japs," *Southern Frontier,* October 1942; *Southern Frontier,* October 1943.

16. U.S. Treasury, Release N, Defense Savings Staff and War Savings Staff Unnumbered Releases, May 1945, File "Interracial Material," NA.

17. "Negroes in the War Bond Program"; Photograph Reference Files, NA.

18. Photograph Reference Files, NA; "Life Insurance Companies Invest Heavily in Bonds," *Southern Frontier,* October 1943. For two close studies of major African American insurance companies, see Alexa Benson Henderson, *Atlanta Life Insurance Company: Guardian of Black Economic Dignity* (Tuscaloosa: University of Alabama Press, 1990) and Walter B. Weare, *Black Business in the New South: A Social History of the North Carolina Mutual Life Insurance Company* (Urbana: University of Illinois Press, 1973).

19. *Southern Frontier,* May 1943, 1; *Southern Frontier,* October 1943.

20. *Southern Frontier,* October 1943.

21. *Southern Frontier,* May 1943; U.S. Treasury, Release N-1489, NA; "$25,800 War Bonds Sold at Negro Rally; $2,250 Pledged," *Paterson Evening News,* 12 April 1943; letter from Clara L. Smith, secretary of Paterson, New Jersey, branch of NAACP, to Odette Harper, NAACP, 24 April 1943, File "War Savings Bonds, 1943–1944," LC.

22. U.S. Treasury, "A Campaign to Organize War Bond Savings Clubs Among Negroes," 1944, Wilson Library Government Center; University of Minnesota, Minneapolis; "1944 Report of Inter-Racial Section," WPP; U.S. Treasury, "Negroes in the War Bond Program," Sixth War Loan campaign booklet, NA.

23. U.S. Treasury, "Campaign to Organize War Bond Savings Clubs."

24. Ibid.

25. Ibid.

26. Ibid.

27. *Southern Frontier,* June 1943; Memo titled "Program Material" from Theodore R. Poston, OWI, to Herbert Plummer, News Bureau, 16 June 1945, NA.

28. "Palmer Memorial Institute 100 Per Cent Loyal in Defense," *Greensboro Daily,* 5 February 1942, newspaper clipping, Photograph Reference Files, NA.

29. *Southern Frontier,* May 1943; Photograph Reference Files, NA.

30. *Southern Frontier,* May 1943.

31. "1943 Report of Inter-Racial Section," WPP.
32. Photograph Reference Files, NA; *Southern Frontier,* February 1942; Letter from Perry B. Jackson, President, Ohio State Association of IBPOE, to Ted Poston, OWI, 21 May 1943, File "Interracial Material," NA.
33. *Southern Frontier,* October 1943; U.S. Treasury, Release N-124, 3 September 1942, File "War Savings Bonds, 1941–1942," LC.
34. U.S. Treasury, Release N-1501, NA; U.S. Treasury, Release N-1496, NA; U.S. Treasury, Release No. 61, 18 October 1941, File "Defense Bonds, 1941," LC.
35. U.S. Treasury, Release N-1529, NA; "1943 Report of Inter-Racial Section," File "Interracial Material," WPP.
36. "1943 Report of Inter-Racial Section," WPP; U.S. Treasury, Release N-1501, NA.
37. *Southern Frontier,* May 1943; "1943 Report of Inter-Racial Section," WPP.
38. "1943 Report of Inter-Racial Section," WPP.
39. Ibid.

Conclusion

1. For an overview of the postwar Savings Bond program, see George Hanc, *The United States Savings Bond Program in the Postwar Period* (New York: National Bureau of Economic Research, 1962).
2. "Planned Spending and Saving," Office of Information, Domestic Branch, July 1944, 4, File "War Savings Bonds, 1943–1944," LC.
3. For a thorough traditional interpretation of postwar consensus history, see Godfrey Hodgson, *America in Our Time* (New York: Random House, 1976). As an example of a more revisionist view, see George Lipsitz, *Class and Culture in Cold War America: "A Rainbow at Midnight"* (New York: Praeger, 1981).
4. For classic studies of the relationship between nationalism and time, see Anderson, *Imagined Communities,* and E. J. Hobsbawm, *Nations and Nationalism Since 1780: Programme, Myth, Reality* (Cambridge: Cambridge University Press, 1990).
5. C. L. R. James, *American Civilization* (Cambridge, Mass.: Blackwell, 1993), 201.
6. Letter from Pickens to White, 27 April 1946, File "War Savings Bonds, 1945–1946," LC; letter from Pickens to NAACP, 11 June 1946, File "War Savings Bonds, 1945–1946," LC.
7. In his *Madison Avenue Goes to War,* Fox makes a convincing case that the administration overemphasized advertising puffery in its propaganda campaign.
8. T. R. Martin, "Inflation: The Second World War," *Current History* 24 (May 1953): 298.
9. Bert G. Hickman, *Growth and Stability of the Postwar Economy* (Washington, D.C.: Brookings Institution, 1960), 79–121.
10. *Time* 64 (13 December 1954): 92.
11. Martin, "Inflation," 299; Thomas, "Lessons of War Finance," 620–29.
12. Martin, "Inflation," 296.
13. Christopher Bliss, "War Bonds: More Delusions of Security," *American Mercury* 72 (April 1951): 432–33.
14. Ibid., 435.
15. Ibid.

★ ★ ★ Index

Adamic, Louis: endorsement of bonds, 97–98
advertising, 48–50; 53–54; in *American Mercury,* 216; in *Crisis,* 152; as free, 82
African Americans: and the "American dilemma," 159–60; attitudes toward war, 131; banks, 14, 144, 189; beauticians, 196; business community, 140–41, 193–98; and civil rights movement, xx, 152–53, 213–14; in fraternal groups, 201; as government employees, 172, 173, 191–92; investment in bonds, 186–205; and Liberty Bonds, 7; and patriotism during World War II, 141, 146, 204, 211; and the pluralistic democracy, 130; racism, xviii; and railroad workers, 193; soldiers, 172, 183–84, 203; World War I, xix, 7, 210
Allen, Willard: and White, 158
American Federation of Labor (AFL): access to social service agencies, 81; role within government agencies, 81; support of bond program, 25, 43. *See* labor
Anderson, Benedict: *Imagined Communities,* 148

Barber, Red: as bond seller, 63
Baseball War Bond League, 63
Beard, Charles and Mary: on Liberty Bonds, 5
Berlin, Irving: as bond songwriter, 62, 64
Black, Hugo: as bond promoter, 175; and Louis, 183
Blum, John Morton: on blacks during World War II, 131–32; on pluralism, xv
B'nai B'rith: role in bond program, 39, 101–2
Bond-a-Month Club, 66
Bonds Float Ships campaign, 84
Bonds for Babies promotion, 43
Bonds for Brides campaign, 43
Books and Authors program, 64
Boy Scouts: of Baltimore 37; and Liberty Bonds, 7–8
Brinkley, Alan: on consensus, xiv, 12; on Morgenthau, 23; on President Roosevelt, 11; on Treasury during war, 23
Brotherhood of Sleeping Car Porters, 193, 194
Brown, Charlotte Hawkins, 199

243

Buck, Pearl, 164; as head of Books and Authors program, 64
Bugs Bunny: as bond seller, 62
Buy a Jeep campaign, 36

Calloway, Cab, 178; "Backin 'em Back," 171
Campbell, D'Ann: on Red Cross, 24
children: farmers, 192; and Schools at War program, 34–37; in Treasury publicity, 72, 190–91
Chinese Americans, 104, 115–16, 119
Churchill, Winston: as bond promoter, 63
college students: apathy toward bond program, 36–37; support of program, 72, 200
Commiskey, Joe, 182
Communist Party: and Pickens, 129, 149; support of bond program, 65, 86
community: as theme in posters, 51
Community Chest War Fund, 81
community theater: and war bond promotion, 64–65
Congress of Industrial Organizations (CIO): black membership in, 133; as catalyst of black activism, 152; picketing, 81; support of bond program, 25, 43; War Relief, 81. *See* labor
consensus: and African Americans, 211, 213; as "American Way of Life," xiv–xv; 13; as pluralistic, 205, 209, 210, 212
Craft, Charles C., 160; and Wilkins, 169
Crosby, Bing: as bond seller, 59
Curie, Eva: petition for bonds, 99
Czechoslovakian Americans, 115

Daughters of the American Revolution: role in bond program, 39
Defense Savings Committees: creation of, 24–25; labor underrepresentation, 81
Defense Savings Program: and African Americans, 167; creation of, 20; versus Liberty Loan campaign, 20; radio promotion, 98; rollout, 127
Defense Savings Staff: advertising policy, 25–26; advertising and promotion program, 48–50; and African American entertainers, 177; bipartisanship of, 21–23; and canvassing, 47; creation of, 10, 20; in

Hawaii, 105; and Pickens, 154; propaganda campaigns, 32; and S. D. Mahan, 167
Dempsey, Jack: avoidance of draft, 184; as bond promoter, 63
department stores: Gimbel Brothers, 101–2; as quasi-official agents of bonds, 47; support of bond program, 66–68
Dies, Congressman Martin: criticism of Pickens, 149
Dietrich, Marlene: as bond salesperson, 97
Double V, xix, 103–4, 168, 173, 175, 185, 186, 202, 204, 205, 211, 214; and African American business community, 141; and Constitution, 147; creation and course of, 136–38; and William Pickens, xxi; rejection by zoot suiters, 132
Douglas, Supreme Court Justice William O.: and Seventh War Loan, 73
Dow Chemical: bond advertising, 80
Du Bois, W. E. B.: on blacks' "special grievances," xix; and Pickens, 128; on "twoness," xix; on World War I, 7

Einstein, Albert: donation of manuscripts to Treasury, 94; endorsement of bonds, 97–98
Ellington, Edward "Duke," xxi, 171, 176, 178, 179–82, 211; parallels with Louis, 182
Ellington, Mercer, 180
ethnic Americans: support of bond program, 94–123

farmers (agriculture): role in bond program, 42, 71, 142–43, 192
Farm Security Administration: Grand Central Terminal mural, 166
Filipinos, 104
Fones-Wolf, Elizabeth: and wartime business community, 79
Four Freedoms: as poster theme, 51; speech, 10; War Bond Show, 67–68
4-H Club, 192
Fox, Frank: on wartime propaganda, xix
Frank Jr., Lew: and promotion of bonds on radio, 97
freedom: as poster theme, 51–52
French Americans, 113–14, 116–17
Future Farmers of America, 71, 192

Index

Gamble, Ted R.: on African Americans' support of bond program, 187; and movie shorts, 61
German Americans, 102–3
Gerstle, Gary: on class, xvi
Girl Scouts: selling of bonds and stamps, 38
Gleason, Philip: on cultural pluralism, xvi–xvii; on democracy, xvi
Golden Gate Quartet, 179
Grable, Betty: and her "bondbardiers," 58
Grandmothers' War Bond League, 41–42; as market segmentation technique, 33
Graves, Harold N., 19; appointment to assistant to the secretary, 21; defense of Pickens, 149; letter from White, 166; and Morgenthau, 47; at Negro Million-Dollar War Bond Dinner, 172; staffing Inter-Racial Section, 154
Greek Americans, 100, 113
Green, William, 164; support of bond program, 25, 89; 164

Hahn, Muriel: *Carmen Jones*, 177
Handy, W. C.: and Eddie Anderson, 178; as bond promoter, 177–78
Hastie, Judge William H.: endorsement of Milton, 154; endorsement of Pickens, 129
Hayes, Helen: as bond seller, 60
Heinz, Mrs. Clifford, 115
Hobsbawm, Eric, 110
Holtz, Merriman, 61
Honey, Michael K., 153
Houghteling, James L.: appointment of Pickens, 127, 154; appointment to assistant to the secretary, 21; on bond sales, 187–88; defense of Pickens, 149; as director of labor relations, 92; as head of National Organizations Division, 78; instruction of deputies, 143; and Inter-Racial section, 130; praise of Pickens, 150
Hughes, Langston, 178; as bond promoter, 175–76
Hungarian Americans, 98, 113
Hunter, Nell: appointment to Inter-Racial Section, 133; and White, 157–58, 160

I Am an American Day, 114

Indian Americans, 105
inflation: bonds effectiveness in stemming, 214, 216; postwar, 217; as threat to wartime economy, 10–12, 28–29, 31; Treasury's overestimation of, 214
Internal Revenue Service: sharing taxpayer list with Treasury, 46
International Business Machines (IBM): bond advertising, 80
Italian Americans, 102–3, 113

Jackson, Chief Petty Officer Graham: as bond promoter, 173, 174
James, C. L. R., 212
Japanese Americans, 104–7, 109
Jeanes Teachers: support of bonds, 139–40
Jewish Americans, 100
Johnston, Gale F.: appointment as Defense Savings Staff field director, 21
Judd, Henry, 82–83

Kallen, Horace M.: theory of cultural pluralism, xv, 95
Kaufman, George: as chair of Treasury's community theater program, 64
Kaye, Danny: as bond auctioneer, 101
Kelley, Robin: on zoot suiters, 131
Kellogg, Charles Flint: on NAACP, 7
Keynes, John Maynard: theory of funding war, 10–14, 28

labor (unions): role in bond program, 42–43, 77–93; as salespeople, 47–48; women's role, 86
Labor Defense Bond Week, 87
Ladies Home Journal: and *Home Front Journal,* 40
Lebanese Americans, 113, 120–21
Lee, Gypsy Rose: as bond seller, 59, 61
Leff, Mark: on sacrifice during World War II, 43–44
Lekachman, Robert: on commercial Keynesianism, 12
Liberty Bonds (Loan), xviii, 3–8, 16, 29; purchase by ethnic Americans, 95; versus World War II bond program, 13, 15, 17–18, 26, 46, 70, 118, 210, 215

Library War Bond promotion, 64
Lichtenstein, Nelson: on ethnicity, 5; on organized labor, 42
Likert surveys, 54
Lipsitz, George, 110
Lithuanian Americans, 98, 113, 115, 117
Louis, Joe, xxi, 171–72; honored by Congress, 183; at Negro Million-Dollar War Bond Dinner 172; 173; 176; parallels with Duke Ellington, 182; 182–84; praised by Willkie, 184; 211
Ludlow, Representative Louis: objection to bond program, 27
Ludwig, Emil: endorsement of bonds, 97

McLean, Charles: visit of teacher colleges, 40
Mad at Jap Club, 71
Maier, Charles S.: politics of productivity, 78
Malcolm X (Little), 131
Mann, Thomas: endorsement of bonds, 97–98
marketing research: advances between world wars, 53; use by Treasury, 54
market segmentation, 33, 209
Meany, George: support of bond program, 87
Merton, Robert K.: on sacredness of bonds, 14
Mexican Americans, 112
Milton, Lorimer D.: appointment to Inter-Racial Section, 154
Morgenthau, Henry (Secretary of the Treasury): and anti-inflation measures, 11; awarding citation to madam, 70; background of, 13; and Cab Calloway, 171; on class divisions, 77; and Defense Savings Staff, 20; and democratic mission of bonds, 46–47, 100, 134; enlistment of European refugees, 97; as "gentlemen farmer," 142; on group affiliations, 32; on ideological role of bonds, 14–15, 25, 27, 70, 143, 171, 187, 202; and introduction of bond program, 19; and Jackson, 174; and joint labor-management committees, 87–88; and Judd, 82–83; and labor support, 89–92; and loan drives, 31; and "new liberalism," 23; opposition to overtime payment in bonds, 72; petitioning Congress, 10; and radio promotion, 48–49; and Razaf, 178; and savings bonds, 8; scrutiny of, 29; and Second War Loan, 164; setting of bond quota, 30; succession by Vinson, 73; support of capital, 12; on tax exempt status of federal securities, 14; and Toscanini, 98; and "the voluntary way," 13; and White, 167, 169; working with banking industry, 46
Murray, Pauli: rejection of war, 139
Murray, Philip (CIO President), 164; name of ship, 85; support of bond program, 81, 87, 89, 92–93
music: and Jackson, 173; at rallies, 172; role in bond program, 64, 98; Treasury Music Project, 178
Myrdal, Gunnar: and "the American dilemma," xiv, 159–60, 213

National Association for the Advancement of Colored People (NAACP): citations from Treasury, 169; endorsement of bonds, xxi, 7, 152–70; growth in membership, 153; payroll savings plan, 157; Pickens as field director, 127–29; Pickens as persona non grata, 149; protest by, 165–69; purchase of billboard space, 163; and Roosevelt administration, 153; and Tuskegee air squadron, 149
National Association of Colored Women: and Liberty Bonds, 7
National Baptist Church: convention, 144; support of bond program, 141–42
nationalism: paradigmic change during World War II, xiii, 211; and pluralism, xvii, 8, 130; and bond sales campaign, 16; and consumerism, 19; and education, 35; in posters, 51; and identity, 104; different interpretations of, 210; elasticity of, 211
National Organizations Division: and Houghteling, 21, 78, 127; creation of, 32; market segmentation techniques, 33; and labor, 78; creation of Inter-Racial Section, 130; pressure to provide sales figures, 165
Native Americans, 108–10
Negro Business League: support of bond program, 140
Negro Methodist Church: support of bond program, 141–42

Index

Negro Savings Clubs, 196–98
New Deal: as anti-capital, 12, 78; and Dies, 149; economic programs of, 11; influence on Defense Savings Program, 20; as legacy, 210; and Morgenthau, 13; move to center during war, 208; Pickens's opposition to, 129; within Pickens's rhetoric, 144; and pluralism, xv–xvi; populism, xvii, 15

Odegard, Peter, 19; on ideological role of bond program, 15–16, 32–33, 88; and Pickens, 146
Office of Emergency Management (OEM): news releases, 135; promotion of bonds on radio, 97
Office of Price Administration (OPA), xvii; creation of, 11; role and criticism of, 24, 43
Office of War Information (OWI): enlistment of blacks' support, 132; and ethnic Americans, 95; and Four Freedoms, 68; material directed to women, 40–41; *Planned Spending and Saving* pamphlet, 207–8; polls, 131; promotion of *Cabin in the Sky,* 181; propaganda campaigns, 32; and radio promotion, 56–57; story for black press, 144–45
Okada, John: *No-No Boy,* 107

Paderewski, Ignace Jan: endorsement of bonds, 97
payroll deduction (savings) plan: among Chinese Americans, 104; as civic affair, 208; creation of, 25; expansion of, 30; and federal government, 192–93; among fraternal and civic groups, 43; at Goodyear and General Tire, 71; and NAACP, 157; number of enrollees, 189; as poster theme, 53; in professional baseball, 62–63; within small businesses, 196; among unions, 88, 90–91
Pickens, William: on absence of sales records, 187; as advocate for administration and black community, 205; on African Americans' support of bond program, 187; and African American press, 135; alienation from NAACP, 149; on America as blacks' homeland, 145–46; appointment to Inter-

Racial Section, 127; background, 128–29; at beauticians' rally, 196; and "black bourgeoisie," 138–39; and black farmers, 142–43; on blacks' economic advancement, 145; and Brown, 199; and business community, 140–41, 198; cellular metaphor, 147–48; and churches, 142; on containing racism, 146–47; criticism of, 148–50; on Double V, xxi; estimating bond sales, 188–89; and Houghteling, 150–51; at Indiana rally, 202; instruction of deputies, 143; "myth and symbol" ideology, 147, 210; at NAACP conference, 154; and NAACP field offices, 160–61; at Negro Million-Dollar War Bond Dinner, 172; and Odegard, 146; on pluralistic democracy, 143–44, 185; as promoter of savings bonds, 151, 169–70; and Tuskegee air squadron, 149; visits black colleges and universities, 139; and White, 156–57, 169–70
Polenberg, Richard: on ethnicity, xvi
Polish Americans, 110–13, 115–16
politicians: support of bond program, 72
Portuguese Americans, 113
posters: featuring African Americans, 156, 158, 165–67; featuring Dorie Miller, 172; featuring George Washington Carver, 175; featuring Joe Louis, 183; foreign-language, 97; savings bonds, 207; themes in World War II bond, 50–53
Poston, Ted: and news releases, 135
Powel, Harford: appointment as Defense Savings Staff information director, 21
prisoners: support of bond program, 69–70, 189–90
propaganda, xvi, xvii, xix; blacks' skepticism toward, 131; and bond program 27, 70, 213; from Coordinator of Information and Office of Facts and Figures, 96; directed to children, 36; as emotional appeals, 17; ethnic-oriented, 100; from Office of War Information, 32; as optimistic in tone, 52; as puffery, 214; on radio, 56–57; on shortwave radio, 99; substitution for blacks' rights, 132; *This Is the Army,* 184
prostitutes: support of bond program, 70
publicity (public relations), 68–71

Puerto Ricans, 107–9

Quiz Kids: as bond sellers, 58

radio: and promotion of bonds, 48, 97–100; as propaganda tool, 56–57
Randolph, A. Philip, 137, 153, 193
Razaf, Andy: as bond promoter, 178
Red Cross, xvii; blood drives, 81; role and criticism of, 24, 43
retailers: support of bond program, 65–68
Rockwell, Norman: "Freedom from Want," xix; role in Four Freedoms War Bond Show, 67–68
Roosevelt, Eleanor: and Grandmothers' War Bond League, 42; and National Council of Negro Women, 133; and Pickens, 151; and Schools at War program, 35
Roosevelt, President Franklin Delano: and baseball, 62–63; and black newspapers, 138; as bond seller, 173; Four Freedoms speech, 10, 51, 67; home-front objectives, 31; and introduction of bond program, 19–20; and Jackson, 173; and Morgenthau, 13, 29; "necessitarian" approach to war, 132; and "one great partnership," xiv, 19; Pickens critical of, 129; and Pickens's praise of, 151; proclamation of I Am an American Day, 114; sensitivity to inflation, 11
Roosevelt, President Theodore: on Americanism, 4
Rose, Billy: as bond purchaser, 101
Rouzeau, Edgar T., 137; 158
Russian Americans, 120

sacrifice: as central wartime theme, 43–44; as theme in posters, 50–51
savings bonds: birth of, 8; investment by banks, 15; Pickens as promoter of, 151; pre–World War II, 9, 214; and rollover of war bonds, 218; and Truman administration, 207; versus war bonds, 46
savings (Defense) stamps: development of, 18; as teaching tool, 35
Schaar, John: on "homeplace" as core of patriotism, 145
Schools at War program, 18, 198, 209; and McLean, 140; as market segmentation technique, 33; opposition to, 214; overview of, 34–37
Scottish Americans, 112
Serbian Americans, 115–16, 118
Shepherd, Marshall, 174–75
Silko, Leslie Marmon: *Ceremony,* 109
Sims, Hilda: *Anna Lucasta,* 177
Sinatra, Frank: "The War Bond Man," 178
Sinclair, Upton: Pickens's support of governor bid, 129
Sitkoff, Harvard: on civil rights movement, 152
Sloan, Eugene W.: appointment as Defense Savings Staff executive director, 21
Slovak Americans, 114–15
Spanish Americans, 99
Studebaker: bond advertising, 80
Swedish Americans, 113
Syrian Americans, 113, 121

Taber, Representative John: objection to bond program, 27
Tarnapowitz, Mrs. Francis P., 115, 120
Thomas, Jesse O.: appointment to Inter-Racial Section, 132; letter to and from Madison S. Jones, 155–56; recruitment of deputies, 143; visits black colleges and universities, 139–40
Tobias, Dr. Channing, 160, 164, 165
Toscanini, Arturo: promotion of bonds, 98
Treasury, United States: advantages in marketplace, 45; and African American notables, 172; citation to Razaf, 178; citations to Jackson, 173; citations to NAACP, 169; and commercial banks, 208; concern of bond redemptions, 73; and debt ceiling, 9–10; and design of World War II bond program, 16–17; and Duke Ellington, 181–82; gain of foreign origin groups' loyalty, 118; hiring of Pickens, 129–30; and inflation, 10; and Liberty Bond posters, 6; Music Project, 178; News Bureau, 99–100; paternalism, 214; personnel of bond program, 20–23; populist mission, 43; public debt, 3; quotas, 188; reception of gifts, 27; refunding of loans, 215; retail practices, 66; retention of Pickens after the war, 151
Turner, Lana: as bond seller, 58

Index

Tuskegee air squadron: 158, 172; and Pickens, 149
Tuskegee Institute: and F. D. Patterson, 212; payroll allotment plan, 139
Tuttle, William: on Native American support of World War II, 109–10; on Schools at War program, 36

Uncle Sam: in bond advertising, 80; in Liberty Bond posters, 6; and movie shorts, 61; in patriotic play, 35

Vanderlip, Frank A., 8
Vanderlip War Savings Campaign, 8
Van Doren, Mark: as bond promoter, 175–76
Van Loon, Hendrik: endorsement of bonds, 97
Vann, Robert L.: and Double V campaign, 137
Vaughan, Leslie: on "100% Americanism," 4
Victory Pig Clubs, 42; 71
Vinson, Fred M. (Secretary of the Treasury): and Victory Bonds, 73

War Activities Committee: and movie shorts, 61
War Bond Day, 69
War Finance Committee(s): African American volunteers, 133; and Chinese Americans, 104; distribution of Curie speech, 99; and ethnic bond rallies, 97; issue of statement, 141; and Arthur T. MacManus, 194; and Negro Savings Clubs, 196; New York State, 161, 163, 165; and posters, 156
War Finance Division, 61; and African American entertainers, 177; and African Americans, 160, 171; and Gamble, 187; and Houghteling, 92; and Negro Savings Clubs, 196; and retail efforts, 66–68
War Savings Staff: and African American entertainers, 177; and canvassing, 47; and foreign-language material, 99; Foreign Origin Section, 114; and Milton Murray, 83; New York, 164, 169; promotion of war bonds, 30, 66; radio announcement, 100; in rural states, 71; and Major C. Udell Turpin, 193
Washington, Booker T.: and America for Freedom bond campaign, 155; versus Du Bois, 128; in OWI story for black press, 145; School 198; ship, 203
White, Walter, xx, 211; endorsement of Milton, 154; endorsement of Pickens, 129; letter from G. E. "Kid" Hilton, 166; letter to and from Carl R. Johnson, 160–61; and Morgenthau, 167, 169; relationship with Pickens, 156–57, 169–70; *A Rising Wind,* 159; supporter of bonds, 153, 158, 162–65
Whitten, John: appointment to Inter-Racial Section, 133; and NAACP, 156
Wilkins, Roy, xxi, 211; and Craft, 169; and Pickens, 154; supporter of bonds, 153, 161–64; telegram to John T. Madden, 168–69
Willkie, Wendell: Pickens's support of presidential bid, 129; praise of Louis and Dorie Miller, 184
Wills, Gary: on Gettysburg Address, 147
Wilson, President Woodrow: on ethnicity, 5; promotion of Liberty Bonds, 26; and World War I, 4–5
Women at War program: as market segmentation technique, 33; overview of, 37–41
World War I: and "100% Americanism," xvi, xx, 4–6, 96; African American veterans, 189; and American identity, 211; bond drives and blacks, xix, 7, 210; and race and ethnicity, 210; rise of consumer price index, 216; spending by navy, 55; versus World War II mobilization, 215. *See* Liberty Bonds
Wright, Richard: *Black Boy,* 175
Writers War Board, 64

World War II: The Global, Human, and Ethical Dimension
G. Kurt Piehler, series editor

Lawrence Cane, David E. Cane, Judy Barrett Litoff, and David C. Smith, eds., *Fighting Fascism in Europe: The World War II Letters of an American Veteran of the Spanish Civil War*

Angelo M. Spinelli and Lewis H. Carlson, *Life behind Barbed Wire: The Secret World War II Photographs of Prisoner of War Angelo M. Spinelli*

Don Whitehead and John B. Romeiser, *"Beachhead Don": Reporting the War from the European Theater, 1942–1945*

Scott H. Bennett, ed., *Army GI, Pacifist CO: The World War II Letters of Frank and Albert Dietrich*

Alexander Jefferson with Lewis H. Carlson, *Red Tail Captured, Red Tail Free: Memoirs of a Tuskegee Airman and POW*

Jonathan G. Utley, *Going to War with Japan, 1937–1941*

Grant K. Goodman, *America's Japan: The First Year, 1945–1946*

Patricia Kollander with John O'Sullivan, *"I Must Be a Part of This War": One Man's Fight against Hitler and Nazism*

Judy Barrett Litoff, *An American Heroine in the French Resistance: The Diary and Memoir of Virginia d'Albert-Lake*

Thomas R. Christofferson and Michael S. Christofferson, *France during World War II: From Defeat to Liberation*

Don Whitehead, *Combat Reporter: Don Whitehead's World War II Diary and Memoirs*, edited by John B. Romeiser

James M. Gavin, *The General and His Daughter: The Wartime Letters of General James M. Gavin to His Daughter Barbara*, edited by Barbara Gavin Fauntleroy et al.

Carol Adele Kelly, ed., *Voices of My Comrades: America's Reserve Officers Remember World War II*, foreword by Senators Ted Stevens and Daniel K. Inouye

John J. Toffey IV, *Jack Toffey's War: A Son's Memoir*

Lt. General James V. Edmundson, *Letters to Lee: From Pearl Harbor to the War's Final Mission*, edited by Dr. Celia Edmundson

John K. Stutterheim, *The Diary of Prisoner 17326: A Boy's Life in a Japanese Labor Camp*, foreword by Mark Parillo

G. Kurt Piehler and Sidney Pash, eds., *The United States and the Second World War: New Perspectives on Diplomacy, War, and the Home Front*

Susan E. Wiant, *Between the Bylines: A Father's Legacy*, Foreword by Walter Cronkite

Deborah S. Cornelius, *Hungary in World War II: Caught in the Cauldron*

Gilya Gerda Schmidt, *Süssen Is Now Free of Jews: World War II, The Holocaust, and Rural Judaism*

Emanuel Rota, *A Pact with Vichy: Angelo Tasca from Italian Socialism to French Collaboration*

Panteleymon Anastasakis, *The Church of Greece under Axis Occupation*

Louise DeSalvo, *Chasing Ghosts: A Memoir of a Father, Gone to War*

Alexander Jefferson with Lewis H. Carlson, *Red Tail Captured, Red Tail Free: Memoirs of a Tuskegee Airman and POW, Revised Edition*

Kent Puckett, *War Pictures: Cinema, Violence, and Style in Britain, 1939–1945*

Marisa Escolar, *Allied Encounters: The Gendered Redemption of World War II Italy*

Courtney A. Short, *The Most Vital Question: Race and Identity in the U.S. Occupation of Okinawa, 1945–1946*

James Cassidy, *NBC Goes to War: The Diary of Radio Correspondent James Cassidy from London to the Bulge*, edited by Michael S. Sweeney

Rebecca Schwartz Greene, *Breaking Point: The Ironic Evolution of Psychiatry in World War II*

Franco Baldasso, *Against Redemption: Democracy, Memory, and Literature in Post-Fascist Italy*

G. Kurt Piehler and Ingo Trauschweizer, eds., *Reporting World War II*

Kevin T Hall, *Forgotten Casualties: Downed American Airmen and Axis Violence in World War II*

Chad R. Diehl, ed., *Shadows of Nagasaki: Trauma, Religion, and Memory after the Atomic Bombing*

Raffaella Perin, *The Popes on Air: The History of Vatican Radio from Its Origins to World War II*

Daniel McKay, *Beyond Hostile Islands: The Pacific War in American and New Zealand Fiction Writing*, foreword by Patrick Porter

Robert Sommer, *The Concentration Camp Brothel: Forced Sexual Labor under Nazi Rule*, translated by Dominic Bonfiglio, foreword by Annette F. Timm

Lawrence R. Samuel, *The World War II Bond Campaign*

www.ingramcontent.com/pod-product-compliance
Lightning Source LLC
Chambersburg PA
CBHW020401080526
44584CB00014B/1116